❦ Action Is Eloquence

Action Is Eloquence
SHAKESPEARE'S LANGUAGE OF GESTURE

෬ David Bevington

Harvard University Press
Cambridge, Massachusetts, and London, England 1984

Publication of this book has been aided by a grant from the Hyder Edward
Rollins Fund.

This book is printed on acid-free paper, and its binding materials have been
chosen for strength and durability.

LIBRARY OF CONGRESS CATALOGING IN PUBLICATION DATA

Bevington, David M.
    Action is eloquence.

    Includes bibliographical references and index.
    1. Shakespeare, William, 1564–1616—Technique.
2. Shakespeare, William, 1564–1616—Dramatic production.
3. Gesture in literature.   I.   Title.
PR2997.G4B48   1984   822.3'3   84-673
ISBN 0-674-00355-1

For my colleagues

Preface

THIS PROJECT grew out of a practical problem I have grappled with over my years as an editor of Shakespeare: when does the editor add stage directions to indicate for the reader what is happening in the theater? Too often the approach has been haphazard. Editors have copied the stage directions of editorial tradition as though they were canonical (most of them are not) and have been reluctant either to question stage business sanctioned by tradition or to detail stage business previously unspecified. The result has been that some kneelings or handclasps or giving of money are noted for the reader, while others are not.

The attempt to remedy this inconsistency proved more difficult than I first thought, as other editors no doubt have discovered. Determining precisely when an action occurs and when it ends (for example, when a character rises from kneeling) is often obfuscated by lack of explicit indications in the text. In fact one cannot always be certain that a stage action occurs at all, even if dialogue and circumstance seem to require it. I was disconcerted to learn that actors and directors, who I had assumed would favor editorial attention to stage business, are wary of the editor's intrusion; providing stage action is in their view the business of the actor or the director, and editorially added stage directions can limit rather than enlarge understanding by being overly specific.

A careful reexamination nevertheless seemed in order, and it led me to this present inquiry. To scrutinize Shakespeare for evidence of stage business is to be struck by his abiding interest in stage picture. Like Montaigne, whose iconoclastic perceptions on the subject of human gesture are quoted a few pages farther on, Shakespeare is fascinated with the communicative power of bodily or facial movement. His profession as a dramatist adds to this more general interest a practical

Preface

concern and opportunity for artistic experiment that extended throughout his creative life span. Although the modern editor may be frustrated
in a search for precise wording that does not claim too much, Shakespeare's texts demand visual realization. Ascents and descents, kneelings, ceremonial processions, joinings of hands, and the like are not
only omnipresent but function as signs of hierarchical relationship,
personal obligation, communal celebration, and a host of other meaningful qualities. Clothing betokens social rank or, conversely, a holiday
inversion of it. Gestures often occupy the central moment of a scene
or signal the reversal of a dramatic action. My aim has been to study
this unspoken language of the theater, and to see how Shakespeare
regards both its capacity and its limitations.

Many are the critical studies that have assisted my task, and I have
tried to record this debt in the notes to this book, but I should like to
name here a few works to which I have returned again and again. Like
others in this recent field of stage-oriented analysis of Shakespeare's
imagery, I am indebted to the pioneering work of R. A. Foakes and
Maurice Charney. George Kernodle's *From Art to Theatre*, for all its
excessive claims on behalf of medieval art and pageantry, is a work too
often neglected today. Along with Francis Fergusson's *Idea of the Theatre*, it has made a great difference in my thinking about the theater
façade as symbolic structure. Bernard Beckerman's *Shakespeare at the
Globe* and several studies by Alan Dessen and John Styan have provided
a wealth of good judgment about Shakespeare's stage and stagecraft.
G. K. Hunter's article on "Flatcaps and Bluecoats" in *Essays and Studies*,
1980, has taught me about spatial relationships in the theater; so has
Keir Elam's *Semiotics of Theatre and Drama*. Barbara Mowat has illu-
minated symbolic traditions of costuming in "The Getting Up of the
Spectacle" (*Elizabethan Theatre*, forthcoming). Thomas Van Laan is
incisive about the concept of role in *Role-Playing in Shakespeare*, and
Lynda Boose about marriage ceremonials in "The Father and the Bride
in Shakespeare" (*PMLA*, 1982). James Siemon's *Shakespearean Iconoclasm*,
then unpublished, came my way at a needful time to clarify my ideas
about Shakespeare's mistrust of visual images. Margery Garber's *Coming of Age in Shakespeare* had the immense usefulness, among other ben-
efits, of sending me to Victor Turner's *Ritual Process*. Ann Slater's
Shakespeare the Director appeared after I had done most of my work, but
I have tried to profit from her instruction by paying attention to the
distinction between authorial and nonauthorial stage directions. Unlike

her, I have said relatively little about Shakespeare's development of visual styles; I do not quarrel with her perception of a development away from the heightened artifice of the early plays to a more "realistic" style of the middle years and thence to a new self-aware sort of artifice in the late phase, but I am more interested in what remains constant throughout that development.

I began work with the help of a term spent at the University of Victoria in early 1981, during which I presented four public lectures on the present topic in what I fear was very rough form. A Guggenheim fellowship in 1982–83 gave me an entire year to read and write. Although none of this work has appeared in print heretofore, I have read portions of it to critically helpful audiences at Beloit College, Bernard Baruch College of the City University of New York, Cornell University, Dartmouth College, Michigan State University, Mount Holyoke College, Nazareth College, New York University, Ohio State University, Reed College, the University of British Columbia, the University of California at Berkeley, the University of Massachusetts at Amherst, the University of Notre Dame, the University of Texas at Austin, the University of Toronto, the University of Washington at Seattle, the University of Wisconsin, and Wittenberg University.

My colleagues, including Edward Berry at the University of Victoria and Wayne Booth and Tom Mitchell at the University of Chicago, have helped open my eyes to critical difficulties. I am deeply grateful to Richard Strier, who gently but thoroughly made me aware of the inadequacies of an early draft and perused a revision as well. Alan Dessen, Joel Fineman, David Kastan, Wayne Shumaker, James Siemon, Jeffrey Stern, and Richard Wheeler have given me invaluable criticism on various chapters or portions of the work. Helen Bevington and Peggy Bevington have read attentively for clarity of argument and expression. My family, and the Ohio farm where I have done so much writing and rewriting, are a source of endless comfort, while the University of Chicago has provided more intellectual challenge than I have been able to meet. None of us can ever fully acknowledge the help we receive, but I can at least say that I grow daily more aware of how communal is the endeavor we call criticism.

❦ Contents

❝ What doe we with our hands? Doe we not sue and entreate, promise and performe, call men vnto us, & discharge them, bid them farwell, and be gone, threaten, pray, beseech, deny, refuse, demaund, admire, number, confesse, repent, feare, be ashamed, doubt, instruct, commaund, encite, encovrage, sweare, witnes, accuse, condemne, absolve, injurie, despise, defie, despight, flatter, aplaude, blesse, humble, mocke, reconcile, recommend, exalt, shew-gladnes, rejoyce, complaine, waile, sorrow, discomfort, dispaire, cry-out, forbid, declare silence and astonishment? And what not? With so great variation, and amplifying, as if they would contend with the tongue. And with our head, doe we not envite and call to-vs, discharge and send away, avowe, disavowe, be-lie, welcome, honour, worship, disdaine, demaund, direct, rejoyce, affirme, deny, complaine, cherish, blandish, chide, yeeld, submit, brag, boast, threaten, exhort, warrant, assure, and enquire? What do we with our eye-lids? And with our shoulders? To conclude, there is no motion, nor jesture, that doth not speake, and speakes in a language, very easie, and without any teaching to be vnderstoode: nay, which is more, it is a language common and publike to all: whereby it followeth (seeing the varietie, and severall vse it hath from others) that this must rather be deemed the proper and peculier speech of humane nature.

—*Montaigne, "An Apologie of Raymond Sebond" (1603)*

Visual Interpretation:
Text and Context

There was speech in their dumbness, language in their very
gesture.

—*The Winter's Tale*

"ACTION IS ELOQUENCE," Volumnia tells her son Coriolanus,
as she urges him to court the plebeians of Rome "with
this bonnet in thy hand" and "Thy knee bussing the stones" (*Coriolanus*,
3.2.75–78).[1] Volumnia's advice epitomizes a central argument of the
present book. Her attitude toward the language of gesture is at once
admiring and cynical. It attributes to visual images an extraordinary
power to move men's minds, a power that words alone cannot claim;
at the same time, it perceives in those visual images a power to deceive.
Volumnia does not speak for Shakespeare, of course, yet his plays and
poems exhibit from first to last a fascination with a theatrical visual
language that is both eloquent and potentially misleading. Even in his
earliest works Shakespeare explores visual statement as the embodiment
of identifiable meaning in which a certain gesture or costume or stage
structure seemingly provides the viewer with a fixed signification, only
to have that viewer later discover that visual language can use this
vocabulary of apparently fixed meaning to suggest something very different.

Visual language poses for Shakespeare, then, a difficulty of interpretation. How are we to read its signals in the theater and not be
misled? Shakespeare's ambivalent attitude of acknowledgment and mistrust is evident when we compare his work with medieval and Tudor
drama. In that drama, as in late medieval art generally, fixed visual
meaning holds an important place. The very concept of an attribute,

by which viewers are able at once to identify the Virgin Mary by a lily or Saint Peter by a key, bespeaks a one-to-one correspondence between *res*, the thing, and what it signifies. Of course the medieval viewer must acknowledge the deceiving wiles of the devil, as colorfully portrayed on the medieval and Tudor stage, but he or she is left in no uncertainty about the visual distinction between good and evil. Theoretical defenses of stage plays, from Thomas Aquinas through those who answered the Lollard antitheatrical polemicists, stress the didactic soundness of dramatic presentation of biblical story: such presentation instructs the unlearned, puts the viewer in mind of the Incarnation of Christ, and stirs feelings of devotion.[2]

Basic to this process of visual instruction is an absolute trust in the signifying function of images. Tudor moral drama, even in the early years of the Protestant Reformation (directed, among other things, at images), makes extensive use of a visual correlation between the spiritual state of the protagonist and his outward appearance. As T. W. Craik has shown, Mankind's characteristic journey of riot and penitence regularly takes the form of extravagant costume followed by the garb of shame and remorse.[3] Since a character's role and his state of mind are expressed by what he wears, an alteration in role or state of mind must take the form of altered outward appearance.

That Shakespeare was profoundly attracted to this idea of certitude in the meaning of images can perhaps best be demonstrated by his use of the convention even when he most devastatingly illuminates its inadequacies. King Lear's journey from regal autocracy through madness to tearful reconciliation with Cordelia is signaled at every crucial turning by what he wears, by his royal robes, by his running "unbonneted" in the storm, by the "lendings" at which he tears and the weeds with which he is madly bedecked, by the "fresh garments" suited to his royal rank in which he is vested at Cordelia's behest.[4] Yet what do these morality-play turnings signify in the face of Lear's last tragedy? What can we tell from the deictic obscurity of Lear's final implied stage direction? "Do you see this? Look on her, look, her lips, / Look there, look there!" (*King Lear*, 5.3.315–316). Othello's resolution to "see before I doubt" (*Othello*, 3.3.196) suggests a terrible sequence of inverted cause and effect in which to see is to doubt. Even when the visual image is redeemed in the late plays, as in Hermione's statue brought to life, the gesture is so fraught with unknowable mystery and hints of forbidden art that Paulina must protest she is unaided "By wicked powers" (*The Winter's Tale*, 5.3.91).

Shakespeare's mistrust of visual certitude is never triumphant. It bespeaks instead a longing for fixed meaning in art and a belief that art cannot communicate and instruct without trustworthy means of signification. Yet it also insists upon a rigorous exploration of the ways in which true art complicates and even defies such a comforting notion of readily perceived meaning. In other words, Shakespeare regularly deconstructs his own art, making it difficult for deconstructionist critics to do it for him. His is an art, as James Siemon has said, that both means and refuses to mean.[5]

This mixture in Shakespeare of desire for certitude and skepticism about it helps define his usage of his dramatic heritage. He makes extensive use of a received visual language, but from the start does so with ironic awareness of its imperfections.[6] The received convention of fixed meaning serves Shakespeare well to define a world of order and meaning, but his purpose in erecting such a milieu is usually to juxtapose this patterned cosmos with his own vision, in which much is inverted or questioned.

The contrast between two worlds in Shakespeare's plays has been observed of late in various contexts. The first world is inevitably that of social order, hierarchy, and place. The second world, set apart from structured society, is the "green world" of Northrop Frye, the festive world of holiday celebrated by C. L. Barber, the "second place" of Alvin Kernan.[7] It is also, as Marjorie Garber has observed, strikingly analogous to the "liminal" or transitional phase of rites of passage as defined by the anthropologists Arnold van Gennep and Victor Turner.[8] Van Gennep's analysis of the rite of passage finds an invariable three-phased process from separation through margin or transition to aggregation or reintegration. Any given ritual usually combines aspects of all three phases. Marriage, for instance, is both separation from one's former family and integration into a new one. Ceremonies of death emphasize acceptance into a new life as well as departure from the old.

The transitional or liminal phase, always present, is of particular interest to drama. It is a period of ambiguity, lying between fixed social customs, and is threatening because of its instability. It is variously likened to death, the womb, invisibility, darkness, bisexuality, wilderness, and eclipse.[9] Those who undergo the transition are novices temporarily lacking position in the kinship system. They are expected to be passive and humble, and to accept arbitrary punishment. Among themselves novices tend to develop an intense comradeship and egalitarianism. Their world of "communitas," in Turner's phrase, is unstructured and undifferentiated, in sharp contrast to the order and ranking of the social system they have temporarily left and to which they will return.

Turner's analysis of the contrast between the structured world and communitas points to a number of features that are highly theatrical and visual, and that may be looked upon as ceremonial vocabularies separating the transitional phase from its more stable opposite. In the liminal world of communitas, for example, distinctions of clothing are left behind for nakedness or simple uniformity of garment. All distinctions of wealth and rank are abandoned; so are those of sex. Kinship rights and obligations are suspended. Silence is treasured in place of speech. The occupants of this world are expected to be humble and obedient, instead of manifesting a just pride of position and obedience only to those who are superior. Expectations of equality, anonymity, disregard of personal appearance, simplicity, and unselfishness sharply distinguish those in transition from their counterparts in the socially unequal, visually differentiated, appearance-conscious, complex, and self-centered world of social order.[10]

The enterprise of this study will be to develop a contrastive vocabulary of visual signals in Shakespeare's plays and poems. The theatrical world is itself a liminal world. Spectators come to it expecting to be worked upon by the artist's magic, and return to their daily lives somehow transformed by what they have seen. Certainly Shakespeare invokes this sense of transforming experience in *A Midsummer Night's Dream* and many other places. Spectators are somewhat like novices, submitting themselves in silence and in undifferentiated communal response to the sacred instruction of a mage. What they see, especially in Shakespeare's plays, hints suggestively at the inversions of wisdom and madness, sagacity and foolishness, so deeply characteristic of the liminal state. Still, the theater, especially Shakespeare's theater, also invokes an image of the world to which the spectators belong in their daily lives, one of observed distinctions and structure. Theatergoing thus serves a holiday purpose; it is a rite of passage to the extent that it transforms normal social values not as revolution but to prepare the

4

participants for a reevaluation of order and a better understanding of its importance in human life.

To such an end Shakespeare needs two visual vocabularies, one of order and one of holiday release where the artist casts his spells. He finds the first vocabulary in the visual conventions of the Tudor stage, as well as in the social norms all around him. The second is to a significant degree his own invention, though generally indebted to notable artists before him. It is a precious gift, for, as Victor Turner argues, the liminal experience is no less essential to human sanity than the structured experience from which it differs. The interrelationship of these two worlds in Shakespeare's art offers insight into the problem of interpretation as well, for the very complexities and uncertainties attendant upon visual interpretation in the artist's liminal world ultimately confirm rather than deny the possibility of meaning in art. The oversimplified equations of object and signification in the conventional vision of structured society are tested and made viable, not destroyed, by the challenge of the artist's vision.

Criticism of "stage picture" or "stage imagery" in Shakespeare is no longer new, though it is recent. Romantic criticism in the nineteenth century concentrated upon character analysis to the virtual exclusion of theatrical analysis, reflecting the disdainful attitudes of many critics toward the contemporary theater, with its ornate verisimilar sets and heavily rearranged texts so much out of touch with Shakespeare's visual practice on a thrust stage devoid of movable scenery. The New Criticism of the twentieth century rebelled against excesses of character study and philological scholarship, but did so in the interests of verbal rather than visual imagery. Critics like L. C. Knights, S. L. Bethell, Robert Heilman, and Cleanth Brooks focused on the plays as dramatic poems containing metaphors and similes that provide a sensuous or pictorial image through words. Methods of analysis originally formulated to examine the poems of Donne or Keats and then applied to the drama sought out iterative imagery chiefly in the words of the text, in "the larger metaphor which is the play itself." Even G. Wilson Knight, while maintaining a major interest in the theater, urged nonetheless that we should see each play as "an expanded metaphor."[11] Caroline Spurgeon, in her famous study professing to tabulate all of Shakespeare's imagery, deliberately excluded stage images from consideration

5

on the grounds that they are not the imaginative source in Shakespeare's mind from which the poetic image is drawn.[12]

Spurgeon thus offered a particularly inviting target to R. A. Foakes and others who, in the 1950s, raised the standard of a criticism based on visual and other "presentational" images in the theater. Since that time theatrical criticism has continually battled with the kind of long-standing antitheatrical prejudice chronicled for us by Jonas Barish, a deep-seated mistrust of masquerading and of spectacle that stems from both Plato and Aristotle and has flourished in Puritan and Romantic opposition to the commercial stage.[13] Correspondingly, the movement toward stage-oriented analysis has welcomed and encouraged presentational developments on the modern stage. Maurice Charney, one of the first to identify "a significant language of gesture and stage properties which communicates meaning to us,"[14] has argued that critical discovery of presentational elements in drama must go hand in hand with a reawakening of the theater itself to its capacity for visual statement. He finds encouragement in the plays of Jean Cocteau and Tennessee Williams, in which the stage's own images are clearly part of the "poetry of the theater," and sees a link between playwriting of this sort and the critical explorations of Foakes, Alan Downer, Paul Jorgensen, and a few other early proponents of stage imagery.[15]

This critical trend begun in the 1950s should be seen as an outgrowth of New Criticism as well as a protest against its narrowly defined concept of image, for both approaches insist on close reading of the text and both focus on imagery. Attention to stage imagery has unquestionably enriched our critical vocabulary and opened new parts of Shakespeare's work to examination. Foakes has illustrated what can be done in *Macbeth*, for instance, when we attend carefully to iterative effects in the theater as a powerful source of imagery: the thunder and the knocking at the gate, the bleeding sergeant and the bloody daggers, the banquets, apparitions, sleepwalking—in short, the stage imagery of noise, blood, and sleep.[16] Charney helps us to focus on the familiar objects and the details of daily life in *Julius Caesar*, things that convey to us as spectators the personal, domestic, and unheroic world of Brutus. In the same play verbal images of sickness and disorder in the body politic are enhanced visually and aurally by vivid firsthand impressions of storm, blood, and fire.[17] Other contributions of this sort, of which there are many, will be cited in subsequent pages. Two anthologies of essays dealing with stage imagery have recently appeared, and the subject has at last received book-length critical treatment.[18] The method is now firmly established, so much so that when I confessed to a friend (also in theatrical criticism) that I was at work on Shakespeare's stage imagery he replied somewhat ruefully, "Who isn't?"

Yet much remains to be done. Despite the new interest in stage picture and despite recent trends in the theater toward thrust stage and presentational direction, preconceptions of verisimilar decorum are very much alive. "Realistic" pictures of Windsor town or Dunsinane Castle or the Forest of Arden emerge in the period costuming and detailed furnishings of the BBC television productions of Shakespeare's plays. (Productions of the *Henry VI* plays and *Richard III* have moved to a more presentational stage—not very successfully, but at least heading in the right direction.) One source of our difficulty in "seeing" stage images as Shakespeare saw them, it has been suggested, may be the medium of film; for film trains our eyes to locate dramatic characters in a fully supplied landscape of which the characters then become a part.[19] That is, film is not ordinarily compatible with a theater in which the characters appear on an essentially bare stage and evoke a sense of location around them by the actors' performance. Historians intent on reconstructing the Elizabethan stage have clung to ornate theories of inner stage and upper stage to facilitate physical change of locale between scenes. Visual interpretation languishes, we suspect, in our verbally oriented classrooms. Ann Slater sees disturbing evidence that, although the need for stage-oriented study of Shakespeare's imagery "has become something of a critical cliché in the past three decades," the approach espoused by Foakes and Charney "appears to be dying a lingering and undeserved death."[20]

One may hope that this warning is too shrill, and at the same time agree that we have reached a time of reappraisal. The manifestos of the first-generation critics of stage imagery, so appropriate to an era of discovery and revisionism, need not be reiterated. When Philip McGuire and David Samuelson undertook to edit a collection of stage-oriented essays on Shakespeare, I am told, their first order of business was to edit out of each contribution a plea for more attention to stage imagery. The point has been made, even if it is not always heeded.

We do need to see where we have come, however. The considerable diversity of approaches to Shakespeare's presentational dimension can perhaps be suggested by the diversity of nomenclature in current use. Some terms like "stage picture" and "stage imagery" are oriented toward theater history or production; others like "visual symbolism," "symbolic action," "visual emblem," and "stage iconography" are focused more on what can be learned from emblem books and iconographic tradition; still others like "visual signal" posit a linguistic and semiotic approach to theatrical signs.[21] Controversy has inevitably erupted among those formerly united against the common enemy of antitheatrical prejudice, especially in the debate among those who look to stage directions and evidence about Elizabethan theatrical conditions versus those who read emblem books.[22] We need to weigh these conflicting claims, and most of all to consider whether attention to stage picture has created its own distorted notion of Shakespeare as purveyor of images.

The dangers are apparent in the work of some enthusiasts for the emblem. Despite remarkably sensitive work by Raymond Waddington and John Steadman, among others,[23] the attractions of emblem hunting have led too often to overreading. Emblems are bookish sources, less immediately available to Shakespeare than the conventions of his own stage. More seriously, emblematic readings tend to cast Shakespeare in the allegorical mode. Some practitioners of emblematic criticism in fact insist that emblematic staging creates for a dramatic character a role akin to personification. The effect of such an emphasis, as James Siemon justly points out, can be to warp our view of dramatic action itself, making of it a kind of visual metaphor. Emblems generate a sense of wider signification by stylizing the individual event. Emblemized stage action becomes timeless, prototypical.[24] Because emblems embody the commonplaces of the age, moreover, finding them in Shakespeare's plays has the effect of suggesting his espousal of conventional thought.

Not surprisingly, apologists for the emblem turn for support to the doctrine of neoplatonism and its insistence on vision as man's surest gateway to knowledge through a direct, immediate, and nonverbal perception.[25] Indeed, neoplatonic thought offered a view of symbolism inherent in artistic representation that found its way into every aspect of Renaissance idealism. At its best, neoplatonism offered a means of reconciling the apparent conflict between symbolism and representation, by insisting that a beautiful literal representation of a person or object could discover ideal form and thus convey the universalized idea embodied in the outward visible shape.[26] Symmetry was perceived to be an expression of harmony, beauty, and goodness. The basic visual sign in God's great hieroglyph was considered to be order itself, in the cosmos and in society. Music offered a powerful model for a harmonious correspondence between the divine and physical worlds.[27]

Such a "poetic of correspondences"[28] found symbolic meaning in color, spatial arrangement, and gesture—on stage as in the public lives of Renaissance men and women. In the life of Queen Elizabeth every use of costuming, jewelry, decoration, or action could be interpreted in the sententious phrases of the emblem. Emblem books, popular in England as on the Continent, encouraged a habit of thought uniting word and picture in a close relationship aptly expressed by the saying attributed to Simonides of Ceos that "painting is mute poetry and poetry a speaking picture."[29] The universal language of emblems appeared in mottoes, coats of arms, mummings, street pageants, morality plays, Lord Mayor's shows, and sermons. The court masque provided a dramatic genre in which pictures and words were closely interrelated, as in the emblem books, by neoplatonic doctrines of correspondence. Even Ben Jonson, who asserted forcefully "that the Pen is more noble, then the Pencill," was ready to acknowledge that "Picture is the invention of Heaven: the most ancient, and the most a kinne to nature." He insisted that "*Whosoever* loves not *Picture*, is injurious to Truth: and all the wisdome of *Poetry*."[30] John Webster too applied the notion of *ut pictura poesis* to the theater in his characterization of "An Excellent Actor," one who knows how to paint with gesture: "by a full and significant action of body, he charmes our attention . . . Hee is much affected to painting, and tis a question whether that make him an excellent Plaier, or his playing an exquisite painter."[31]

Pervasive as this symbolic mode of thought undoubtedly was, we must realize its limits as well as its merits for dramatic interpretation. Elizabethan dramatists spoke of their art as chiefly verbal, acceding to the view of Aristotle's *Poetics* that spectacle in drama is inferior to character and plot. Thomas Heywood, for example, deplored "Anticke gesticulations, dances, and other Mimicke postures, devised onely for the vulgar, who are better delighted with that which pleaseth the eye, than contenteth the eare."[32] Calvinist attacks on the theatrical nature of the Roman Mass added polemic intensity to some Englishmen's mistrust of ornate visual displays.[33] Icons were suspect. Visual symbolism embodied in emblem literature tended therefore to represent a traditional view, a received idea of fixed symbolic meaning in art, that for Shakespeare could only express one side of a dialectic between symbolism and mimesis.[34]

Despite the attempts of neoplatonic thought to bridge the worlds of symbolism and representation, emblems and emblematic devices in Elizabethan public pageantry tended to emphasize the symbolic and stereotypical. Emblems interpreted *ut pictura poesis* literally, as Judith Dundas has argued, joining picture and poem by literalizing metaphor in the form of a picture.[35] Staging devices in Tudor drama and public pageantry brought this visual sententiousness directly into Shakespeare's theatrical heritage. In his own drama, on the other hand, as in the best of his contemporaries, Shakespeare gives substance to picture by incorporating it in a mimetic fiction. He uses sententious commentary to reveal character, never simply to express the moralizing "sentences" so deeply ingrained in Elizabethan commonplace wisdom and even in the educational curriculum. By devoting what had formerly been emblematic picture-making to an imitation of nature, as Dundas says, Shakespeare "has turned the truth of emblem to living experience." Our search for *topoi*, or emblematic commonplaces, in his works must not "lead to a form of categorizing which may prevent us from seeing what is there."[36] We must see that the traditions of visual symbolism so prevalent in Shakespeare's culture serve him well because they express the limits as well as the colorful richness of conventional symbolism. Shakespeare often invokes the symmetrical harmony of the cosmos and society latent in symbolic picture in a context of dramatic mimesis that leaves him free to explore his own more iconoclastic vision.

Occasional excesses of enthusiasm are natural to a new critical approach; our first response is to revel in Shakespeare's preoccupation with visual imagery, to find images everywhere and catalog them, to read them literally in the conventional symbolic terms they seem to represent. Early students of Shakespeare's physical stage, like students of the emblem, have erred in this generous direction. George Reynolds and W. J. Lawrence, for example, have paid too much attention to large stage properties and stagecraft.[37] Reynolds presents us with a stock list of scenic effects dependent not on painted scenery but on movable properties such as thrones, pulpits, beds, trees, forests, gardens, caves, rocks, tents, altars, barriers and lists, tombs, and the like. Evidence in stage directions and in Henslowe's *Diary* does point to the existence of such properties, to be sure, but too great an emphasis on them can misleadingly suggest that Shakespeare relies on such devices to invoke symbolic locale and all the metaphoric values of correspondence that we find in emblematic tradition. Glynne Wickham is another scholar whose invaluable erudition is sometimes pressed into the service of reading Shakespeare and his dramatic contemporaries as allegorists of the stage who employ a rich medieval legacy of theatrical properties not unlike those used in tournaments, street pageants, and cycle drama.[38] Like some emblemists, then, these historians of the physical stage occasionally exalt the iconic in Shakespeare in such a way as to literalize the metaphor, reading in it the conventional terms of the received tradition.

Investigation of the visually symbolic nature of the Elizabethan stage can nonetheless be valuable if we bear in mind the medieval thrust of that symbolism and regard it as a conservative idea to which Shakespeare can respond iconoclastically, rather than as a limiting force of tradition to which he is bound. George Kernodle's *From Art to Theatre* illustrates both the dangers and the potential of the approach. His argument that symbolic meaning on the Renaissance stage may well have owed something to conventions of medieval and Renaissance art is vulnerable, as Bernard Beckerman observes, on the grounds that the medieval tradition it claims as a source was interrupted in England by the Reformation.[39] Unquestionably, Kernodle's emphasis on the symbolic and conventional, like that of emblematic investigators, sometimes invites too iconic a reading of Shakespeare's art and sees him implicitly at least as the last of the medieval dramatists. Still, we do need to know what the visual theatrical conventions were that Shakespeare inherited, and Kernodle is an excellent place to begin.

Insisting that "theatre is one of the visual arts,"[40] Kernodle invites us to consider the Elizabethan stage itself as a visual symbol capable of organizing space like the dimensions of a painting. With its boldly thrust platform, its flanking vertical pillars painted to represent marble, and its overhanging heavens rich in symbolic decoration, all so impressive in its Renaissance decor that Elizabethan spectators marveled at the "painted" theater and its "stately-furnished" scene,[41] the façade inevitably frames the action that appears in its midst and defines relationships between upper and lower, downstage and upstage, left and right. It is especially adept at suggesting, according to Kernodle's argument, a set of visually symbolic locations found alike in medieval art and in street pageantry or masques at court: tower, castle, throne, pavilion-tomb, arch or doorway, ship, mountain (or cave), and garden (bower, tree, fountain, well, hedge with gate).[42] At times the stage makes use of movable properties like those studied by Wickham and

Action Is Eloquence

Reynolds to achieve its symbolic effects, but Kernodle's emphasis is on the ability of architectural detail and spatial dimensions and framing to invoke many of the locations that are necessary to Shakespeare's plays.

One of Kernodle's best observations is that the rich architectural background of the Elizabethan stage façade can serve for both exterior and interior locations, much as an architectural screen can be used in medieval art to frame a Last Supper or an Annunciation whether the scene is placed outdoors or inside. Elizabethan stage architecture, Kernodle argues, is wonderfully versatile in facilitating rapid shifts from exterior to interior locations because of the tradition in medieval and Renaissance art that allowed exterior architectural detail to be applied indifferently to exterior and interior scenes. Whether or not Kernodle is right about the source in art of this visual idea, he is certainly right that the versatility of shift from exterior to interior on Shakespeare's stage gains visual support from a façade that is not merely neutral in appearance. With its two or more doors and a gallery above, the Elizabethan stage possessed the means (in Andrew Gurr's apt phrase) to "provide the imagination with the exterior doors and balcony of a house or the interior doors and gallery of a great hall."[43] Architectural detail could prove itself at once flexible and specific, adaptable to outside or inside and yet visually graphic and plausible for both.

This way of regarding the Elizabethan stage and its physical dimensions as an essential part of stage picture is instructive, so long as we bear in mind the dangers of too emblematic a reading of the resulting tableau. The architectural background, as in medieval art, does function like a setting or foil for a jewel. The columns on stage frame the action and support the heavens above. The associative quality of this façade enhances the visual impression of a castle exterior, a city wall under siege, a royal pavilion for a tournament. Nevertheless, as we shall see, such an ordered world can bear witness to action that undercuts the hierarchical assumptions physically set forth in the theatrical building itself. In dramatic context, visual symbolic statement is qualified and tested. Kernodle and Wickham are invaluable if we recognize the limits of the world they find embodied in the picturesque Elizabethan stage.

Other critics like Beckerman and G. K. Hunter have found ways of demonstrating how Shakespeare's theater and his company could communicate meaning visually in a symbolically rich environment without surrendering to the inertia of emblematic statement. One valuable insight has been that of showing how Shakespeare's actors established a sense of location in a theater at once devoid of scenery and yet not visually neutral, and how they changed that sense of location from scene to scene without actually shifting from main stage to "inner stage" or "upper stage" as used to be supposed. The actors' essential strategy, according to this line of interpretation, was to build scenes around themselves, inviting spectators to adapt stage and architectural decor into a quickly varied series of imaginative landscapes with the actors at the focal point. The actors, Beckerman tells us, "did not regard the stage as a place but as a platform from which to project a story, and therefore they were unconscious of the discrepancy between real and dramatic space."[44] In Hunter's phrase, the Elizabethan actor created "realities" around him, "relying on the simple primary qualities of *above*, *below*, and (no doubt) upstage and downstage." The Elizabethan theater required its actors to "make their presence real by claiming position in that field of force that the open stage represents."[45]

Such creation of theatrical space in the absence of scenery demanded a clearly understood set of conventions—what Hunter calls "a vocabulary of visually registered movements."[46] The actors, using this vocabulary, could establish locale for any scene by their mere presence as well as by their conversation; to see Cleopatra on stage is to realize that we are in Egypt, and a royal entourage accompanying a king announces a presence chamber.[47] Shakespearean localization is capable of being concrete (before the gates of a town, for example), or indeterminate (somewhere in Scotland), or something in between (within the city of Rome); in any case, its visual signals rely more on spatial relationships than on verisimilar properties or sets. The gates of a town are suggested by the stage doors leading into the façade, by defenders in the gallery above, by attackers on the main stage below, and perhaps by scaling ladders—but not by walls painted to represent stone. As Beckerman argues, "The audience is not expected to identify the stage with a particular location but to understand that it functions as a token of Troy or the Danish palace or the Forest of Arden."[48]

When large stage properties are used (though more sparingly, in the view of Beckerman and others, than Reynolds and Wickham suggest), they signal locale much as the actor does, not by fitting into a complete landscape or a setting already established through scenery but by defining through theatrical language the space around them for purposes of a scene. Lawrence Ross observes of Desdemona's bed in Act 5 of

Othello that it is not part of the room furnishings but "physically and expressively the center of the action and so placed as to be inseparable from it."[49] After being thrust or carried on, such properties claim "their relationship to the world around them."[50] The doors on Shakespeare's stage are similarly employed not in an illusionistic way to lead to some fixed understood offstage location throughout the play, except perhaps in the early neoclassic *Comedy of Errors*; the attempt to stage *Troilus and Cressida* with one door representing Troy throughout the play and one representing the Greek camp has been shown to be impossible.[51] Symmetry often takes precedence instead, allowing characters to confront one another "*at several doors*" even when one has left the stage in pursuit of the other shortly before, and might then be supposed to re-enter from the same offstage location.[52]

Spatial relationships of "within" or "above" are crucial to a definition of location in the sparing use of the "enclosure" or "discovery" space (once called the "inner stage") and the gallery above the stage doors (formerly called the "upper stage").[53] These spaces do not serve as acting areas for entirely separate scenes, but as acting stations visually associated with the main stage. Actors in the gallery over the stage always relate themselves to others below on the main stage,[54] and the discovery space invariably opens its action out onto the larger acting arena lying before it. Vertical relationships also define the spatial significance of the trapdoor, with its connotations of the underworld,[55] and the "heavens" above the stage through which, in two late Shakespearean plays, the gods descend from or ascend into their "palace crystalline" with its "marble pavement" and "radiant roof" (*Cymbeline*, 5.4.113–121; see also *The Tempest*, 4.1.72 ff.).

Cumulatively, recent scholarship has done much to provide us with a suggestive vocabulary of visual signals by which the Elizabethan stage and its actors can provide a meaningful stage picture. The theater is anything but the bare plain platform sometimes supposed. It can offer a symbolic locale for the action it encompasses. Within its façade lies that which is to be concealed and discovered; the façade itself can at times signify the fortifications of a city or castle, with a place above for actors to appear as though on the walls of a besieged place; its gates open as though into a city or tower or inner room. The architecture of the stage is an appropriate background for exterior or interior scenes. The open stage, with heavens above and hell beneath, is an essential part "of a vision of man's central place in a cosmos of dignity and order."[56] Even here, however, we must be careful not to assume that Shakespeare uses such iconic richness for straightforward effect. He certainly exploits the resonances of order and vertical hierarchy in his stage, but often as a devastatingly ironic backdrop to the action. When Hamlet reminds us of the "majestical roof fretted with golden fire" that is a part of what we see in the theater, he does so in a speech that also disparages humanity as a "quintessence of dust" (*Hamlet*, 2.2.296–309). We will see similarly in Chapters II and III that the conventions of costume and gesture inherited by Shakespeare function in much the same way; Elizabethan commonplaces of human behavior provide him with an acting tradition in which costume and gesture are put on according to an expected decorum of fitting gesture to meaning,[57] and yet Shakespeare transcends convention by using it to represent, sometimes ironically, the ordered world of Elizabethan orthodoxy in all its predictable external form. As with emblematic action, we must guard against acceptance of visual conventions at face value. Only when they become part of a complex interplay of picture and text can they add vitally to our comprehensive understanding of Shakespeare's artistry.

Studies in the semiotics of theater and drama can help clarify the task of interpreting stage action, first by calling attention to its pervasiveness as a language and second by defining how its "symbolic" function relates to that of verbal language. Semioticians like Tadeusz Kowzan and Jiří Veltruský agree upon the simple but overwhelmingly important fact that "everything is a sign in a theatrical presentation," and "all that is on the stage is a sign."[58] The very circumstance of appearance on stage suppresses practical function in favor of a signifying role. Gesture in the theater is essentially synecdochic or metonymic, substituting the part for the whole or the sign for the thing signified, and it is above all deictic in that it often shows rather than describes, explains, or defines.[59] Through theatrical convention, stage action stands for "something other than itself."[60] Space is not neutral but potentially fillable; the distances between actors, and between actors and audience, crucially affect our perception of relationships, just as proximity or distance in real life is ruled by a complex set of conventions.[61] Gestures can indicate intentionality and attitude.[62]

Is gesture, then, a language no less capable of utterance than verbal speech? In the outspoken view of Jerzy Grotowski, gesture is nearly everything in the theater; it is a pure and primitive element capable of escaping linguistic thought, a "preverbal" source of feeling that is in fact the origin of theatrical expression. Antonin Artaud too does battle with the classical view of gesture as a mere accessory of speech; reversing the usual hierarchy of Aristotle's *Poetics*, he maintains that the most significant dimension of drama is the concrete language of the stage itself.[63] Between the extremes of logocentrism and gestural primitivism, however, most semioticians regard gesture as neither subservient to nor totally independent of verbal language.[64] Gesture cannot be segmented to the extent that speech can be segmented; it has no clearly definable repertory of gestèmes (the gestural equivalents of phonemes). Even if it is not tightly organized to produce invariably the same impression, gesture does nonetheless have a vocabulary of its own. A child learns to coordinate gesture and speech and to read visual signals. The language of gesture can demonstrate, in the context of speech, the four "modalities" of language: affirmation, interrogation, command, and request. It certainly possesses rhythm and deictic expressiveness.[65] In the theater it can both reinforce and diverge from verbal language, and indeed the range of interplay is subtle.[66] Stage imagery can use iteration, recurrency, and cumulative effect in much the way that verbal imagery forms a network of images.[67] Contrasts of word and visual image can be used to differentiate main plot from subplot, public scenes from private. We can have shifting contexts and multiplicity at one point, synchronism and mirroring at another.[68] Adding the visual dimension to our vocabulary of image patterns increases markedly our awareness of the subtlety and range of Shakespeare's achievement as poet and as theater poet.

Understandably, criticism of stage imagery during its first thirty years has tended to overstate its case. The first impulse has been to point out, enumerate, classify, call attention to a neglected language in Shakespeare. One discovers that Shakespeare, as professional dramatist and actor, is constantly aware of his visual effects. A natural consequence is to claim a unique power for visual imagery, and even to assert its primacy over verbal imagery. Criticism has usefully proceeded to analyze how visual language works, how it employs sources and devises patterns, and sometimes the claims have been exaggerated. Most worrisome is the tendency to see Shakespeare as an iconist, one who exalts the visual in neoplatonic terms and accordingly gives special place to the allegorical, the symbolic, the emblematic, the traditional. Before proceeding to detailed analysis, we would do well to ask what claims

Shakespeare himself makes for the visual in his dramatic art, and especially what limits he acknowledges in such a language of the theater.

Shakespeare has left us no body of theoretical writing about his art. Still, one finds everywhere in his writings a sense of his fascination with wordless actions that can speak through their own language of gesture. In what sense is it fair to speak of this wordless action as a language? Does it have its own grammar, its own rhetoric? What can it do, in Shakespeare's view, that verbal speech cannot do? What are its limits? In what ways do these two languages of the theater resemble each other, and how do they differ as modes of communication?

The first claim to which Shakespeare directs his attention is that of persuasive eloquence. A primary rhetorical capacity of spoken language, in the view of classical rhetoricians, is its ability to change minds; does gesture embody a similar power? Shakespeare's characters frequently assert that it does, and that indeed the persuasive force of action is at times unmatchable by words alone. "The silence often of pure innocence / Persuades when speaking fails," declares Paulina in *The Winter's Tale*, as she undertakes to determine whether the sight of the newborn Perdita can alter Leontes' wrath against mother and child (2.2.41–42). The unspoken fact of helplessness and innocence will, she hopes, present through picture a case for mercy more forceful than the conventional *topoi* of persuasive rhetoric could muster.

Paulina's confidence in the rhetoric of action is undercut, however, in at least two ways: she is ready enough to talk when occasion demands, and in fact her gesture does not persuade the King to reaccept Hermione and Perdita. The image in the theater is visibly arresting for us as spectators, but its rhetorical effect on its intended object, Leontes, is questionable. Paulina's sententious appeal sounds wise and convincing out of context—images have a special authority to change men's minds— but in context the reality mocks her attempt. Volumnia's "Action is eloquence" testifies to the persuasive power of images in a similarly wry contextual way by deploring the motive and by anticipating Coriolanus' failure to act as he is bid.

As a consequence, the rhetorical use of gesture and image to persuade is especially prominent in extreme situations when rational discourse breaks down. The English history plays and the Roman plays, with their interest in political rhetoric, offer repeated instances of dramatic conflict for which words prove inadequate. "Speak thou for me and tell them what I did," says Richard of Gloucester as he shows his brothers and allies the Duke of Somerset's severed head (*3 Henry VI*, 1.1.16). No action could more starkly signify the extent to which parliamentary debate and negotiation have given way in England's civil wars to reciprocal violence. In *Julius Caesar*, too, conspiracy turns to elemental gestures of defiance when petitions and other means of orderly redress have been rejected by the mighty Caesar. "Speak, hands, for me!" cries Casca, as he and the other conspirators stab Caesar (3.1.76). Gesture of this sort begets gesture, and in the ensuing violence Mark Antony proves himself a master of gestural eloquence. Claiming (falsely) that he has "neither wit, nor words, nor worth, / Action, nor utterance, nor the power of speech / To stir men's blood," he shows the populace sweet Caesar's wounds, "poor poor dumb mouths," and eloquently bids them speak for him. Antony succeeds (in part through clever speech) in putting "a tongue / In every wound of Caesar" (3.2.220–228). Of course Antony's rhetoric is masterful in its very disclaimers of rhetorical ability. The body of Caesar does not change as it lies in formal state; the way it "speaks" is determined by Antony's presentation. We can see that, in its use of both gesture and words, Antony's oration cleverly exploits the rhetorical *topos* of substituting gesture for speech, "action" for "utterance." A similar rhetorical substitution is at work in Macduff's challenging of Macbeth: "I have no words. / My voice is in my sword" (*Macbeth*, 5.8.6–7). Persuasive gesture cuts through to swift and violent conclusions.

Along with persuasive power, another attribute of silent eloquence to which Shakespeare directs our attention is its presumed ability to portray certain emotions with an expressiveness that spoken language cannot always match. When in *The Two Gentlemen of Verona* Proteus and Julia mournfully take leave of each other on the eve of Proteus' enforced departure for Milan, Julia's silent exit says more to Proteus than words could do:

> What, gone without a word?
> Ay, so true love should do; it cannot speak,
> For truth hath better deeds than words to grace it. (2.2.16–18)

The proverbial character of this sententious last line suggests the extent to which Proteus is being used by Shakespeare to express a commonplace of human experience: gestures and actions can signify feeling with an aptness that can only be approximated by words. Persuasiveness is not at issue here, for no attempt is made to change minds; instead, Proteus testifies to a kind of decorum, in which wordlessness is especially suited to the intensity and pathos of Julia's situation. A sheltered young woman, on the verge of parting from the young man upon whom her happiness depends, cannot even begin to say what she feels. She must rely on simple gesture to convey the directness of grief.

For all the commonplace wisdom of this view of gesture as enunciated by the thoroughly conventional Proteus, the most intense expressions of this sort in Shakespeare are conveyed to us verbally. Shakespeare paradoxically uses his finest writing to exalt the eloquence of the non-verbal. The reunion of Leontes and Polixenes in *The Winter's Tale*, we are told, was "a sight which was to be seen, cannot be spoken of" (5.2.43–44); that is, language cannot adequately convey the intensity of the experience derived from firsthand seeing. Shakespeare does not stage the "sight" for us, as he could easily have done, perhaps in order to save his most powerful theatrical effects for the reunion of Leontes and Hermione in the next scene. He chooses instead to assert the impossibility of conveying through words what the combined joy and sorrow of the reunion was like. "I never heard of such another encounter," says one gentleman, "which lames report to follow it and undoes description to do it" (ll. 57–59). Moreover, we hear that the reunion itself was characterized by wordlessness. The two kings spoke more in gestures than in words: "There was casting up of eyes, holding up of hands, with countenance of such distraction that they were to be known by garment, not by favor" (ll. 47–50). So too with the reunion after so many years of Leontes and Camillo: "They seem'd almost, with staring on one another, to tear the cases of their eyes. There was speech in their dumbness, language in their very gesture" (ll. 12–15).

Shakespeare chooses, then, to convey the impact of a scene through reporting the language of gesture. He emphasizes gesture in a scene we do not see, and stresses the inadequacy of language in words that are eloquent and moving. The paradox does not deny Shakespeare's attentiveness to the language of action. He does show us the reunion of Leontes and Hermione in the play's final scene, and builds the action around a seeming statue that comes to life—a stage image that expresses the idea of rediscovered marital happiness and forgiveness with an intensity that words seem unable to supply. The participants, at any rate, are struck by the expressive failure of words. "I like your silence," says Paulina, as she unveils the seeming statue of Hermione, "it the more shows off / Your wonder" (5.3.21–22).[69] Still, throughout the last scenes of *The Winter's Tale* Shakespeare seems intent on exploring the limits of the very gestural language he sets before us.

Shakespeare is perhaps quizzical in his presentation of traditional claims for a visual language as uniquely persuasive and as expressive of deep emotion. The claim that gesture has a special theatrical power rests on firmer ground, since it is in the theater that gesture makes use of an array of visual effects sharply differentiating drama from poetic and solely verbal forms of artistic expression. Shakespeare repeatedly calls our attention to the capacity of visual signals for generating moments of extraordinary theatrical tension, when a protagonist's choice hinges on a gesture and the reversal of the play's action seems poised before us in briefly silent tableau. Isabella's choice to kneel or not to kneel in Act 5 of *Measure for Measure* must determine the fate not only of Angelo and Mariana but of nearly every character on stage. The repeated urgings from Mariana and from the Duke to embrace or reject mercy suggest a visual balancing of moral choice on stage and a dramatic silence as Isabella hesitates and then finally kneels. Volumnia, in the last act of *Coriolanus*, shows her mastery of theatrical effects by her awareness of gesture and its signification. She knows that the somber costume she wears, her expression, and her supplicating posture must speak volumes to the proud son from whom she now begs Rome's safety. "Should we be silent and not speak," she declares, "our raiment / And state of bodies would bewray what life / We have led since thy exile" (5.3.94–96). Her kneeling before her own son, and her resolution to be "hush'd until our city be afire, / And then I'll speak a little," culminate in one of the most moving silences in all Shakespeare: Coriolanus *"holds her by the hand, silent"* (ll. 181–182).[70] The climactic scenes in both plays are, to be sure, anything but wordless; the language moves us deeply[71] and reminds us that visual and verbal effects collaborate in the theater. Nonetheless, Shakespeare here chooses a stage action to carry the immediate burden of the play's moment of reversal.

The immediacy of theatrical performance also gives some plausibility to the claim that visual signals in Shakespeare's theater demonstrate and inform. Shakespeare seems to press the claim for a deictic function, for example, when characters first encounter one another, or when constraints forbid the use of explanatory language; on such occasions gesture and expression become a necessary means of communicating information. Shakespeare's characters repeatedly emphasize how gestures can demonstrate before words are spoken, though paradoxically the way the gestures are verbally described is important in determining what we see. "The business of this man looks out of him" says Octavius Caesar of an Egyptian who comes to him from the defeated Cleopatra (*Antony and Cleopatra*, 5.1.50). "What a haste looks through his eyes!" exclaims Lennox of the Thane of Ross, who arrives in haste from the Scottish battlefield at Fife (*Macbeth*, 1.2.48). King Lear's Fool, confronted by Goneril with her "frontlet" on, need not hear her speak to know her displeasure: "Yes, forsooth, I will hold my tongue; so your face bids me, though you say nothing" (*King Lear*, 1.4.191–193). In fact, the Fool does not hold his tongue. When in *1 Henry VI* the antagonists of York and Lancaster first come face to face in the Temple Garden of London, they find they must resort to a symbolic way of expressing the vast differences that reasoned discourse cannot bridge. "Since you are tongue-tied and so loath to speak, / In dumb significants proclaim your thoughts," says Plantagenet as he plucks a white rose; Somerset plucks a red rose, and the Wars of the Roses at once assume a tangible reality (2.4.25–26).[72] Shakespeare is plainly aware of the potential of gesture for providing information about character, mood, and situation, though these examples once again stress in context the possibility of misinterpretation and the need for verbal elaboration.

Shakespeare's ambivalent attitude toward the language of gesture is evident in the rich vocabulary he uses to convey the effective action of the visual sign. In its visible and nonverbal function it acts as verbal signs do to link the signifier with the thing signified in a certain and meaningful relationship; Shakespeare's characters variously refer to the signifier as a sign, symbol, token, image, type, figure, mark, significant, ostent, and likeness. At the same time Shakespeare's numerous metaphors for the visible sign invest it with a sense of mystery, ciphering, and even troublesome prophecy: it is a badge, beacon, herald, messenger, pursuivant, post, title-leaf (title page), cognizance, favor, scutcheon, cipher, abstract, key, index, map, portent, warrant, seal, stamp, and livery. In its action the visible sign is capable of both clarification and ominous import: it portrays, proclaims, expresses, tells, speaks, shows, says, indicates, means, and the like, but also ordains, bodes, argues, blazes forth, bewrays, foretells, promises, signifies, feigns, attests, and presents. The visible sign enables us to behold, know, judge, and decipher. This extensive terminology suggests the seriousness of Shakespeare's interest in and commitment to non-verbal communication, even while it outlines the complexity of his response.

These claims for a visual language—that it is at times uniquely persuasive; that it is expressive of deeply emotional situations like parting and reunion when words seemingly fail; that it can produce arresting theatrical effects at moments of discovery or reversal; that it functions deictically or demonstratively to inform viewers about identity, character, intention, or mood; and that it utilizes a rich vocabulary defining the visual sign and its functions—are ultimately rhetorical claims. They use the language of rhetorical analysis; although visual effects "speak" through a medium different from that of speech, they act much as speech does, to persuade, move, command attention, and inform. Shakespeare views these conventional claims with positive interest but also with quizzical disillusionment. The claim of persuasive power is to a degree vitiated by evident failures, so that visual persuasion serves best in extreme situations when reasoned discourse has broken down. The affective power of gesture to reflect moments of keen emotion seems undeniable, and yet the very effects of gesture must at times be rendered to us in words. The attempts of Shakespeare's characters to conceive of gesture as a language sometimes have the paradoxical effect, in context, of creating a disjunction between language and vision, whereby language is used as a figure for precisely that which calls vision into question. Shakespeare speaks about gesture in such a way as to set a limit on the range of visual representation.

If we pursue in further detail the analogy between spectacle and speech as defined by Shakespeare, we find a problematic gap between the conventional and reassuring thesis of reliably communicated meaning on the one hand and the reality of misperception on the other. Shakespeare examines the capacity of gesture to perform the various tasks expected of verbal language—to instruct and delight through figural devices of language that include personification, extended metaphor, synecdoche, and metonymy—only to discover that the readily understood conventions upon which the transmission of meaning depends are potentially deceptive. The rhetoric of visual language has in fact a special capacity to deceive, though spoken language too can be used to mislead. Such are the conclusions, at any rate, that we are invited to derive from Shakespeare's detailed comparisons of painting and poetry in *The Rape of Lucrece* and *Timon of Athens*.

Lucrece's encounter with a painting or tapestry of the Trojan War[73] is for her an intensely painful experience, because she must interpret it in the light of what she has just suffered at the hands of Tarquin. Shakespeare's interest in the difficult process of interpretation is everywhere apparent in his narrator's sympathetic but analytical report of what the painting tells Lucrece and us. The narrator speaks of the work of art as telling, showing, expressing, and ciphering what the artist hopes to convey, while the viewer's task is to observe and interpret these signs. For example, the soldiers in the crowd listening to Nestor's oration bear "signs of rage" in their angry red faces and threatening gestures (l. 1419). In the "art / Of physiognomy" used to portray Ajax and Ulysses, one might behold how "The face of either cipher'd either's heart; / Their face their manners most expressly told" (ll. 1394–97).

In this task of interpreting, the narrator seems at first to rely on a reassuring fixity of meaning between the signifier and the thing signified. Such an assumption of strong correlation between gesture and meaning would appear indeed to be essential to the success of a visual language. The viewer is able to "cipher" the heart, we are told, because the face expressly "tells" about manners. The red face is a predictable "sign" of rage. In similar fashion the narrator relies on a conventional vocabulary of gesture to convey to his viewer the instructive contrast between idealized age and youth: "In great commanders grace and majesty / You might behold, triumphing in their faces; / In youth, quick bearing and dexterity" (ll. 1387–89). Nestor's fabled skill at oratory is recognizable in his every movement as he encourages the Greeks to fight, "Making such sober action with his hand / That it beguil'd attention, charm'd the sight" (ll. 1403–4). The "mild glance" of "sly Ulysses" shows "deep regard and smiling government" (ll. 1399–1400). Conversely, baseness and ignoble bearing take discernible form in those "Pale cowards, marching on with trembling paces, / Which heartless peasants did so well resemble / That one would swear he saw them quake and tremble" (ll. 1391–93). The laboring pioner (digger of mines) is plainly identifiable by his appearance, "Begrim'd with sweat, and smeared all with dust" (l. 1381). These signs are informational about social class and occupation, or expressive of emotion; in either case a one-to-one correspondence establishes the connection between sign and meaning upon which the communication of intent must evidently rest.

One assumption underlying the narrator's hopeful belief in readily understood correlation in meaning is that individuals belong to specific classes or types from whom the viewer expects a conventional sort of behavior. Generals are graceful and majestic, orators skillful in the use of "sober action" with the hand, peasants are "heartless," pioners sweaty and dusty. These conventional signs work like the fixed epithets of poetic language: just as a particular gesture goes hand in hand with a certain social class or age group, fixed epithets yoke generic adjectives to nouns and proper names. The painting shows pioners who are recognizable by their sweaty and dusty complexion; the poem alludes in fixed epithet to "the laboring pioner." Physical details from the painting similarly find their correspondence in the generic adjectives assigned to famous persons: the epithets "sly Ulysses," "grave Nestor," "bold Hector," and "doting Priam" underscore a decorum of types both in Shakespeare's poetic language and in the painting upon which these generalized epithets are based.

Convention also governs the interpretation of emotion through apposite signs: rage is associated with red or pale faces and with threatening gestures, cowardice is linked to trembling. These expressive signs act through a kind of artistic shorthand. Red faces and the appearance of trembling are only the outward and most obvious signs of inner emotion, but in a painting or poem they signal a more complex state of mind, to be imagined through the viewer's or reader's own experience. The eyes are especially revealing: Ajax's eyes seem to roll with "blunt rage and rigor," whereas "sly Ulysses" is known by his "mild glance." The artist can suggest through the shorthand of visible signs a universal human experience such as growing old and careworn: in Hecuba's wrinkled cheeks the artist has "anatomiz'd / Time's ruin, beauty's wrack, and grim care's reign" (ll. 1450–51).

As David Rosand argues, the shorthand devices of synecdoche or metonymy are common in the visual arts, as they are in poetry. By showing only part of his subject and inviting the viewer to imagine the rest, the artist "creates the ideal situation for the beholder's self-projection, for his participation in the living fiction of the image."[74] Drama too must continually resort to synecdoche in its visual images, by allowing a wall to stand for a castle and a few soldiers for an army. *Lucrece*'s narrator is especially aware of synecdoche and its rhetorical function in the painter's depiction of Achilles' spear:

For much imaginary work was there,
Conceit deceitful, so compact, so kind,
That for Achilles' image stood his spear,
Grip'd in an armed hand; himself, behind,
Was left unseen, save to the eye of mind.
    A hand, a foot, a face, a leg, a head,
    Stood for the whole to be imagined.   (ll. 1422–28)

In many ways, then, the narrator seems satisfied with the rhetorical capability and reliability of visual signs. He insists on their power of showing and ciphering—that is, of communicating meaning—and enumerates the conventions of typical gestures by which age, rank, occupation, and temperament are to be discovered. He discovers a rhetoric of visual signs that prominently includes synecdoche and metonymy. The rhetorical analysis of actors' gestures was in fact a commonplace of the Renaissance; actors were often compared to orators, and their way of illustrating or ornamenting speech could be described in the language of rhetoric much as music was analyzed in terms of anaphora, antistrophe, antimetabole, and the like.[75]

All this seeming promise leads to a serious disillusionment. Even the narrator perceives that the "conceit" of synecdoche used to portray Achilles through his spear is "deceitful" (l. 1423), and to Lucrece the painting's apparent certainty of meaning is simply illusory. To her eyes the artist has so well succeeded in making Sinon look smoothly plausible, has labored so successfully with his skill "To hide deceit" and give a "harmless show" to the perjurer, that she is unable to find a correspondence between appearance and inner substance. The discrepancy appalls her because it reminds her of Tarquin, armed "With outward honesty, but yet defil'd / With inward vice." Apart from her personal misfortune, moreover, the problem of illusion presents a challenge to visual art itself. The "signs of truth" in Sinon's "plain face" so mislead Lucrece that she can only conclude "the picture was belied" (ll. 1506–33, 1545–46). The artist has succeeded too well in hiding deceit. Lucrece's experience suggests two fundamental difficulties: first, that art's very skill in creating illusion can be turned against the goal of communicating clear meaning, and second, that the extraordinary power of visual language to move and persuade renders it all the more dangerous when it is used for deception.[76]

In the poem, to be sure, the riddle of illusion is controlled by Shakespeare's verbal use of point of view. We are not deceived about Sinon or Tarquin because the narrator tells us their true character, and the dramatic irony or discrepant awareness enables us to see how deception works on others. In visual terms, nevertheless, the lack of correspondence between form and substance remains disturbing; for it is upon the doctrine of correspondences that so much depends in constructing a language of nonverbal communication. The potential for visual deception is of special concern to the visual artist, whether in the studio or in the theater. Shakespeare poses for himself in this early tragic poem a challenge with which his art, especially his tragic art, will be increasingly concerned.

In a late and bitter play, *Timon of Athens*, Shakespeare returns to a comparison of painting and poetry with the same distressing perception of a gap between conventional theories of visual communication and the realities of misinterpretation and deceit. The Painter and the Poet, who so aptly summarize the so-called *paragone* debate over which of the two gives more valuable service to society,[77] are themselves craven flatterers whose purportedly didactic works are intended to win Timon's patronage. Their conventional instruction is lost on him who stands most in need of art's wise teaching. By the time Shakespeare wrote *Timon*, the *paragone* debate had more or less resulted in a draw; apologists for the visual arts, countering deeply held suspicions of sensuousness and idolatry in art with neoplatonic arguments in praise of sight as man's most noble and spiritual sense, had assured the stature of the artist to the extent that sketching was acknowledged to be a proper pursuit for a gentleman.[78] Shakespeare does not take sides in the debate. He allows the two figures to air Renaissance commonplaces about the relationship between visual and verbal art, then surrounds the two arguments with a despairing context in which the commonplaces appear deficient.

Despite the rivalry of Painter and Poet and the different media in which they work, the two share certain fundamental concepts about art. Both are at least nominally committed to an ethical purpose. The Poet's work is an allegory about the slipperiness of Fortune. The Painter deals in the same language of exemplum: "A thousand moral paintings I can show," he boasts, that will deal with the subject "More pregnantly than words" (1.1.95–97). The aim does not differ; the contention concerns which art form can claim superiority in bringing home to the viewer or reader the truth of the theme proposed. Painting and poetry are also alike in that they deal with personification and extended metaphor; they share a commitment to teaching through illustrations that simultaneously delight. They share too a preference for mythological and traditional subjects, such as a medieval commonplace about Fortune or (in *Lucrece*) the Fall of Troy.

In the contest for expressive eloquence through which to move and persuade, the Poet seems to concede to the Painter a special intensity, a "mental power" that shoots forth from the painted eye and an "imagination" moving so in the painted lip that, in the Poet's words of praise, "To th' dumbness of the gesture / One might interpret" (ll. 33–37). The Painter's visual images are taken in by the observer's eye and impressed upon the memory with a special clarity and speed, thereby "tutoring" nature and rendering the Painter's touches "livelier than life" (ll. 38–41). Even here, however, the Poet's very readiness to praise his rival for the expressive qualities of his art bespeaks a common interest in the forceful eloquence of image, whether visual or verbal. Pictorial art has a special vividness and impact, but the Poet too uses images to move and persuade by means of the *energeia* so much praised in Sir Philip Sydney's *Defence of Poesy*.

The result of a shared commitment to instruction, delight, and persuasion, all expressed in terms of mythological or allegorical subject matter, is that painting and poetry can borrow to a large extent from each other's vocabulary. The Romantic era of Lessing dwelled on the difference between painting's use of figures and color in space and poetry's use of articulate sound in time,[79] but to the Renaissance world, as exemplified in the *paragone* debate of *Timon*, the sister arts were closely related. The Painter and Poet predictably accept as beyond question the famous parodox of Simonides, iterated as we have seen in many iconographic and mythological treatises of the Renaissance, that painting is mute poetry, and poetry a speaking picture.[80] The Poet's way of interpreting the painting of his rival is to note how it can "speak" through silent gesture, expression, and object. The painting is successful, in the Poet's view, because its meaning can be confidently grasped by the discerning interpreter and expressed in moral sententiae. The Poet's best praise for the painting is that its language functions like his own.

Just as the Painter's work succeeds because it is "mute poetry," the Poet's work succeeds because it is a "speaking picture." It too deals in images that move and teach more effectively than do abstract arguments. The poem is displayed for the Painter's approval, as though it were a painting to be examined and interpreted. Its allegorical images are highly visualized: a "high and pleasant hill" upon which the artist has "Feign'd Fortune to be thron'd," the base of the mount filled with all degrees of men laboring up the slope (ll. 68–69), and the like. The poem is dominated by three emblematic objects, "This throne, this [figure of] Fortune, and this hill" (l. 78), all laden with ethical meaning. The Poet's method is to search out images that provide a visual equivalent of his theme: in order to stress the fickleness of Fortune, and the arduousness and danger of seeking her favor, he selects as his dominant images those that suggest climbing and falling, elevation and casting down. Even in its principles of organization the poem resembles Renaissance painting to a degree, for its narrative mode reminds the Painter and us of many Renaissance or medieval paintings in which we simultaneously behold in a single work of art a number of scenes in sequence, to be seen as a whole and yet read in a chronological and sequential way. The *paragone* debate in *Timon* illustrates the conventional linking of the sister arts in Shakespeare's day,[81] though we should plainly be warned by the fact that these truisms are enunciated by such flattering spokesmen.

Like the narrator in *Lucrece*, both Painter and Poet take as their most axiomatic assumption the ability of art to communicate through fixed correspondences connecting signifier and thing signified. This correlation depends on readily understood truisms about human behavior. The Poet's representative figures are quickly grasped because they are types. His flatterers use characteristic gestures, filling the lobbies of Fortune's favorite with "tendance," raining "sacrificial whisperings in his ear," venerating even his stirrup as they help him to his horse, and so on. The aspiring climber is himself generic, one whose person "would be well expressed / In our condition" (ll. 81–87). The Poet, like the Painter, uses appropriate gestures in accordance with a theory of decorum; the expected and soon-grasped correspondences between image and meaning are the key to correct interpretation.

For all these bland assurances of cooperation between the arts and of a common interest in reliable correspondences of meaning, the debate in *Timon* is devastatingly pointless. In context we see that their fine neoplatonic truisms have encouraged the Painter and Poet to bring forth works that are hollow ceremonial forms. Their ability to achieve a "pretty mocking of the life" (l. 38) takes on a double meaning, of imitation and of travesty. Their allegories, warning how "Feign'd Fortune" from her hilltop first beckons and then spurns the aspiring mortal who heeds her siren song, are wholly misinterpreted by Timon. He sees the artists' gifts as tributes to his greatness and as petitions for his bounty, rather than as instructive mirrors of human conduct.[82] We as spectators, to be sure, see the point of the warning, and indeed can use it as an anticipatory structuring device for the play as a whole; as in *Lucrece*, Shakespeare explores the paradox of misinterpretation without surrendering control of his own point of view. Still, in his portrayal of two inferior and self-serving artists, the very conventionality on which reliable interpretation would seem to depend is turned against the enterprise, since convention has become mere artifice. When Shakespeare most wishes to criticize the myth of correspondences, he chooses allegory as the kind of art most given to complacent generalities.

Shakespeare's insistence on the complexity of visual communication, on its seeming promise of clearly perceived meaning and its capacity to misinform, is thus evident in his work both early and late. However much he may have deepened his understanding (and ours) of the dilemma as he continued to write, the problem held his attention in his earliest work. *Titus Andronicus* graphically illustrates his preoccupation at the very start of his career with visual signaling and its limitations. The play has fared ill at the hands of critics, yet has achieved notable success when staged,[83] suggesting that its visual images in the theater are essential to what it has to say. Indeed, the play has responded best to interpretation attuned to its stage picture. Lawrence Danson and Clark Hulse, for instance, see *Titus* as a play about silence, and about the inability of Titus' family to achieve adequate expression for overwhelming emotional needs.[84] Lavinia, bereft of hands and tongue, must find a means of revealing what has happened to her. Her father, conversely, must learn to decipher a new language of action forced on his family by their tragic plight. Only a language of action can begin to express their suffering and provide some measure of revenge.

Viewed in this light, the gruesome stage pictures of dismemberment for which the play has received much adverse criticism are anything but gratuitous. They give visual form to a tragic dilemma of communication. The hands and the tongue are our chief means of speaking to others—through gesture, writing, and speech. How is the mutilated Lavinia, "*her hands cut off, and her tongue cut out*" (2.4.1), to tell her family what she has suffered and from whom? The problem of wordlessness

29

is inherent in Shakespeare's Ovidian source, the tale of Tereus and Procne, and seems to have been an important element in attracting Shakespeare to the story.

Titus and his kinsmen attack the problem of learning a new visual language with assumptions like those in *Lucrece* and *Timon*; they expect to find a correspondence between the "signs and tokens" (l. 5) employed by Lavinia and a perceivable meaning. The language must have its own vocabulary, albeit partly unfamiliar, of blushes, tears, sighs, winks, nods, and the like. Titus' eagerness to master this new language is apparent in his efforts at interpretation. He begs of Lavinia "some sign how I may do thee ease." What then do her mute gestures mean when she rejects her brother Lucius' handkerchief, offered her when she sobs and weeps? Titus is sure he can interpret correctly:

> Mark, Marcus, mark! I understand her signs.
> Had she a tongue to speak, now would she say
> That to her brother which I said to thee:
> His napkin, with his true tears all bewet,
> Can do no service on her sorrowful cheeks.   (3.1.143–147)

Her very incapacity to speak becomes for Titus an opportunity; she is a "map of woe, that thus dost talk in signs" (3.2.12), and her language requires no more than a perspicacity in determining a correlation between sign and meaning:

> I can interpret all her martyr'd signs.
> . . . . .
> Speechless complainer, I will learn thy thought;
> In thy dumb actions will I be as perfect
> As begging hermits in their holy prayers.
> Thou shalt not sigh, nor hold thy stumps to heaven,
> Nor wink, nor nod, nor kneel, nor make a sign,
> But I of these will wrest an alphabet
> And by still practice learn to know thy meaning.   (ll. 36–45)

As they press on, however, Lavinia's kinsmen learn that meaning is not easily discovered. They are repeatedly perplexed. "What means my niece Lavinia by these signs?" asks Marcus as she runs after young Lucius with his books under his arm, one of them being Ovid's *Metamorphoses* (4.1.8). "Why lifts she up her arms in sequence thus?" "Give signs, sweet girl, for here are none but friends" (ll. 37, 63). And in fact

30

Lavinia cannot communicate her awful truth through gestures alone. She must rely on a device that seems both crude and obvious, writing the name of her attackers in the sand with Marcus' staff *"in her mouth"* and guiding it *"with her stumps"* (l. 78). This stage action is itself eloquent testimonial of the limits of nonverbal communication.

All of Titus' family must learn the inadequacy of conventional gesture to express the terrors of their suffering. Titus, deprived of one hand by another mutilation, can no longer tear his hair or beat his breast in a usual icon of grief; he must instead, as Marcus suggests, grotesquely rend his silver hair with one hand only, while gnawing with his teeth the other mangled stump (3.1.260–261). He and Lavinia, lacking their hands, "cannot passionate [their] tenfold grief / With folded arms," in another expected gesture of sorrow. Titus has only one poor right hand "to tyrannize upon my breast," while Lavinia, lacking hands entirely, cannot strike her breast "thus to make it still," and so must "Wound it with sighing" and "kill it with groans" (3.2.6–15). The Andronici are driven to the limits of verbal and visual speech and still find those means of expression too short of what they feel. Titus' seemingly mad behavior is a response to this extremity, for conventional language of gesture or word no longer satisfies. Although he concedes the truth of his brother's observation that "Now is a time to storm," Titus laughs rather than weeps; his laughter "fits not with this hour" (3.1.263–265) and is thus expressive of a profound sense of dislocation that ordinary grief cannot remedy.

Because no conventional language of word or gesture seems able to convey the enormity of the family's tragic experience, Titus is propelled toward the shocking visual devices that constitute the play's catastrophe: Titus with his one good hand cutting the throats of Chiron and Demetrius, "Whiles that Lavinia 'tween her stumps doth hold / The basin that receives [their] guilty blood" (5.2.182–183); Titus as cook serving to Tamora the blood and ground-up bones of her sons baked in a pastry; and the rapid series of stabbings in which Lavinia, Tamora, Titus, and Saturninus fall. When the civilized restraints of verbal and visual discourse fail, the revenger resorts to action that is increasingly unexpected and savage. As D. J. Palmer observes, the extremities of horror and suffering in *Titus Andronicus* "seem to stretch the capacities of art to give them adequate embodiment and expression."[85] Shakespeare appears to be testing the limits of his resources, both poetic and dramaturgic, in this early play. Wordless communication is a dire necessity forced on the Andronici by the ravages they have endured; it is also imperfect, crude, violent, distressingly inadequate. Words and gestures fail in different ways, but the failure of gesture is here the more distressing, because to the Andronici it cannot provide a substitute for speech as they had once hoped; instead it too comes to represent a total breakdown of communication and a resort to simple destructiveness. The wanton catastrophe of the play is by its very crudeness and non-verbalized antagonisms a means of articulating "unspeakable woes."[86]

Shakespeare's expectations from a theatrical language of gesture are paradoxically hopeful and skeptical. We should not minimize the attractions for him of traditional theories of correspondence. Like spoken language, the language of gesture seems at first to depend on a correlation between appearance and identity of inner substance. Correct interpretation requires, or would seem to require, a series of understood conventions through which signs are joined to what they signify. Age, social class, rank, function, and attitude should reveal themselves through characteristic gestures, costumes, expressions, or speeches. Just as a decorum of type presumably enables poetry to speak in fixed epithets, gestures communicate through expected and plausible attributes. In the relative simplicity of this idealized model we can see how the communicative process insists on convention as a means of ensuring that the artist's or poet's intent will be correctly perceived. The shorthand of synecdoche enables the dramatic artist, like the poet, to expand the thing represented through appeal to the viewer's imagination. The devices of gesture are rhetorical devices, appropriate to the orator as to the actor.

Still, gesture's very eloquence is such that it has a special power to misrepresent through illusion. Moreover, the conventions upon which a theory of correspondences rests emphasize the typical in human behavior to such an extent that signs appear doomed to trivial effect. The allegories and traditional symbols thus manufactured become the vapid playthings of sycophants and poetasters. Burdened with such a critical failure, bereft of power to express the real horrors of which humanity is capable, conventional gesture retires in favor of action that is dislocated, idiosyncratic, and misunderstood.

At every point in Shakespeare's career, in every genre, his characters express both the need for a reliable language of visual signs and a sad awareness of its potential for distortion. Characters whom we like, even those who are obliged for a time to rely on visual duplicity, are instinctively drawn to the notion of correspondences; virtue ought to be recognizable on its face, and appearance ought to be an instantaneously recognizable index to inward emotional state or to identity. Archbishop Scroop in *Richard II*, for example, explains his sorrowful looks to the King by appealing to a correspondence in nature itself as the basis for postulating a correspondence between his own feelings and his outward expression: "Men judge by the complexion of the sky / The state and inclination of the day. / So may you by my dull and heavy eye" (3.2.194–196). Yet what are we to make of such conventional interpretation of signs in a play that chronicles the deposition of a lawful king and that repeatedly mocks Richard's rhetorical question, "Is not the king's name twenty thousand names?" (l. 85). Another weak king, Henry VI, can assert the doctrine of correspondences in his interpretation of Duke Humphrey's countenance—"in thy face I see / The map of honor, truth, and loyalty" (*2 Henry VI*, 3.1.202–203)—but what avails this sentiment to a king who is repeatedly duped and who allows Humphrey's enemies to prevail against him?

Shakespeare's exploration of neoplatonic assumptions about correspondences leads him to the heart of the problem. Even if one allows vision the primacy over spoken language to which neoplatonism is committed, vision remains capable of error. Outward beauty ought to signify virtue within, according to neoplatonic theory, but in fact it often fails to do so. Viola in *Twelfth Night* says as much when she commends the "fair behavior" of the captain who has helped her ashore at Illyria. She is persuaded in this case that the captain truly has "a mind that suits / With this thy fair and outward character," even though she is wisely aware of the hazards of interpretation by means of outward show: "nature with a beauteous wall / Doth oft close in pollution" (1.2.47–51).

The reading of visible signs is uncertain too because we are such fallible readers. The marks of Richard III's villainy seem unambiguous enough—the hunched back and the teeth with which he was born, as Henry VI says, "To signify thou cam'st to bite the world" (*3 Henry VI*, 5.6.54). Still, Richard is able to deceive his victims into believing him a loyal brother, a passionate wooer, a pious recluse, and the like. One difficulty is that ugliness need not always signify villainousness, despite the neoplatonic notion of correspondences. Hubert in *King John* may seem at first to be what the King accuses him of being, "A fellow by the hand of nature mark'd, / Quoted, and sign'd to do a deed of shame," simply because of his villainous appearance (4.2.221–222), but young Arthur is able to soften Hubert's heart with love and appeals to sympathy.

Shakespeare's stance on the neoplatonic equation of beauty and goodness is consistent with his observations on the language of signs in the theater. The optimistic view, based on the idea of correspondence between true being and its visible form and including the neoplatonic equation of beauty and goodness, validates the process of communication through which we can hope to recognize characters' identities, discover states of mind, and thus begin to understand what the author wishes to convey to us through instruction, delight, and the persuasive eloquence of visual forms. The negative view casts doubt on the very enterprise of communication, for it finds in deception and misinterpretation a sign of fallen human nature and hence a strong possibility that the speaker's intent will not be correctly perceived. It is this dichotomy of hope and disillusionment that we must study further in detailing Shakespeare's language of gesture for the stage.

II
The Language of Costume and Hand Properties

Montjoy You know me by my habit.
King Henry Well then I know thee. What shall I know of thee?

—*Henry V*

COSTUME and other appurtenances worn or carried by actors are more important to theater than their external nature might suggest. As with all other theatrical signs, stage costuming takes on a special meaning in the illusionistic world of the theater; a costume is "clothing which means something."[1] Specialized costume, as Lord Raglan observes, is as old as ritual itself, so much so that ritual cannot be said to exist without it: "nowhere in the world is anyone allowed to take a prominent part in any ritual unless he is dressed for it."[2] In the ancient history of costume we can discern the very origins of drama in magical rite, for the wearing of animal skins and masks was one of the ways that early man attempted to induce game to come within range of the hunter.[3] "Sympathetic magic" of this sort was an early form of mimesis in the dances that primitive man regarded as indispensable to all rites of passage.[4]

The religious drama that emerged from ritual in Attic Greece and in medieval Europe was, in James Laver's phrase, a "blend of magic and decoration,"[5] retaining the power and mystery of incantation while moving toward the richly decorative style that we associate with later and more self-consciously sophisticated art. The visual decor of that religious drama, as of all religious art, was deeply symbolic. Costuming and other visual effects in such drama were by their nature ancient and traditional, calling upon associations that a religious audience might not always have recognized but that were nonetheless inherent in the celebratory and worshipful occasion uniting audience and performers. Renaissance drama remained meaningfully in touch with this symbolic tradition of costuming although, as we shall see, the ordered and hierarchical world that this tradition represented came into conflict with an unstructured and saturnalian world represented by a very different sort of costuming, that of antiritual.

Costuming on the Renaissance stage did indubitably lend itself to symbolism and to decorative splendor. The visual sumptuousness was important because the theater building itself, although pictorially impressive, provided no scenery. Shakespeare's acting company, like other Elizabethan acting companies, spent lavishly on costumes, both esoteric and familiar. Henry Wotton's account in 1613 of the play called *All Is True* about the reign of Henry VIII (presumably Shakespeare's play) notes the "extraordinary circumstances of pomp and majesty, even to the matting of the stage; the Knights of the Order with their Georges and garters, the Guards with their embroidered coats," and the like.[6] Philip Henslowe's *Diary* is a rich source of information on elaborate costumes including such items as "A scarlett cloke with ii brode gould Laces: with gould buttens of the sam downe the sids," "A crimosin Robe strypt with gould fact with ermin," "A velvett dublett cut diamond lact with gould lace and spang," and many more.[7] The actors evidently made use of fine apparel that had originally belonged to aristocrats and gentry. According to Thomas Platter, writing in 1599, it was "the English usage for eminent lords or Knights at their decease to bequeath and leave almost the best of their clothes to their serving men, which it is unseemly for the latter to wear, so that they offer them for sale for a small sum to the actors."[8] The emphasis on contemporary dress in the theater was not simply a matter of style, but of actual source. This circumstance engendered a remarkable sense of closeness among the Elizabethan theater and the world of London and the court to which the acting companies addressed their plays.

The relation of costuming in Shakespeare's plays to this exterior contemporary world, as in the plays of other Elizabethan playwrights, was twofold: costuming symbolized an ordered universe of hierarchical rank and moral choice between good and evil, but it also celebrated a festive world of release from constraints. The first aspect emphasized didactic meaning and convention, using costume and hand properties to indicate status or role, and changes of costume and hand properties to signify alteration of status or role in the stages of a spiritual journey.

The Language of Costume and Hand Properties

The second aspect emphasized narrative event, theatrical illusion, metamorphosis, and entertainment, using change of costume or hand properties as a device of disguise or plot complication. Costume was the primary visual embodiment of these divergent impulses.

Overt allegorical costuming was rare on the Elizabethan stage; Shakespeare's *"Rumor, painted full of tongues"* in the Induction to *2 Henry IV* reminds us by its exceptional character of the scarcity of morality types elsewhere. Nevertheless, the contemporary and familiar stage dress of Shakespeare's plays did more than mirror the social world from which it was derived. By stressing visible distinctions in rank at a time when sumptuary laws, though still recognized, were in a decline, Shakespearean costuming invoked a hierarchical system of order and degree. Traditional associations of certain trades with characteristic tools bespoke a world in which persons were defined less by their individuality than by their social status.[9] Typing according to visible signs of rank and function had been a staple of medieval and Tudor drama, and its continued employment on the Elizabethan stage emphasized ideas of decorum and of identification of role through conventional signs. Audiences were often able to recognize a character's status and function, in Shakespeare's plays and in those of his contemporaries, by appearance alone. G. K. Hunter lists a number of stage types such as midwife, nurse, ambassador, counselor, senator, Turk, master of a ship, herald, sergeant, devil, nymph, and Irishman for whom the dramatic context seems to require visual identification on stage before the action can be comprehended.[10] Inventories of costumes from Henslowe's *Diary* and similar sources indicate a recognizable convention of costuming for Jew, Spaniard, Italian, Amazon, huntsman, ghost, invisible character, and others.[11]

At the same time, use of contemporary costume on Shakespeare's stage encouraged quite a different theatrical world—one of illusion. The actors, even when sumptuously dressed in the garments of hierarchy and degree, played at social roles outside the everyday sphere of most Londoners, and thus enacted a vicarious escape from vocation.[12] The actors' escape into a world of royal splendor and romance, through the medium of dress and hand-held possessions, engendered a recurrent carnival atmosphere in the theater wherein class differences were minimized; theatergoing was holiday.[13] If such a release from constraint was evident even in the use of hierarchical dress, it was much more so in Shakespearean costuming of disguise and theatrical metamorphosis.

Action Is Eloquence

Victor Turner provides anthropological perspective on this contrast between costuming of the hierarchical system and costuming of the holiday world.[14] Turner's idea of a liminal world of communitas (referred to in Chapter I), a transitional and ambiguous world in any rite of passage when the novices have been separated from their previous status as children or unmarried persons and have not yet been reassimilated into their new status as young adults or married persons, has important consequences for costuming. Temporarily lacking position in the kinship system and set apart from the norms and rituals of their usual stable existence, the novices are thrown together in an egalitarian comradeship that expresses itself in nakedness or uniformity of clothing. All sartorial differentiations by sex or social rank are minimized. Disregard for personal appearance is common.

Yet since they are undergoing a ritual process, the novices cannot be said to lack costume. Theirs is instead a costume of nonstatus and antistructure, and it has significant affinities to costuming in Shakespeare's world of release from constraint. Disguise, bisexuality, role reversal, and invisibility are all qualities connected with the liminal world, in Shakespeare as in Turner's social rituals. The undifferentiated garments of the forest dwellers in *As You Like It*, nakedness and disavowal of ceremonious costume in *King Lear*, young women dressed as young men in the comedies, the invisibility of the fairies in *A Midsummer Night's Dream*, veiling, masking—all belong to a liminal and festive antistructure. So too does the liminal ritual, reflected in *Lear* and elsewhere, of humbling the mighty through revilings and divestings, and of elevating for a time the underprivileged. Turner gives us two radically different costuming modes, both related to ritual: the one hierarchical, the other offering a reversal and a profound critique of the first.

Historically considered in Renaissance terms, the dual function of costuming can be traced to a duality of costuming practice in Tudor drama. On the one hand, the morality play tends to stress symbolic and hierarchical aspects of order. The world of antistructure is incorporated, to be sure, in Mankind's escapades with his roistering tavern-mates and Vicelike companions, but a didactic assertion of order remains paramount. Because instructional meaning must remain unambiguous, costuming signals are self-proclaiming and sharply differentiated. As Barbara Mowat observes,[15] the spectators are led through the fiction or "game" of the drama toward the "earnest" lying beyond it and clearly

38

perceive changes of garment as signals of change in the spiritual life of the protagonist. Villains may of course disguise themselves as virtuous, but spectators can never fail to equate each sign with its corresponding spiritual reality. Interpretation is therefore sure, and the entire spectacle is profoundly supportive of the idea of correspondences in the cosmos as in the social and moral order.

Neoclassic drama of the Inns of Court and indoor courtly or humanist performance, on the other hand, is more comfortable in the liminal world of dramatic illusion. Costume change and disguise are often the elements of a romantic plot, rich in discrepant awareness. If, following Mowat's suggestion, we contrast John Redford's *Wit and Science* (1539–47) with the Inns of Court's sprightly version of Ariosto's *I Suppositi* (translated by George Gascoigne as *Supposes* in 1566), we see in the first play a seeker of knowledge who puts aside his scholar's robe in a symbol of self-betrayal until at length he is penitentially restored to his gown of knowledge, and in the second play a young wooer who adopts and then doffs a scholar's robe in the interests of sexual intrigue and out-witting of parents. Although the visual shape of the two plays is similar, one invites us to ask "What does it mean?" whereas the other entertains us with "What will happen next?"[16] Both plays use costume change to signal alterations in the status of the protagonist, but the emphasis in *Supposes* is on holiday and inversion. Our sympathies are directed toward the young in their courtship and their defiance of authority. They are most interesting to us in their transitional status; its uncertainties and even dangers entertain us, and the lovers' arrival at a structural reso-lution, though necessary for dramatic closure, is more a framework than the raison d'être of the play. Costume accordingly emphasizes inverted status, ambiguity, and surprise. Interpretation is not didac-tically motivated. The play abounds in visual deception, putting the-atrical entertainment and illusion ahead of certainty of meaning.

This contrast should not be overstated. Popular and courtly drama borrowed significantly from each other, just as the Elizabethan age made a concerted attempt to reconcile the aims of symbolism and representation. We see a blending of the two traditions of costuming in the drama of Lyly, Marlowe, and Greene,[17] and it was to this mixed tradition that Shakespeare was heir. Nevertheless, its dual character did provide him with two contrastive modes of costuming, one em-phasizing the visually symbolic and the other the illusory.

A major consequence for Shakespeare of the divergence between

moral symbolism and neoclassic illusionism is that his costuming expresses potentially contrasting views of character and identity. On the
one hand, the hierarchical concept of decorum forcefully declares that
characters are to be vested according to social function, status, age,
and sex; it is fitting that old men dress soberly and that carpenters carry
woodworking tools. Change of costume signals a change of role or place
in the social order, and with such a change of role comes a change of
identity. The moral consequences of error often take the form of a
sartorial lowering of status; the protagonist, like the Mankind figure of
the morality play, changes garments to express a fall that may lead
through repentance to eventual acceptance of self and a resumption of
the outward form that originally signified the character's identity and
role. The change thus portrayed is often distressingly real. Even when
other characters in the play disguise themselves, like the tempting Vice
of the morality play, the moral consequences and spiritual transformations resulting from such deception are profound.

In the illusionistic tradition of costuming, on the other hand, the
adoption of disguise and eventual revelation of self are apt to indicate
a journey of mistaken appearances in which the disguising figure, either
through choice or through circumstances beyond his or her control, is
misunderstood. Here the throwing off of disguise is not a regenerative
act stemming from within but a restoration of appearances to their
original; servants and masters once more dress in their proper garb and
young women are discovered to be who they really are and not the
young men they have impersonated or the false women they have been
accused of being. Hand properties such as rings and jewels can serve
functions like those of costuming, by signifying change of status or
revelation of true identity.

We can examine Shakespeare's divergent pattern of costume in the
way he uses a richly detailed visual vocabulary of social distinctions.
Both Elizabethan custom and contemporary staging provided him, as
we have seen, with an extensive array of conventions signaling gra-
dations in order and degree. Shakespeare's own plays make impressive
use of these signs. Regalia, badges of office, and elaborate garb are
everywhere used to identify royal persons or aristocrats and to distinguish them from untitled gentlemen, members of the professions, and
commoners. Sizable retinues escorting figures of importance augment
the visual impression of exalted rank. In pictorial terms Shakespeare's
staging idiom of opulence and decoration sums up a long tradition of

medieval and Tudor drama, as well as art, in which visual splendor is a sign of rank.[18]

Shakespeare exploits the conventional thrust of this received tradition. Outwardly at least, the visual signs of order and degree appeal to ideas of decorum and type. Signals are unmistakable and are quickly read by onstage observers. When two gentlemanly bystanders in *Henry VIII* observe certain countesses marching in the coronation procession of Anne Bullen, for example, they need only take notice that the marchers have on "*plain circlets of gold without flowers*" to identify the wearers' rank; the women are countesses because, as one gentleman explains to his companion, "Their coronets say so" (4.1.36–54). No words could speak more clearly the salient fact of rank. Such unambiguous interpretation bespeaks a symbolic language of costume in which correspondence between sign and meaning is paramount. Identity is defined by role and status.

Yet Shakespeare virtually never stages royal pageantry without qualifying commentary. Spectacle is to him a primary sign of structure, and as such it identifies only the normative world to which the opposite realm of the dispossessed offers an essential perspective. Surely it is no coincidence that *Henry VIII*, a play preeminently defined in visual terms by ceremonial pageantry, is also a play of ceaseless political rise and fall, of vestiture and divestiture, of public greatness and private obscurity. The order of coronation for Anne Bullen makes us especially conscious of rank with its identifying regalia; the Lord Chancellor marches "*with purse and mace before him*," the Earl of Surrey with a "*rod of silver with the dove*," and so on in an extraordinarily elaborate stage direction. A major point of such splendor is to make visual demonstration of a worldly grandeur that must in time suffer an eclipse.

The falls of Wolsey and the rest are signaled by a stripping away of the regalia that have defined a brief elevation to power. Wolsey, outmaneuvered by his own cleverness and brought to bay by his enemies, is at last forced "To render up the great seal presently" (3.2.229). Earlier, his entrance into the trial of Queen Katharine has been impressively heralded by "*a Gentleman bearing the purse, with the great seal, and a cardinal's hat*" (2.4.0). In his farewell to Cromwell and to the world, he professes that "My robe, / And my integrity to heaven, is all / I dare now call mine own" (3.2.452–454). Queen Katharine's most sumptuous procession is, ironically, to her divorce trial. We last see her plainly lodged and poorly attended, near death, her spirit fixed on a vision of six "personages," whose white robes, garlands of bays, and palm branches employ the iconography of an entrance into heaven rather than into the world of affairs. The "*spare garland*" they hold over her head replaces the royal crown of which she has been bereft (4.2.82). A similar divestiture through the stripping away of identifying regalia is to be found in *2 Henry VI*, where Duke Humphrey's prophetic dream that "this staff, mine office-badge in court, / Was broke in twain" (1.2.25–26) is brought to fulfillment by his enemies' connivance. In *Richard II* and *1 Henry IV* we are reminded several times how the Earl of Worcester broke his staff of office in King Richard's time to signify his resignation as High Steward.[19]

Shakespeare visually presents the Fall of Princes, that highly iconic tradition of the *Myrroure for Magistrates*, through symbolic stage actions that simultaneously evoke conventions of splendor and warnings of worldly instability. Richard II nicely captures the polarity when he learns that he must yield "the name of King" to Bolingbroke; Richard will "give [his] jewels for a set of beads" and his "gay apparel for an almsman's gown" (*Richard II*, 3.3.146–149). In the anticeremonial of Richard's deposition, so daring in its inversion of structure that it had to be excised from the early quartos, Richard particularizes his divestiture: he gives "this heavy weight" of the crown from off his head and the "unwieldy scepter" from his hand, washing away with his tears all sacred balm and forswearing all "pomp and majesty" (4.1.205–212). The scene is a fitting reversal for a play that commences with the colorful pageantry of royal judgment and trial by combat, only to end with the irregular funeral procession of a king who has been meanly kept in a prison and murdered.

The antithetical balance in Richard's divestiture gives visual definition to a contest that is everywhere apparent in Shakespeare's costuming distinctions between the privileged world of court and the outcast world of those who have fallen or fled. Courtly finery is a sign of rank, but it is also a token of pride that must be brought low. Eleanor of Gloucester in *2 Henry VI* "sweeps it through the court with troops of ladies, / More like an empress than Duke Humphrey's wife," and the "duke's revenues" on her back are a sure indication of the threat she poses to her husband's position (1.3.77–80). Such outlandish fashions are frequently denounced in Shakespeare for their continental origin and their extravagant costs, as in John of Gaunt's anger at the "Report of fashions in proud Italy" to which Richard II and his sybaritic favorites pay too great attention; in Mercutio's humorous lectures against Frenchified "fashion-mongers" who "stand so much on the new form that they cannot sit at ease on the old bench"; in the Duke of Norfolk's characterization of the French at the meeting of Henry VIII and Francis I as "All clinquant, all in gold, like heathen gods"; in Portia's satire of her unwelcome suitors' attire as from every part of Europe; and so on.[20] These patriotic and traditional attitudes, common also in medieval and Tudor drama,[21] do not gainsay that the perquisites of rank have a justifiable place in Elizabethan society, but they do equate those signs with a social elite that is too often corrupt and unfeeling.

Conversely, the unstructured world of exile subjects persons of rank to costuming differences that are arrestingly visible on stage. Duke Senior's deeply felt address to his "co-mates and brothers in exile" in *As You Like It* needs to be savored in the context of the scene's opening stage direction: the Duke and his lords enter *"like foresters"* (2.1.1), in sharp contrast to the pomp and circumstance attending Duke Frederick in alternating scenes at the palace. In their appearance in Act 2 scene 7, Duke Senior and his lords appear *"like outlaws"*; the term is almost equivalent to *"like foresters"* and classes them in terms of sumptuary regulations with the outlaws of *The Two Gentlemen of Verona* or the foresters in *Love's Labor's Lost* and *3 Henry VI*.[22] Not only are the Duke and his men visibly of lower rank than their counterparts at court; their uniformity of dress, their refusal to observe distinctions, and their professed disregard for appearances all show them to be inhabitants of the undifferentiated and egalitarian world of communitas. Duke Senior's expected resumption of his ducal robes at the end of the play is no less a sign of the restored harmony that characterizes aggregation (in van Gennep's term) or a return to a revivified hierarchical structure.

Casual dress or partial undress is sufficiently unusual for figures of importance that it becomes pronouncedly marked as a dramatic gesture. Since all ranks seldom appear bareheaded on the Elizabethan stage,[23] indoors as well as outdoors, the absence of crown or coronet for a person of rank is especially symptomatic of dislocation. When Lear runs "unbonneted" in the storm (*King Lear*, 3.1.14), the fact is deplored by his supporters as self-evident proof of his radically lowered status and mental imbalance. Hamlet, we are told, wears "No hat upon his head" when he visits Ophelia's apartments in visible distress and is immediately taken to be mad, as he intends (*Hamlet*, 2.1.76).[24] Crowns can be wrongly appropriated, as well. The visible sign of Claudius' mortal offense against old King Hamlet is that the younger brother "Now wears his crown" (*Hamlet*, 1.5.41). Edward IV, in *3 Henry VI*, is urged by his brother Richard to "tear the crown from the usurper's head," that is, from the head of Henry VI (1.1.114), in a gesture of civil conflict that anticipates the literal physical grappling for the crown between Richard II and Henry Bolingbroke in Richard's scene of deposition (*Richard II*, 4.1.182). The crown accompanies King Henry IV even when he is abed and dying; its removal from his pillow by Prince Hal visibly expresses the transition of power and the troubled circumstances under which the change of leadership occurs (*2 Henry IV*, 4.5).

Garments other than crowns can also show the unstructured implications of informal dress. The ailing Henry IV in *2 Henry IV* enters "*in his nightgown, alone,*" to bewail in soliloquy the troubles of a monarch; the unusual character of his dress emphasizes the lateness of the night through which he is watching and the solitary burden of his kingship (3.1).[25] Julius Caesar appears during the terrible storm preceding the assassination "*in his nightgown*" (*Julius Caesar*, 2.2), and in the previous scene Portia chides her husband Brutus for walking "unbraced" in his orchard in the raw cold morning (2.1.262). The parallel circumstances of these two great counterparts remind us that we see them thus at home, in surroundings of domestic intimacy. After the murder of Duncan in *Macbeth*, in another disrupted domestic setting, those who are rudely aroused in their nightwear to learn of their King's death are bidden to "put on manly readiness / And meet i' th' hall together" (2.3.134–135). The murderer himself wears a nightgown; his motive is to suggest that he too has been caught unprepared by the frightful irregularity of the event, but manifestly the disruption of orderly appearances has more far-reaching connotations.

The size and sartorial splendor of royal parties are indexes not merely of status but of reduced or suddenly altered circumstances. From Gonzalo's remarks in *The Tempest*, for example, we gather that the garments worn by Alonso's party are those they took with them to a royal wedding in Africa, and that this ceremonial attire has been miraculously unspoiled by salt water (2.1.64–73). The wearers are decidedly overdressed for the desert island on which they have been cast. The striking dissimilarity between their appearance and that of Prospero's bizarre entourage is enhanced by the considerable size of Alonso's train, for it includes not only Gonzalo, Adrian, and Francisco, who together with Antonio and Sebastian are called "lords," but also the unspecified "*oth-*

ers" and *"etc."* referred to in the Folio stage directions (2.1, 3.3). Conversely, when Prince Florizel, in *The Winter's Tale*, shows up at Leontes' court in Sicilia with "But few" in his train, "And those but mean," the King knows that something is amiss, and Florizel is driven to cover the gross irregularity with a lie (5.1.92–93). Octavius is affronted when his sister comes to him from her negligent husband, Antony, with an inadequate train. "You are come / A market-maid to Rome," he protests with some exaggeration, since she in fact enters *"with her train"* (*Antony and Cleopatra*, 3.6.38–51).

Livery or other identifying marks of important households are especially valuable in the theater as a means of distinguishing factions in a dispute or occupants of contrasting dramatic worlds. The servingmen of the feuding Duke of Gloucester and Bishop of Winchester in *1 Henry VI* face one another at the Tower of London in the blue coats and tawny coats appropriate to their distinct functions as servants to a nobleman and servants to a prelate of the church (1.3). The conflict between King Lear and his elder daughters centers on the size of his retinue to be sustained in the daughters' households; the antagonism between Kent and Oswald is sharpened by the perception that one is recognizably in the service of Lear, the other of Goneril. The visual contrast between Egypt and Rome in *Antony and Cleopatra* is less to be found in the protagonists than in their followers, for Cleopatra is accompanied by a large retinue of women, soothsayers, *"Eunuchs fanning her,"* and other exotic members of *"the train"* (1.1.10), whereas Antony, like Octavius and Pompey, is attended by soldiers, staff officers, lieutenants, and military associates. Liveried costume is thus rich in information not merely about identity but about wavering loyalties, changing affiliations, declines or elevations in fortune, and other matters of dramatic conflict.

Like aristocrats, persons of comfortable wealth or professional status appear on Shakespeare's stage in the contrasting garb of structured and unstructured worlds, but the terms of the polarity are different. Costume of social respectability is especially normative and unmarked in Shakespeare's theater; doublet and hose, cloaks, swords, and the like are presumably much in use and need no comment. When notice is taken, on the other hand, it usually points to inversion: young women disguised as men, masters exchanging places with servants, and young gentlemen passing themselves off as schoolmasters.

Because respectable attire normally connotes a middle social position, wealth, professional accomplishment, and the like, it naturally invites parody of its self-seriousness in the holiday world of saturnalian escape. This kind of inversion is eminently suited to comedy; the graver falls from fortune characteristic of aristocratic protagonists in the world of tragedy yield here to transformations that are comically irreverent. Whenever these transformations occur, they hold respectability and position up to the consideration that they are only illusory, like costume itself. Such costuming inversion is therefore inclined to be metadramatic, calling attention to the theatrical metaphor. It belongs to the liminal world above all in its delight in paradox, substitution of foolishness for sagacity, confusions of social rank, and so on. It upends kinship rights and obligations, reverses distinctions of sex, temporarily bestows property on the dispossessed, misappropriates systems of nomenclature, and mocks pride of position.

The transformations in *The Taming of the Shrew*, for example, capitalize on the extent to which clothes can make or unmake a gentleman. This cheerful mocking of respectability is especially marked in the plot of Bianca and her wooers, taken from Gascoigne's translation of Ariosto's *I Suppositi* where, as we have seen, a neoclassic emphasis on theatrical illusion lends itself to inversion. The bourgeois society of Padua, where appearances are everything and where eligible daughters are auctioned off to the highest bidder, invites exploitation by those who are clever enough to manipulate its outward forms. Accordingly, when Lucentio's "color'd hat and cloak" adorn his servant Tranio, this "bravery" is enough to signify that the new and supposed Lucentio is to be obeyed by his fellow servants and is to be accepted as a plausible wooer for Bianca. The part of Tranio invites parody of respectable mannerisms on the part of the actor. No less absurdly, Lucentio is able to disguise himself as a schoolmaster merely by acquiring *"the habit of a mean man"* and a "small packet of Greek and Latin books," while Hortensio passes for a musician simply because he carries (or, on one occasion, wears wrapped around his head) a musical instrument. In the plot of Petruchio and Kate, concern with fashion is also satirized; much of Kate's "taming" takes the form of disciplining her self-indulgent appetite for "ruffs and cuffs and farthingales and things," scarves, fans, beads, and other such "knav'ry" (4.3.55–58). She has come to know herself when she can throw her own cap underfoot as a gesture of submission to her husband's authority.

All theater relies on games of illusion, of course, but the joke in *The*

Taming of the Shrew is turned against everything that respectable attire comes to represent. Not surprisingly, the comic denouement requires the use of a Pedant, recognizable as "a mercatante, or a pedant, / I know not what; but formal in apparel, / In gait and countenance surely like a father" (4.2.63–64), who is foisted upon the credulous and status-conscious citizens of Padua as Vincentio of Pisa, father to Lucentio. Vincentio himself, proclaimed by his habit to be "a sober ancient gentleman," is the spokesman at last for a sane perception of true rank. His vigilant eye is required to expose Tranio as no more than a servant dressed in "A silken doublet, a velvet hose, a scarlet cloak, and a copatain [high-crowned] hat" (5.1.61–69). His dignity ushers in a return to a normal state in which a gentleman can in fact be identified by what he wears; but throughout most of the play, including the frame story of the beggar Christophero Sly turned lord for a day, the inversions of attire subject mercantile and gentlemanly respectability to the comic irreverence that it too often deserves.

These comic strictures against respectability are partly neoclassic in origin, to be sure, and perhaps need to be qualified with the perspective of a play like *The Merry Wives of Windsor*. The costumes and properties of this play, while resolutely bourgeois, are more endearingly presented. Of course the comfortable materialism is there, not only in the visible wealth of the Ford household but in incidental mention of "chimney" and of "press, coffer, chest, trunk, well, vault" (4.2.47–54). Still, it is the intruder into this world who is more the *alazon*, or impostor, than those who typify the community and its mode of dress.[26] Falstaff's attempt to seduce Mistress Ford by offering her "the ship-tire, the tire-valiant, or any tire of Venetian admittance," the "semicircled farthingale," and other such items of latest fashion, fails because she is satisfied with her present life. Her contentment is summed up in her comfortably bourgeois look; she will settle for "A plain kerchief, Sir John; my brows become nothing else" (3.3.49–57). Mistress Ford's appearance on stage, plainly in accord with this view on proper attire, thus defines not merely her social class but, more important, her attitude toward her domestic life. The intruder Falstaff is appropriately punished for his scorn of bourgeois domesticity: he is stuffed into a buck basket used for laundry, disguised as a woman of the neighborhood in "thrumm'd hat," muffler, kerchief, gown, and the like, and tricked into playing the part of scapegoat in a fairy mock ritual of purification. Thereby does the domestic world of Windsor gain its revenge.

Action Is Eloquence

We encounter a more complacent world of bourgeois comfort in *Romeo and Juliet*, where Capulet, head of a dignified and ancient household, is continually bossing servants "*with napkins*" who are to do away "with the joint-stools, remove the court-cupboard, look to the plate" (1.5.1–7), or is directing the efforts of three or four servingmen "*with spits and logs, and baskets*" who are to assist at the festivities for Juliet's wedding (4.4.13). These bustlings, ironically misdirected, serve chiefly to define the structured social order of kinship obligations and property rights from which the young lovers flee into the ambiguous nighttime world of mutuality ("I have night's cloak to hide me from their eyes") and the abandonment of systems of nomenclature ("What's in a name?") so characteristic of liminality. Capulet is compassionately viewed by Shakespeare as well-meaning if choleric, but his appurtenances and visible wealth inevitably cast him in a blocking role.

Women in Shakespeare have a special propensity for the liminal world by virtue of their powerlessness, their humility, their silence, unselfishness, obedience, acceptance, perceptiveness, and simplicity— all qualities demanded of the novice in the transitional state of rites of passage.[27] Not all women behave thus, of course, but the expectation of such a role enables women to serve in Shakespeare's plays as especially discerning critics of the predominantly male world of order and rank. Women assume disguise frequently in Shakespeare and, because their disguises often comprise male attire, the incongruity of manner and appearance offers refreshing insight into the pretentions of gentlemanliness. Rosalind in *As You Like It* appears "caparison'd like a man," yet lacks "a doublet and hose in [her] disposition" (3.2.191–199). Imogen in *Cymbeline* adopts the mannish swagger that belongs to "doublet, hat, hose, all / That answer to them" (3.4.165–171); but she, like Viola in *Twelfth Night*, must timorously take up the swords and rapiers that young gentlemen brandish at one another. When Portia in *The Merchant of Venice* descends from her mountain retreat at Belmont into the competitive legalistic masculine world of Venice, her lawyer's gown and imposing sheaf of documents enable her not merely to pass for a learned young man but to shame with her pert mimicry the mercantile hard bargaining for which Venice is legendary. Young women in disguise as men are adept at puncturing the illusion of male sobriety and competition. Rosalind as Ganymede and Viola as Cesario instruct their men, providing them a fresh perspective available only by means of

48

such outsiders' precepts, whereas men disguised as women (notably Falstaff in *Merry Wives*) are merely intruders.

In their private lives as well, women visually define through their clothes and hand properties a world alternative to that of men. Through clothes women express their attitudes of acceptance or defiance toward male authority, their longing after adventure, or their dissatisfaction with domesticity. They are the managers of large households and are ordinarily in charge of the keys; when keys are in the custody of men, such as Shylock or Master Ford,[28] the suggestion is one of mistrust or jealousy. To a remarkable extent women's domestic roles center on the making, wearing, and sewing of clothes or embroidery. The use of needle and thread helps portray their largely passive role (especially in the history plays), their vulnerability to male stratagems, their perseverance, their reliance on one another.

Sometimes the business of needle and thread is reported rather than directly staged, as in *Pericles*, where we learn that Marina earns her livelihood even among thieves and bawds "with her neele" (5, Chorus), or in *The Taming of the Shrew*, where Baptista Minola bids his favorite daughter Bianca "Go ply thy needle"—that is, return to your usual occupation—in order to avoid the spite of her shrewish sister (2.1.25). Helena reminds Hermia, in *A Midsummer Night's Dream*, of the closeness of their childhood friendship by recalling how they "Have with our needles created both one flower, / Both on one sampler, sitting on one cushion" (3.2.204–205). At key moments, on the other hand, we are actually shown women at their needle in a token of the hearth and of marriage not unlike that of Penelope's tapestry weaving in *The Odyssey*. Queen Katharine and her women appear before us in *Henry VIII*, after Katharine's public trial, "*as at work*" (3.1); one of the women has a lute as the others occupy themselves. The domestic tranquillity thus shown is Katharine's sole comfort and refuge in the face of divorce and the persistent intrusions of Cardinals Wolsey and Campeius. In *Coriolanus*, ironic juxtaposition is even more abrupt: Volumnia and Virgilia, mother and wife of the protagonist, "*set them down on two low stools, and sew*" while they debate whether Coriolanus should seek honor in war or the embracements of the marriage bed (1.3). Other dramatists use the device as well: in the anonymous *Thomas of Woodstock* (ca. 1591–94), the Queen and her noble ladies sew "*shirts and bands and other linen*" for distribution to the poor (2.3). The action is symbolic and traditional, having been

49

associated with the Virgin Mary in medieval iconography,[29] but what is noteworthy in Shakespeare is its consistent use as a commentary on the predominantly male world of structure.

Religious costuming and properties also serve a liminal function in Shakespeare. As Turner has demonstrated, religious orders share many characteristics of the transitional state in rites of passage. The homogeneity of many religious communities, their denial of ownership of property, their anonymity and sexual continence, their acceptance of pain and suffering, and their mystical claims of a kind of supernatural folly all establish them as belonging to a sacred "outsiderhood."[30] The importance of this group without status, and the necessity of its critical perspective toward the structure-bound social order, are so widely recognized that religious communitas is often given a permanence and structure of its own (as in the monastic orders) to allow it to survive and continue. Yet an established communitas, something of a contradiction in terms, can take on the characteristics of what it is supposed to criticize.

This paradox of religious outsiderhood gives Shakespeare ample material for a dual view of religious costuming. It also creates anxiety about interpretation, for, in the area of moral and religious instruction where images ought most to provide clear signification, hypocrisy of appearances is most notorious.[31] A prelate should be one "whose white investments [vestments] figures innocence," as Westmorland says of the Archbishop of York in *2 Henry IV* (4.1.45), and indeed the religious robes of the friars in *Romeo and Juliet* and *Much Ado about Nothing* betoken men whose sympathy with young lovers oppressed by parental authority is apparent even in the friars' naiveté and inexperience. On the other hand, Shakespeare uses traditional color symbolism to denounce the "scarlet robes" of Cardinal Beaufort in *1 Henry VI* or Wolsey in *Henry VIII*. Scarlet in this pejorative religious sense is common in Renaissance drama, as for example in the costuming of the lecherous elders in Thomas Garter's *Virtuous and Godly Susanna* (1563–69).[32] No doubt the scarlet gown is itself an unambiguous signal of hypocrisy in Protestant England, but it nonetheless undercuts the idea of correspondence between religious exterior and inner piety. Certainly the familiar black clerical gown can be variously interpreted. The Clown Feste in *Twelfth Night* exploits its unsavory reputation when he puts on "this gown and this beard" to mimic Sir Topas the curate, pointedly wishing he were "the first that ever dissembled in such a gown" (4.2.1–

6). Yet several clerics in Shakespeare deserve our trust, and even "dissembling" in a friar's gown may be well intended, as is that of the Duke in *Measure for Measure*.

The ambivalence of meaning in religious objects can be seen in Shakespeare's use of books of devotion. In traditional medieval and Renaissance iconography they are attributes of the Virgin Mary, various saints, and pious patrons.[33] Robert Greene attests to the proverbial piety of those who carry such books when he observes of a person, "he was religious too, neuer without a booke at his belt."[34] Shakespeare knows how to invoke these conventional associations in a reported scene, as when we learn that "A book of prayers" lay on the pillow of the two innocent nephews of Richard III and almost changed the mind of a thug sent to murder them (*Richard III*, 4.3.14). On stage as well, a connotation of innocence betrayed by violence informs the scene of Henry VI's death, for he is at his "book" when Richard of Gloucester arrives at the Tower of London to murder this genuinely pious man (*3 Henry VI*, 5.6.1).[35] Shakespeare uses such traditional symbolism on occasion, then, to suggest the world of the meek who are oppressed by worldly insolence.

This traditional symbolism is nonetheless prone to villainous misuse that challenges the very premise of fixed symbolic meaning. Richard III, having murdered the pious Henry, soon learns himself how to "get a prayer-book in [his] hand" and appear "*aloft, between two Bishops*" when he wishes to hoodwink the Lord Mayor and some citizens of London with his seeming piety (*Richard III*, 3.7.47–98). Ophelia in *Hamlet* pretends to study a book of devotion when she is set as a bait for Hamlet by her father and Claudius. As Polonius observes, "with devotion's visage / And pious action we do sugar o'er / The devil himself" (3.1.47–49). Shakespeare's ambiguous use of such signals reflects sharp difference in his own age about the validity of icons and the proper use of vestments. Whether he uses religious images traditionally to signify pious behavior or ironically to signify deceit, the effect is generally critical of structured society, for truly pious persons eschew social status in the name of religious brotherhood, whereas pious frauds are persons of the social order perverting religious icons to their corrupt use. Beneath the illusory nature of images, the religious ideal is one that does indeed criticize the social order from its outsider's vantage.

Sartorial restrictions in Renaissance England were directed against the lower classes. However unsuccessfully the elaborate sumptuary regulations of the time may have been enforced, their intent was to keep the underprivileged in their place. "Serving men and other yeomen taking wages may not wear cloth in their hose above 2s. a yard," read one Henrician Act, "nor hose garded or mixed with any other things that may be seen through the upper part of the hose, but with the same cloth only."[36] Visual distinctions between classes were considered essential to the preservation of hierarchy. Such a language of differentiation inevitably makes its way into Shakespeare's plays, and its nominal function is to support order and degree. At the same time, we must remember that Shakespeare's theater is itself a place of holiday and of escape by the actors from sumptuary regulation. The interplay between structure and holiday is omnipresent in Shakespeare's use of commoners' dress. Persons of rank use the language of lower-class dress condescendingly, to typify and to demean as well as simply to label. Yet such a language is theirs, not Shakespeare's, and to the lower classes the language of costume is sometimes an expression of inversion, escape from restraint, even defiance. Costuming defines for the commoner his role in society, but alternatives in dress hold out to him a means of enacting an escape from vocation not unlike that of the actor in the theater.

In the Tudor theatrical tradition inherited by Shakespeare, sartorial distinctions in rank are often accorded their face value. A character called Art in *All for Money* (1576–1577) enters "*with certeyne tooles about him of diuers occupations*," and in *The Three Ladies of London* (ca. 1581) Simplicity appears "*like a Miller, all mealy, with a wand in his hand.*"[37] This is the kind of simple metonymy used by the creator of the painting in *The Rape of Lucrece*, and it lends itself to an easy notion of correspondences. In a decorous world a craftsman should identify himself by the signs of his trade—an apron, a handicraft tool, an apprentice's flat cap.

Shakespeare, though fully conversant with this tradition, uses it instead as a reductive language expressing hostility or a sense of superiority on the part of a wellborn speaker toward his social inferiors. Menenius sarcastically refers to the plebeians in *Coriolanus* as "apronmen" (4.6.98). Cleopatra is no less caustic at the expense of the "Mechanic slaves / With greasy aprons, rules, and hammers" who will gape at her in Rome in Caesar's triumph (*Antony and Cleopatra*, 5.2.209–210). Hubert, when he wishes to describe the astonishment of the populace at various prodigies thought to indicate the troubled times of

King John, speaks of a smith who stood "with his hammer, thus, / The whilst his iron did on the anvil cool," listening openmouthed to a tailor "Who, with his shears and measure in his hand, / Standing on slippers, which his nimble haste / Had falsely thrust upon contrary feet," tells news of a French invasion (*King John*, 4.2.193–198). For the most part, these images, reported or imagined rather than staged, tell us more about the speakers' attitudes than about plebeian conduct in the plays where they occur. The language of typicality in costuming is a received tradition and something of a cliché, suited more to defamatory rhetoric than to visual theatrical use.

The hostility is often satirical, indulging in abusive overstatement. Petruchio in *The Taming of the Shrew*, adopting a choleric hyperbole to "tame" his wife Kate, comically berates a tailor with invective derived from his trade: "thou thread, thou thimble, / Thou yard, three-quarters, half-yard, quarter, nail! . . . thou rag, thou quantity, thou remnant!" (4.3.106–111). Falstaff jests at Feeble, the woman's tailor, in *2 Henry IV*, by "pricking" him down for conscription and by asking him if he will "make as many holes in an enemy's battle as thou hast done in a woman's petticoat" (3.2.154–155). Tradesmen to Falstaff are "whoreson smooth-pates" who refuse him credit and "do now wear nothing but high shoes, and bunches of keys at their girdles" (1.2.37–39). The flat caps prescribed in London ordinances[38] are not infrequently associated in Shakespeare's plays, as in the work of other Elizabethan dramatists, with cowardice, vacillation, and unwarranted social aspiration. Minor functionaries come in for a good deal of such comic abuse at the expense of their bureaucratic or menial functions, like the arresting officer in *The Comedy of Errors* described as "A devil in an everlasting garment . . . One whose hard heart is button'd up with steel . . . a fellow all in buff" (4.2.33–36). Jailers and keepers are associated with bunches of keys, cords, hot irons for torturing, and chains.[39] Servants and waiters are condescendingly identified by the apron, as in *2 Henry IV* (2.2.163–164), and by napkin, trencher, and plate.[40] Women of lower station are apt to be sartorially identified in terms of a caricatured item of clothing or jewelry, like the "pink'd porringer" on the head of a haberdasher's wife in *Henry VIII* (5.4.47) or the "chains" and "jewels" worn by Doll Tearsheet in *2 Henry IV* and by other "bona robas" (2.4.47). Various country folk are laughed at for their shepherds' garb, the "clouted brogues" on their feet (*Cymbeline*, 4.2.215), and the "ballow" or cudgel that serves as a rustic weapon (*King Lear*, 4.6.242).[41]

For all this seeming endorsement of visual distinctions in rank and the practical use both in Shakespeare's society and on his stage that such statements exaggeratedly reflect, Shakespeare's actual costuming effects in the theater can often express saturnalian release. When commoners' garb calls attention to itself, in fact, the circumstances are apt to be irregular. "Is this a holiday?" the tribune Flavius accosts the "idle creatures" of Rome who have entered as *"certain Commoners over the stage"* to rejoice in Caesar's triumph. "What, know you not, / Being mechanical, you ought not walk / Upon a laboring day without the sign / Of your profession?" Why does the carpenter appear without his "leather apron and [his] rule," or the cobbler without his "awl" and "neat's leather" (*Julius Caesar*, 1.1.1–25)? The departure from prescribed costuming is perceived by the alarmed tribunes as a sign of disorder. Jack Cade's rebellion in *2 Henry VI* employs aggressive mirth too on the subject of clothing from a lower-class viewpoint. Cade jokes that he is himself a "clothier" who means to "dress the commonwealth, and turn it, and set a new nap upon it," while Dick the butcher undertakes to labor in his "vocation" by cutting the throats of sin and iniquity, and Smith the weaver cuts the threads of life. John Holland deplores the fact that "The nobility think scorn to go in leather aprons" (4.2.4–29). The ending of the rebellion is at hand when the rebels are bidden to fling up their caps in a gesture of request for clemency.

Costuming thus provides a language both of acquiescence to hierarchy and protest against it. The protest, like transitional behavior in any rite of passage, has its dangerous, inauspicious, anarchical aspect. It is a time of licensed obscenity, and it attracts the outlawed and the downtrodden, those dwelling on the margins of social order.[42] It must be circumscribed lest it become too threatening, and so it partakes of those rituals in which the perennially inferior in the social order are temporarily given a symbolic or make-believe elevation in status. Cade's fantastic posturings are of this sort, at once genuinely alarming and so gross that they can only be regarded as a self-defeating parody of the social order. The exaggerations paradoxically reinforce the reality of, and the need for, structure. Escape from vocation through costuming is as necessary to enlightened order as is prescribed custom itself.

We have been examining ways in which Shakespeare uses traditional distinctions in costuming to characterize the structured social order, while he simultaneously contrasts that structure with a holiday world of costume featuring disarray in dress, divestiture of tokens of rank, exchanging of garment by master and servant, transsexual disguise, illusory use of religious vestments and icons, and lower-class protest against sumptuary legislation. Polarity in costuming also functions in Shakespeare on the level of plot, directing our attention to changes in characters' attitudes and fortunes as they move back and forth between the world of status and that of undifferentiated communitas. Here the emphasis is on journey and return. Let us look at the plot function of certain costuming devices and hand properties in Shakespeare, noting how they possess a symbolic value expressive of their owners while they also operate at the surface value of narrative event, entertaining through games of illusion and inviting us to wonder what will happen next. They harmonize, in other words, symbolic and practical aims, in the spirit of those Renaissance artists who refused to allow a valid distinction between symbol and representation.

The seemingly mundane business of writing and misdirecting love letters, for example, so amusing and so essential to the plot of *Love's Labor's Lost*, tells us a good deal about the young men and their need for a more mature understanding of their own emotions. The movement signaled by the love letters is essentially from contract to perjury and from innocence to complicity until eventual discovery brings about clarification. The play's fascination with words and oaths centers on the way in which the characters protest their good intentions in writing, and the plot device of misdirected or overheard missives is expressive of imperfectly understood relationships, efforts at concealment of emotion, and self-delusion.

The play begins with the signing of a contractual oath by the young lords of Navarre's court. Each agrees to abstain from love, and subscribes his name "That his own hand may strike his honor down" (1.1.20). Order and law are given control over passion and feeling; the structured world is one of statutes and regulations. Transparently, however, the regulations cannot long be enforced, because they fail to take into account the realities of human feeling. When structure attempts to build a defensive wall around presexual innocence, it is destined to collapse through its own absurdity. Berowne foresees that "Necessity will make us all forsworn" (l. 148), and so it proves. The first breaches of contract occur among the below-stairs characters. Costard is reported to the King by Don Armado's first letter to have "sorted and consorted, contrary to thy established proclaimed edict and continent canon . . . with a child of our grandmother Eve, a female" (ll. 252–258). Armado is then fittingly caught in his own trap by a letter intended for the country wench Jaquenetta but delivered in error to the Lady Rosaline, revealing Armado's own malfeasance. Armado is shown to be guilty by the evidence of his own hand; the dramatic process of discovery, working through the device of the letters, unveils the truth of forsaken promises. Men are natural perjurers in this play, and the evidence of their handwriting is a comic nemesis by which they undo themselves and stand revealed for what they are. Yet because these revelations allow men to confront their own natures more candidly in the holiday world of concealment and exposure, their perjuries are ultimately benign in effect.

Certainly the young lords gain comic perspective on themselves through the scene of discovery in which their perjuries are proclaimed to one another.[43] The action is carried by a series of hand properties, written love sonnets, that offer visual proof against the authors. "*Enter Berowne, with a paper in his hand, alone*," the scene begins (4.3). The King follows "with a paper" which he reads and then drops surreptitiously, for Longaville too enters "reading" and festooned "like a perjure, wearing papers," that is, with a spare sonnet tucked into his hatband.[44] His guilty appearance calls to Berowne's mind the legal custom of attaching to a committed perjurer's breast the papers involved in and setting forth his offense. Together, these three offenders suggest to Berowne "The shape of Love's Tyburn" (l. 50), a triangular gallows used in public executions. Dumaine, the fourth to arrive, is in his turn visually identified by the sonnet he carries. Each must then blush as his accuser steps forth "to whip hypocrisy" and to show how each "perjur'd" lord is prone to "break faith and troth" or "infringe an oath" (ll. 139–153). Berowne, the last to be exposed, receives his comeuppance in the form of a letter sent by him to Rosaline but delivered by Jaquenetta and Costard into the King's hand. Berowne tears the letter but cannot deface the evidence: "It is Berowne's writing, and here is his name" (l. 199).

Throughout, letters and documents visualize the action of comedy in exposing the folly of love to curative laughter. The tidy world the young men have constructed of contracts and prohibitions is invaded by a holiday world of illusions and misdirected missives, all suggestive of awakening sexual interest that is by its nature disconcerting. The process of discovery, conveyed through the revelations of perjury, enriches the structured world to which the lovers must return by giving them a more measured sense of language and a tolerance for innocent folly. A similar function of letter writing might be explored in *The Two Gentlemen of Verona*, as an expression of estrangement and misunderstanding; in *The Merchant of Venice*, where letters express through visual means a central opposition of love and vengeance; in *Twelfth Night*, in which letters and their interpretation are a vehicle of satirical exposure; or in *Cymbeline*, where letters play a central role in testing the protagonists and in revealing the will of the gods.

Rings and jewels are especially expressive in Shakespeare of a comparable journey between structure and holiday. Because they enjoy a uniquely personal relationship with their possessors, such tokens are closely identified with those who wear them, both on the level of plot and as symbolic meaning, and become a visual means of revelation of the wearer's identity.[45] Their misplacement into undeserving hands expresses in stage action a betrayal, misunderstanding, or other form of estrangement. Conversely, rightful ownership or restoration to the true possessor betokens constancy or renewal of a pledge. The bestowing of these tokens is usually accompanied by the swearing of an oath whose validity is then directly expressed in terms of the physical possession and transfer of the object. By this means, plot function is made coincident with symbolic function.

The exchanging or misdirecting of such tokens is an essential device of plot complication in romantic comedy, and identification of the rightful owner is frequently a means of revelation and of restored harmony; that is to say, these tokens express a movement through complexity toward comic discovery and reversal. Love tokens are often the embodiment on stage of the generic form of romantic comedy. They assist the viewer in following the complication and clarification of the plot, and simultaneously they represent through synecdoche the progression of the characters through confusion and other forms of testing to restoration of identity.

The close relationship of rings to the wearer's identity is especially clear in plays featuring two rings, for here we see symbolized the contrasting views of the self that arise from the morality tradition of moral transformation on the one hand and from the illusionistic tradition of impersonation on the other. Shakespeare was attracted to this duality early in his career and gave it prominence in *The Two Gentlemen of Verona*. The ring bestowed on Proteus by Julia becomes a token of his faithlessness to her and the seriousness of his moral decline. He attempts to woo Silvia with the ring, but in doing so he entrusts the ring to Julia disguised as "Sebastian," thereby enabling Julia to know his perfidy and seek to disarm it. The action suggests a benign comic irony by which man is saved from his own capacity for evil. Thus Proteus' ring makes a journey representative of his inconstant wanderings in love and eventual return to unmerited forgiveness. Conversely, the ring given Julia by Proteus never leaves her finger. It tells a story of constancy and patient suffering and is an important means of revelation of her identity in the final act. The progress of Proteus' ring denotes moral error and spiritual conflict; Julia's ring tells a story denoting misunderstood innocence that proceeds through disguise to eventual confirmation of inner truth.

For all its apparent simplicity, and its resemblance to plotting devices in early romances and Tudor plays like *Clyomon and Clamydes* to which Stephen Gosson and others took vigorous exception,[46] this plot of two rings neatly demonstrates Shakespeare's craftsmanship in adapting a narrative convention to the visual demands of the theater. The tangible reality of the rings is essential; they betoken qualities of their master and mistress that ultimately cannot be hidden. Because the rings are a witness of their owners, the moment of their most significant stage use is fittingly also the moment of discovery and reconciliation.

The parallelism and contrast of two rings in *All's Well That Ends Well* expresses in a later and more complex play a similar attraction and conflict between an erring male protagonist and his innocent beleaguered wife. The ring of the husband suggests a journey of self-betrayal leading to repentance, while that of his wife tells a story of maligned virtue forced to disguise itself until at last truth is revealed. Bertram's ring, his own "gem" conferred by testament from generation to generation "Of six preceding ancestors," clearly betokens his ancestral honor. When he basely offers it in exchange for Diana's chastity, she properly responds, "Mine honor's such a ring. / My chastity's the jewel of our house, / Bequeathed down from many ancestors" (4.2.45–47). The fact of Diana's possession of Bertram's ring seems a clear demand for justice in the final scene of confrontation: "That ring's a thousand proofs" (5.3.195–198). Through the ironies of the plot, nonetheless, the ring serves as an instrument not of vengeance but of restoration: when Helena reclaims this ring from Diana and offers it to her wayward husband, along with his letter containing his vow to marry the woman who can obtain the ring from his finger, the contractual reunion of husband and wife is manifest in the tokens used to express it.

Helena's ring, meantime, is a gift of the King of France and is thus endowed with magical promise of rescue from extremity. Helena places the ring on Bertram's finger during their nighttime assignation so that, as Diana tells Bertram in her role as the woman Bertram thinks he will sleep with, "what in time proceeds / May token to the future our past deeds" (4.2.62–63). The ring does leave Helena's finger, but only to be given to one who may then be held accountable for his act of generation with her. Whereas the first ring plot deals with Bertram's serious moral lapse, that of Helena deals in illusion, in manipulation of appearances by a heroine who has been misunderstood but has never fallen. The two rings thus both reflect and to an extent reconcile the duality in the play's problematic ending, that of a moral legalistic obligation made necessary by man's fallen nature and a promise of restored trust in goodness.[47]

The essential feature of the ring as stage property is that it is so closely identified with its owner's true self. Diana makes this point when she insists, "Mine honor's such a ring." So does Iachimo in *Cymbeline* when he proposes in a wager to win both Posthumus' ring and the lady who gave it him—"she your jewel, this your jewel" (1.4.153–154). The eventual clearing of Imogen's reputation is coincident with the public disclosure of this ring and its companion bracelet, wrongly in Iachimo's possession but conceded by him to be the tokens "of the truest princess / That ever swore her faith" (5.5.418–419). To part with such a ring from one's finger is to part with the dearest aspect of one's life, as Bassanio freely acknowledges in *The Merchant of Venice*: "O, then be bold to say Bassanio's dead!" (3.2.185). Portia, for her part, has given to Bassanio "This house, these servants, and this same myself" when she bestows upon him "this ring" (ll. 170–171). The gift of ring is a gift of self, even if the transaction also involves a considerable transfer of wealth and an upgrading of Bassanio's social status. Portia playfully teases Bassanio about the ring by requesting it of him in her disguise as a young lawyer who has saved Antonio's life, but she knows that his choice of friendship proves him worthy of a lasting contractual bond. Plot device and symbolic function merge; Portia tricks Bassanio into bestowing the ring on his own wife, just as Proteus unknowingly gave his ring to Julia and Bertram his ancestral ring to Helena. The ring is thus a token of the woman especially, whose patient resource-fulness tricks the man into a chaste union that his worst instincts have resisted but that he welcomes in spite of himself. In Gratiano's con-cluding bawdy jest about "keeping safe Nerissa's ring" (5.1.307), the sexual significance of the ring is perfectly blended with ideas of friend-ship, fidelity, bond, and mutual submission.[48] These rich associations are not simply part of an image pattern in the language of the play, but describe an actual stage property that is the focus of important stage business and a visual means of clarifying the story for spectators.

Rings, love letters, and other tokens thus are practical stage objects that can express their owners' wayward or innocent natures, and the eventual recovery of the owners' original selves through penitence or public vindication of innocence. Changes of costume similarly accom-plish a dual objective in Shakespeare's plays, displaying a versatility of symbolic effects that is commensurate with the visual splendor and variety of Elizabethan stage dress. Two metaphors are dominant in the expressive function of costuming change, that of journey and that of metamorphosis. One is derived chiefly from the tradition in medieval and Tudor drama of rapid and easy costume change signifying a turning toward worldly dissipation or conversely toward repentance. Costume changes here are visible signposts of a spiritual journey from fall to eventual recovery.[49] Because they are unambiguously didactic, these signposts confirm the idea of correspondences so necessary to a struc-tured view of social and moral order. The journey is usually both spiritual and literal, as signaled by the convention of donning or doffing of traveling boots.[50] The use of costuming for metamorphosis, on the other hand, is derived chiefly from the illusionistic tradition of neo-classic theater and from prose narrative sources in which disguise is the stuff of romantic plotting. The motifs of masking, veiling, and the like as prevalent plot devices invite us into a world of transition, am-biguity, and confused sex distinctions. These devices are characterized by entertaining event, narrative suspense, surprise, and sudden change of direction. The visible change in a character's situation is a matter of surfaces rather than of inward turmoil.

As with rings and jewels, these dual traditions of costume change offer rival insights into the complex relationship between role playing and identity.[51] As signs of order and place in the structured world of moral order, costumes also transmit information about alterations in a character's social or moral status. Since actors begin their roles, in the

The Language of Costume and Hand Properties

Elizabethan view, by donning an appropriate costume, they might be expected to shift into new garments when something of moment happens to the characters they are playing. Costume is a primary means of defining role, on stage as in society, and so change in costume becomes a primary means of denoting change in role. On the other hand, the holiday use of disguise encourages spectators to regard costume change as illusory, and to perceive that the character's inner self is no more changed than is the actor in the theater. A marked feature of the disguise plot in Shakespeare is the moment of revelation, in which the character recovers his or her original outward form and thus proclaims a restored and reaffirmed identity. Costume change therefore can become a sign either of essential inner alteration or of the outward vicissitudes of fortune. One pattern is tragicomic, the other romantic. Both posit a return to one's original self as the necessary completion, in comedy, of the fictional journey or transformation. In a paradox that must have appealed to an age that inspired Spenser's "Cantos of Mutability," change of costume in comedy ultimately affirms the unchanged inner substance of what a person is. To try out different parts as an actor might do is to rediscover one's essential role—that is, one's identity.

The Tudor morality play presents with unusual visual clarity the costuming pattern of spiritual journey and soul struggle. Its archetypal plot of ensnarement in sinful behavior and eventual penitence is represented in visual terms by disfigurement and then cleansing, or by sartorial decadence and reform. Whether or not the protagonist recovers a state of well-being (and the potential for tragic conclusion is always there, as in *Enough Is As Good As a Feast* or *The Conflict of Conscience*),[52] the journey produces strong inner conflict and distress. The adoption of wanton finery bespeaks a real degeneration of character, from which the protagonist can recover only by an equally abrupt change in himself. The repentance that manifests itself in sober costume is a rebirth and rediscovery of self, but one that involves the change of heart needed for the acceptance of grace rather than a dispelling of misunderstanding.

Shakespeare reveals an awareness of this pattern of clothing change in his *Henriad*. Prince Hal twice discovers that his sojourns in the tavern produce in him something very like the sartorial transformations of the Prodigal Son. Hal himself jestingly speaks in *2 Henry IV* of his visual metamorphosis "From a prince to a prentice" as a "low transformation" and a "heavy descension" (2.2.165–167). The apron he puts on, so patently a sign of tapsters and other laboring professions, casts him into a recognizably inappropriate role. He conceives of his transformation as a disguise, of course, and in *1 Henry IV* anticipates the day when he will proclaim his reformation; he will show himself in battle, "His cushes on his thighs, gallantly arm'd," and reveal himself to be his father's true son (4.1.105). Yet to the extent that he is really attracted to Falstaff's company, especially in the first play, and is attempting to have it both ways with a disguise that bears some resemblance to the blackened face and fool's garments of the protagonist in *Wit and Science*, Hal reveals in his changes of costume a complex progression of states of mind. His final public epiphany in *2 Henry IV* as the young King Henry V, exemplar of justice and majesty, is less an unmasking than an emergence of something created out of experiment and conflict. Costuming can mark the stages of trial and error as well as the revelation of character.

The contrary impulse of illusionism in costume change manifests itself in the romantic disguise plot, with its emphasis on revelation of the true self through discovery or recognition. Unveiling, unmasking, and removal of disguise are all, on Shakespeare's stage, literal devices of discovery. Structurally they are often reserved for the climactic moment of *anagnorisis*. As such, these gestures serve at once to resolve the complications of the plot and to reveal hidden identity and motive. The last act of *Measure for Measure* is a tour de force of such revelations through costume, as Mariana unveils herself at her husband's bidding, the Duke is unhooded, and Claudio is unmuffled. Discovery brings with it renewal and the fulfillment of one's true role without misconception or hindrance: Mariana finds her place as the loyal wife whom Angelo once discarded, the Duke asserts a new authority untarnished by slander, and Claudio is brought to life as the brother once thought dead.[53] Hero too, in *Much Ado about Nothing*, is born anew through unmasking and becomes "another Hero," the slander that besmirched her reputation having perished with her discarded attire. The symbolic death and rebirth, so characteristic of rites of passage,[54] records Hero's movement from the structure of her sheltered life at the start of the play through the dangers of transition to a new family integration. "As surely as I live, I am a maid," she insists, for identity is integrally dependent on her role as unspotted virgin (5.4.63). Unmasking restores her true identity and her proper role; what is discarded is not a part of her but an appearance of unchastity, a garment deceptively worn, like the clothing used by Margaret in her clandestine rendezvous with Borachio.

The manipulations of appearances by Shakespeare's resourceful heroines are a necessary part of their struggle to vindicate themselves and show wherein they have been misperceived. Rosalind, in *As You Like It*, stage-manages a scene in which her resumption of her accustomed garb performs the seeming miracle of restoring a daughter to her father and the lovers to each other. The revelation of Viola's true self beneath her male attire in *Twelfth Night* uncovers a wife for Orsino in the supposed young man he has taken for his dearest friend. Unmasking, unveiling, and the putting aside of disguise share a positive connotation in Shakespeare of dispelling pretense, misunderstanding, and willful withdrawal, as when Olivia puts aside her veil in *Twelfth Night* and discovers what it is to fall in love. The gesture of removing the mask is one of giving up defensive self-concealment in favor of open acknowledgment of feelings.

The two functions of costume change, as expressive of inner conflict and of innocence at last revealed, are most apparent when they are juxtaposed in a single play. Much as two rings belonging to wavering protagonist and long-suffering heroine are contrasted in *The Two Gentlemen of Verona* and in *All's Well That Ends Well*, the play of *Cymbeline* assigns one costuming tradition to Posthumus Leonatus and the other to Imogen.

Posthumus' changes of clothing employ a language of spiritual fall. His journey, as he changes outwardly from exiled British gentleman to seeming Italian soldier of fortune to forlorn British peasant warrior and back again, is a painful odyssey of lost faith, attempted murder, suicidal longing for oblivion, renunciation, and the seeking of forgiveness. The Italian costume he wears suggests something of what he has gone through in Italy, in the company of Iachimo. His return to his original appearance does not clear away misapprehensions so much as it acknowledges failure and seeks opportunity to begin anew.

Imogen, meanwhile, sets aside her "laborsome and dainty trims" in favor of the unfamiliar costume of men (3.4.165) for reasons that are external to her character. Because she is wrongly suspected of infidelity, she must undergo a transformation and a journey that mirror the misunderstandings under which she suffers. Being misunderstood, she must appear to be other than what she is. The false perception thrust upon her in large part by male jealousy, possessiveness, and self-hatred is an illusion that can be dispelled only by Posthumus' acknowledgment of the wrong he has done Imogen. Her removal of disguise thus enables her both to clear her reputation and to complete the education of her deceived husband. The play's climactic moment of recognition resolves the travails of husband and wife simultaneously in the unmasking and reconciliation.

In both patterns, that of Posthumus and that of Imogen, the staging device of costume change becomes a metaphor not merely of change but of a transformation that necessarily returns to its point of origin. The experience in both is of a journey into the liminal world of anonymity and inversion. Although, as we have seen, the morality tradition of soul struggle puts more emphasis on the unambiguous didacticism of a moral structure while the neoclassic tradition of illusion is more at home with ambiguity, Shakespeare combines the two in such a way as to preserve the best features of each. His is a synthesis in which the morality tradition preserves its moral seriousness without heavy-handed didacticism, while the neoclassic tradition preserves its playful entertaining illusionism without surrendering to ambiguity. A character dons a disguise or otherwise changes costume to make a journey that is both symbolic and literal; the disguise is removed or the original costume is resumed to signify the return home, the affirmation and acceptance of self. As in rites of passage, discovery of one's essential identity, both personal and social, is arrived at through a process of change that brings new awareness but not a wholly new person. Metamorphosis is fulfillment, in this benign journey of self-discovery. The tragicomic and the comic merge as waywardness turns to penitent forgiveness and as misunderstanding is dispelled.

In tragedy, on the other hand, the patterns refuse to merge or to restore the characters to a renewed self-awareness. Shakespeare's darker tragic vision is one in which change is too often destructive. Inner conflict leads to an unrecoverable fall, as in late Tudor morality plays concerning protagonists who are predestinately damned;[55] misunderstandings about true worth, created by illusion, are dispelled too late. The moment of *anagnorisis* is not one of identity restored but of irreversible catastrophe belatedly understood. In such a fallen world, Shakespeare shows how the costuming conventions of journey and metamorphosis, with their comic and romantic resonances, can be used to create expectations that are devastatingly unfulfilled. As he was later to do in *Cymbeline*, he pairs and contrasts in *King Lear* two patterns of costume change by juxtaposing the stories of Edgar and Lear. The restorations that ought to accompany the recovered garments of each are instead inverted and destroyed.

Edgar, like Imogen, undergoes both a journey and a resort to disguise that are thrust upon him by an undeserved slander. He adopts the seeming role of outcast that his father's anger and his brother's envy have provided for him. In his remarkable series of transmutations from eldest son to madman, peasant, Cotswold rustic, anonymous challenger in arms, and finally successor to the kingship, we see many features that belong to an essentially comic pattern of disguising: the resourceful inventiveness of the disguiser, the opportunity for observation of manners from a vantage of concealment, the expectation of return, the dramatic revelation of identity through the removal of disguise, and above all Edgar's need to recover his true role as loyal son. "In nothing am I chang'd / But in my garments," he tells his father, and the speech points to Edgar's eventual hope of vindicating himself in the eyes of the parent who has disinherited him (4.6.9–10). In this tragedy, however, it is not true that "The worst returns to laughter" (4.1.6). To pronounce even such a guarded hope is to invite further disaster. Edgar's revelation of self to his father is mocked by the bursting of his father's heart, and his entry into royal succession calls forth a lament for "The weight of this sad time" (5.3.328).[56] Edgar perseveres to the end of his saga and reclaims his lost identity from Edmund as "Edgar, and thy father's son" (l. 172), only to find his achievement mocked by the catastrophe that surrounds him.

Lear's resumption of his kingly role after his descent into misfortune is even more savagely undercut. The visual pattern is clearly one of fall and recovery rather than of disguising and revelation. The play's first scene not only sets in motion Lear's tragedy but establishes the royal splendor that he will lose, the robes and ornaments, the dukes and princes in attendance. The divestiture of these tokens of rank visually marks his descent into wretchedness and loss of sanity, as he attempts to "unbutton here" and seek out the "bare forked animal" beneath all courtly finery, conducts an imagined trial of his daughters with a "robed man of justice" (really Edgar) at his side, and runs away from his attendants fantastically bedecked with weeds.[57] The putting of "fresh garments" upon him in preparation for his awakening and reunion with Cordelia (4.7.23) seems an unmistakable signal of recovered hope and reconciliation. As with Posthumus, the moment of restored identity through costuming brings with it deep contrition, forgiveness, and reaffirmation of a role to which Lear's garments give mute but vivid testimonial. In this play, however, the self is recovered only to be lost again. The role of kingly father, so preciously bestowed on Lear by his daughter, is at the last an empty form and a painful reminder of what is no longer. Tragedy can thus reverse the function of the dual costuming traditions used by comedy.

The relation of costuming to identity and role thus explores most eloquently what Shakespeare has made out of the theatrical tradition of his day. He uses a dual pattern, inherent in Elizabethan ideas of costume as well as in the theater, to portray an antithetical opposition between the ordered hierarchy of status and holiday escape from vocation. Costuming moves diversely toward structure and toward release as it depicts both high station and divestiture of rank, respectability and saturnalia, social differentiation and protest against inequality. Most of all, polarity in costuming enables Shakespeare to record the journeys and transformations through which his characters undergo liminal experiences essential to proper definitions of identity and role. They recover their better selves by turning to repentance and acceptance of frailty, or they uncover their true selves by setting aside false illusions. Costuming change marks the deepening and chastening experience through which they pass, and it celebrates the successful conclusion of a journey of recovery or vindication. It may also, in tragedy, signal the failure of such a quest.

In either case, Shakespeare insistently acknowledges the dangers of superficiality inherent in visual labeling through costume. He finds he must modify conventions of visual identification, invert them, or set them in ironic contexts. He nevertheless returns again and again to visual identification as an essential confirmation of a continuity in human nature transcending the illusion of change. The final emphasis then in his language of costume is on clarification and on meaningful communication rather than on ambiguity. The characters who invite our sympathy in Shakespeare, whether in comedy or tragedy, are seen at last to be what they appear. As they resume the garments in which they first appeared on stage, Shakespeare's characters often can say in effect what John Webster's greatest stage creation says of herself, "I am the Duchess of Malfi still."

66

❧ III

The Language of Gesture and Expression

Action is either a certaine visible eloquence, or an eloquence of
the bodei, or a comely grace in deliuering conceits, or an
external image of an internall minde.

—Thomas Wright, *The Passions of the Minde in Generall* (1630)[1]

J UST AS SHAKESPEARE inherited and shaped to his use a tradition
of identifying character types through their clothes and hand
properties, so also was he familiar with the widespread assumption that
types of emotion could be identified through appropriate gesture and
expression. The many handbooks of the period, like that of Thomas
Wright quoted above, begin with the idea that passion and action are
closely linked, that action is an outward form of an inward state. The
stereotyping impulse that we find in Elizabethan attitudes toward clothing applies to gesture and expression as well: in the same way that
social status and occupation require certain apparel and badges of
profession, states of feeling require certain unvarying manifestations in
the visage and use of the limbs.

A common attitude informs both sets of assumptions, for both place
considerable stress on the concept of role; a person plays a set part in
the social organism, and that role prescribes certain outward forms.
Gesture is something put on, like a garment, to enable one to fulfill a
social role. The idea of decorum dictates that a given emotion is appropriate to a given situation, in a form that is carefully prescribed,
just as wearing apparel must be regulated by sumptuary legislation.
Expression of emotion often takes on a public or social character, especially in rites of passage like marriages and funerals, where the formal
function of giving vent to emotion outweighs the importance of individual response.

Action Is Eloquence

Shakespeare reveals everywhere his familiarity with the basic assumption of Elizabethan theories of behavior that emotional states and their outward manifestations are closely linked. He is aware of the commonplace idea that one can read emotion through its visible signs and that meaning can be reliably determined. Although the many disagreements on matters of detail among the various handbooks preclude serious accuracy in the method, the generally accepted attitude is what matters. It offers Shakespeare a conventional language of gesture built upon his spectators' ready acquaintance with a lore of gesture and expression.

As with the conventional language of costuming, Shakespeare is not unattracted to this readily understood means of communication. Its shorthand offers him artistic efficiency, and its presumed certitudes speak to a hope that language in the theater can instruct as well as delight. At the same time, Shakespeare's own observations of emotion are assuredly not derived from textbooks.[2] The precepts codified in the handbooks on psychology can do little more for him than outline preset and typical attitudes toward visible forms of emotion. As such, they are useful to him in delineating the structured and ceremonial world of civilized intercourse, where role playing and decorum predominate. The lore of gesture and emotion enables Shakespeare to show predictable responses, useful for instance when dramatis personae describe verbally the gestures of others on or off stage. Verbal descriptions of emotion rely necessarily on convention; they become set pieces, characterizing the speaker's perception more than the action itself.

To Shakespeare, the language of conventional lore speaks for a world of correspondences, comforting in its assumptions about meaning but imprecise and even misleading in its generality. It cannot follow him into the world of personal emotion, silence, nuance, spontaneity, and discovery of inner self. Its inadequacies are especially marked in such liminal experiences as falling in love, suffering a private sorrow, or facing death. Instead, its function is to represent typical and social expressions of emotion, with which Shakespeare contrasts the inner emotions of individual experience. As with costuming, Shakespeare needs two theatrical languages for the gestures of emotion.

The conventional gestural language of Shakespeare's age owed its visually predictable character to the assumption that gesture and emotion were generated by fixed physiological processes. Theorists from

Aristotle, Lucius Apuleius, and the first-century rhetorician Palaemon to Pietro d'Abano, Albertus Magnus, and Giambattista della Porta all stressed medical doctrine of the humors as a way of accounting for alterations in emotional states. An English writer like Joseph Hall could speak of anger as something very physical, a "shaking of the hands and lips, palenesse, or rednesse, or swelling of the face, glaring of the eies, stammering of the tongue, stamping with the feet, vnsteady motions of the whole body, rash actions which we remember not to haue done, distracted and wilde speeches."[3] Physical symptoms like these were believed to arise in response to a number of factors: the balance or imbalance in the body of the four humors, diurnal and seasonal cycles, sex, age, heredity, exercise, and still others. The language of gesture was thought to be universal, because any given passion was assumed to produce the same physical effect on all who experienced it.[4] Like any language, it could be abused by villainous practitioners of deception, in the theater or elsewhere, but this potential did not gainsay the accuracy of the language in its intended state. It lent itself readily to notions of decorum, in which groups or classes of people were thought to behave according to type.[5] The theory of humors pointed toward characteristic body types: the sanguine person, for example, was expected to be of medium height and inclining to plumpness, with soft skin and golden or amber hair, ruddy of complexion, graceful of movement, cheerful and melodious of voice.[6] Persons might accordingly be judged by their complexion: a ruddy person was to be trusted, a dark-complected person not; a ruddy person was apt to be wise, a dark person lecherous, a pale person peevish.[7]

The face in particular, because of its expressiveness, offered a way of knowing a person's heart and mind. Thomas Wright argues the case as follows:

> The heart of a man changeth his countenance, whether it be in good or euill: for in anger and feare we see men, eyther extreame pale, or high coloured; in melancholy and sadnesse, the eyes are heauy; in ioy and pleasure, the motions of the eyes are liuely and pleasant, according to the olde prouerbe *Cor gaudens exhilarat faciem*, a reioycing heart maketh merry the face. And questionlesse wise men often, thorow the windowes of the face, behold the secrets of the heart.[8]

The eye was above all an *"Index* of the *Minde"*[9] and accordingly was of special significance to the physiognomer, as it was to the dramatist.

The advantages to an Elizabethan dramatist of a conventional set of relationships between feeling and gesture were manifold. Gesture proved itself able to take on in the theater the symbolic character of language itself; it was, as William York Tindall says of symbolism of every kind, "a visible sign of something invisible . . . an outward device for presenting an inward state."[10] Dramatists and actors found they had at hand a way of suiting action to emotion in a language based on universally understood conventions. The language was accessible to all audiences, for, despite the "scientific" claims of the theorists, its traditions were widely disseminated in popular lore and in literature, both dramatic and nondramatic. Moreover, the notion of illustrating emotion through suitable gesture accorded with prevailing views of rhetoric. Gesture was ornament, employed equally by the actor in the theater and the orator in the public assembly. As Thomas Wright expresses it, "In the substance of externall action for most part oratours and stage plaiers agree."[11] The great classical rhetorician Cicero gives authority to the dictum that "by action the body talks, so that it is all the more necessary to make it agree with the thought."[12] Sir Francis Bacon, in his essay "Of Boldnesse," deplores the fact that "action" or gesturing should be esteemed by most orators above invention and elocution, and that "that Part of an Oratour, which is but superficiall, and rather the vertue of a Player; should be placed so high, aboue those other Noble Parts"; but Bacon concedes reluctantly that visual persuasion is certain to succeed so long as "the Foolish part of Mens Mindes" is taken in by the potent effects of gesturing.[13] Even those who mistrust gesture, then, acknowledge its centrality both to oratory and to the oratorical art of acting.

Many of these apparent advantages, however, tend to limit gesture to a formal and symbolic function better suited to a public and role-conscious world of correspondences than to private experience. To see gesture as a branch of rhetoric, one in which acting is put on like a garment by the actor or orator in accordance with an expected decorum,[14] is to stress the public function of gesture and its subservience to speech. Gesture becomes ornament, best capable of portraying external and typical features by which the viewer is to recognize the generic behavior of groups or classes. George Whetstone reflects such a reductive and classifying notion in his complacent formulation that

"graue olde men, should instruct: yonge men, should showe the imperfections of youth: Strumpets should be lasciuious: Boyes vnhappy:
and Clownes, should speake disorderlye."[15] John Bulmer's *Chironomia*
(1644), in which every imaginable emotional state is associated with a
particular configuration of the speaker's hands,[16] testifies both to the
continued popularity of this classificatory line of thought about gesture
long after Shakespeare's time, and to the ultimate absurdity of quasi-
scientific precision in dealing with a phenomenon of potentially infinite
nuance.

Whether Shakespeare's acting company employed a "natural" acting
style in contrast to the "formal" style of their predecessors has been
much debated, though too often the debate has lapsed into unproductive
exercises in relative judgment.[17] Surviving records of spectators' responses even from the medieval and Tudor drama, which to our taste
often seems stylized, formal, and naive, in fact uniformly praise the
actors for credible, persuasive, and affective imitation of the characters
they represented.[18] Shakespeare, like Hamlet, undoubtedly preferred
to have his actors "hold, as 't were, the mirror up to nature" rather
than "tear a passion to tatters, to very rags" (*Hamlet*, 3.2.9–22); but in
saying so, Hamlet simply expresses the aim of all actors in all ages,
who perennially correct what they perceive to be the formal strutting
and bellowing of their ancestors.

If we could reconstruct in all its detail an authentic Shakespearean
performance as seen in 1600, no doubt it would strike us as quaintly
formal to the extent that its acting conventions would reflect a hierarchical society and a symbolic mode of thought very distant from our
own. The outdoor Elizabethan stage, with spectators on all sides at
varying distances from the actors, placed a premium on bold delivery
and large scope. A splendid façade at their backs encouraged the actors
to exploit symbolically pictorial effects in costuming and stage movement. The repertory system and its extraordinary demands for so many
new plays meant that the actors, able to spend little time on new visual
arrangements of the cast on stage, fell back instead on conventions of
blocking that made considerable use of symmetry.[19]

Still, our sense of distance from such Elizabethan conventions is only
relative. Shakespeare's own interest in banishing all easy and old-fash-
ioned appeals to "barren spectators" is undeniable. The most balanced
appraisal, that of Bernard Beckerman and John Russell Brown, is that
Elizabethan acting was at once ceremonious in a conventional frame-

work, romantic in dramatizing high passions, and epic in its scope and elevation of tone. It was passionate, socially mimetic, virtuoso, imaginative, individual, embracing a kind of heroic naturalism.[20] It was, in short, both formal and natural. It reconciled those diverse impulses much as Renaissance neoplatonism sought to reconcile symbol and representation. Endowed at once with symbolic and verisimilar qualities, Elizabethan acting provided Shakespeare with a dual language capable of rich and complex interplay. His essential strategy, this chapter argues, was to link such a duality to the dialectical contrast between a structured world in which formal decorum is supposed to express social function (though it can be hypocritically employed) and a more private world in which gesture is individually capable of protest against established norms.

One formal characteristic of the conventional gestural language Shakespeare inherited from earlier dramatists and from the truisms of his age is the tendency toward schematic contrasts. Age and youth, for example, are defined by their opposition to each other. Humans were thought to grow dry as they aged, and hence to incline toward phlegmatic and choleric behavior. The "dry hand," wrinkled skin, palsy, and the like, were believed to betray the hot and dry temperament within.[21] Conversely, youth was thought to enjoy a natural moisture and warmth that manifested itself in a damp hand, softness, plumpness, and a ruddy or blushing countenance. These oppositions leave little room for accommodation between age and youth.

Shakespeare's characters make use of these typical and reductive symptoms of age and youth, but in dramatic context we recognize such statements as commonplaces meant to exaggerate or criticize and thereby characterize the one who is doing the mocking. Ursula cuttingly identifies the aged Antonio at a masked ball in *Much Ado about Nothing* by the "waggling" of his head and his "dry hand" (2.1.109–112). Age, she implies, cannot be concealed by a mask. Hamlet taunts Polonius by pretending to quote from a book to the effect that "old men have grey beards, that their faces are wrinkled, their eyes purging thick amber and plum-tree gum, and that they have a plentiful lack of wit, together with most weak hams" (*Hamlet*, 2.2.198–201). The Lord Chief Justice in *2 Henry IV* can find no better way to upbraid Falstaff for his folly than by castigating his pretensions to youth when he is "written down old with all the characters of age . . . Have you not a moist eye, a dry hand, a yellow cheek, a white beard, a decreasing leg, an increasing belly? Is not your voice broken, your wind short, your chin double, your wit single, and every part about you blasted with antiquity?" (1.2.178–183). Thersites in *Troilus and Cressida*, we are told, makes the "faint defects of age" his "scene of mirth" as he mimics the seniority of Nestor by affecting "to cough and spit, / And, with a palsy fumbling on his gorget, / Shake in and out the rivet" (1.3.172–175). These are not directions for the actors, but satiric vignettes. The language is not intended to describe what we see on stage; indeed, the dry hand is hardly a visible sign in the theater, and Thersites' parody is not staged to our view. We do see Antonio, Polonius, and Falstaff and perceive that they are old, but the scornful speeches about their age tell us more about the speakers' attitudes than about what age looks like in the theater. The speeches, with their conventional and derogatory symptoms, use stereotype as a dramatic effect with which to mock the mundane reality of aging.

The conventional signs of youth conveyed to us in dialogue are no less reliant on stereotypical symptoms, directed toward moralistic commonplaces and not easily detected in the theater. Youth is itself a sign of wantonness. Venus in *Venus and Adonis* proclaims her concupiscent nature by her "soft and plump" flesh, her "marrow burning," and her "smooth moist hand" (ll. 142–143). Iras' claim that her warm and moist hand is a token of chastity provokes derisive laughter from Charmian in *Antony and Cleopatra*, for Charmian knows that "if an oily palm be not a fruitful prognostication, I cannot scratch mine ear" (1.2.54–55). Paris, in *Troilus and Cressida*, appeals to the assumption that the natural moisture and heat of youth are influenced by gluttony and indolence in his teasing description of Pandarus: "He eats nothing but doves, love, and that breeds hot blood, and hot blood begets hot thoughts, and hot thoughts beget hot deeds, and hot deeds is love" (3.1.128–130). Othello, finding his wife's hand to be warm and moist, interprets this as evidence of proneness to sensual pleasure. "This argues fruitfulness and liberal heart," he warns her; "Hot, hot, and moist" (*Othello*, 3.4.38–39). These diagnoses are too easy, and are based on signs not visible in the theater—most of all the warm, moist hand.

The contrastive signs of age and youth, then, serve not as a guide to stage action but as a series of ironic contexts. Falstaff is of course whitebearded and fat as the Lord Chief Justice describes him, but the main effect of the speech is to contrast Falstaff's age with his mischievous and irresponsible qualities of youth. Thersites' derision at Nestor's seniority in years, for which Nestor ought to be respected, is a sign of deteriorating morale in the Grecian camp. A major source of Othello's tragic error is that he allows himself to think stereotypically about Desdemona, and to judge her by the conventional expectations of Venetian society. The signs of age and youth are too simple and too defamatory to be directly informative.

Similar dangers apply to another schematic contrast, that of sex stereotyping. As with age and youth, Renaissance psychology invited an antithetical approach to sexual differentiation. Sex was thought to be, along with age and heredity, one of the "natural" determinants of temperament and hence of gesture and expression, as distinguished from the "nonnatural" causes like exercise, sleep, air, and food. Women were regarded as naturally phlegmatic, fleshy, and soft; their moist temperaments inclined them to tears and to passions that were quickly engendered, but as quickly dissipated. Men were as a whole more dry and hot, and therefore braver, more choleric, more intelligent.[22]

These commonplaces encourage the view that men's tears and sighs are "womanish." Friar Laurence says as much when he rebukes Romeo for his unmanly grief at his banishment: "Unseemly woman in a seeming man" (*Romeo and Juliet*, 3.3.112). In context, however, most uses in Shakespeare of this sex-stereotyped attitude adopt a skeptical stance toward the convention and sympathize with men who find weeping necessary. Henry V's insistence to Katharine of France that "I cannot look greenly, nor gasp out my eloquence" may seem at first like the chauvinistic remark of one who comes as conqueror to woo, but the main thrust is to belittle the exaggerated signs by which young men proclaim their lovesickness. Henry cannot die for love (*Henry V*, 5.2.144–153). Rosalind in *As You Like It*, who is similarly unpersuaded that people really die for love, is gently laughed at by Celia for weeping in her disguise as Ganymede: "have the grace to consider that tears do not become a man" (3.4.2–3). Mercutio in *Romeo and Juliet* congratulates Romeo for conquering his hapless longing for Rosaline, exclaiming "Why, is not this better now than groaning for love? Now art thou sociable, now art thou Romeo" (2.4.87–88), but Mercutio understands nothing of Romeo's new attachment for Juliet in which an equality of "grace for grace and love for love" breaks down the conventional differences of sex. Mercutio's own male aggressiveness, pitted against that of Tybalt, sets in motion a quarrel in which Romeo feels he must

74

eschew the feminine signs of tenderness and yielding learned from his love: "O sweet Juliet, / Thy beauty hath made me effeminate, / And in my temper soft'ned valor's steel!" (3.1.112–114). Romeo's "womanish" tears are thus a visible sign of the conflict in him between a stereotypical maleness so characteristic of the family feuding and a secret relationship of self-discovery wherein Romeo can learn to acknowledge feminine qualities in himself.

Shakespeare's tragic heroes must learn a similar lesson, though not in time to avert the catastrophe generated at least in part by masculine aggression. Othello weeps twice, once when he confronts Desdemona with his certainty of her guilt and again when he learns too late of her innocence. His tears can thus suggest his loss of self-control and of his military occupation, but they also bespeak at last a tenderness and regret that ameliorate to a degree his crime. They acknowledge the "woman's part" in him that he has repudiated and destroyed.[23] Brutus' stoicism prompts him to withhold his tears on the occasion of his wife's death and of Cassius' untimely end, but even he gives way at last to such grief "That it runs over even at his eyes" (*Julius Caesar*, 5.5.14). The gesture must indicate far more than awareness of military defeat and the imminence of death for one who is indifferent to fortune's blows; the tears generously acknowledge that Caesar's wronged ghost, who has appeared to Brutus at Philippi, must be expiated.

King Lear's weeping chronicles a turning in him from masculine defensiveness to softer emotions worthy of one who suffers. At first his tears shame him as unbefitting his status as ruler and patriarch. He counts it a defeat that "women's weapons, water-drops," should "Stain my man's cheeks." It galls him that Goneril can "shake my manhood thus" and cause "these hot tears" to "break from me perforce" (*King Lear*, 1.4.294–295, 2.4.277–278). The tears that accompany his belated and brief reunion with Cordelia, on the other hand, mark an acceptance in him of the gentler side of his nature that he has so long repressed.

Shakespeare's men in wartime weep with surprising frequency—in *Antony and Cleopatra*, throughout the first historical tetralogy, and in *King John*—at the mutual agony of civil strife.[24] Gonzalo is reported to weep in *The Tempest*, Jaques in *As You Like It*, and Antonio in *The Merchant of Venice*.[25] Male weeping on stage is always perceived as strikingly out of keeping with male temperament as conventionally described, and yet it is not rare. That men weep in disregard of strictures against doing so is a sign that they have come to terms with the feminine side of their natures. They have learned through tragic experience that dependence and vulnerability, however much they are disapproved of in Renaissance stereotypes of male behavior, are generous emotions.[26] By reversing the language of conventional lore, Shakespeare has found a stage vocabulary suited to the intensely personal experience of characters whose journeys of self-knowledge and suffering transcend the boundaries of ordinary event.

Of course Shakespeare's characters do not always eschew the stereotypical on stage. Especially in the comedies, both men and women in love (men particularly) often conform to the commonplaces of Renaissance psychology; that is part of what is so endearingly funny about their affliction. Shakespeare is at once mistrustful of labels and aware of their potential for the theater. His young lovers are apt to neglect their appearance or else dress fastidiously, and display every predictable sign of love melancholy. Shakespeare uses conventional signals of love sickness, in other words, to exaggerate and gently ridicule. Moreover, he controls our point of view toward the comicality of such behavior by putting observation of it into the mouths of women, servants, bystanders—occupants of the liminal world of "outsiderhood."[27] Women, because they are less demonstrative and in possession of a more subtle range of gesture than men, are enabled to comment on the absurdity of love's posturing. Especially when, as strangers in transsexual disguise, they enter into the male world, their function becomes that of mocking or criticizing stereotypical behavior.

We learn relatively little from stage directions about lovers' gestures in Shakespeare, but much from the observant commentary of women. Rosalind in *As You Like It*, for example, describes for Orlando the typical distraught young lover she would not have him be: one who features a lean cheek, a "blue" and sunken eye (referring presumably to dark circles under the eye), a beard neglected, and the like. If Orlando were to play the role of melancholy lover to the full, she mockingly instructs him, "your hose should be ungarter'd, your bonnet unbanded, your sleeve unbutton'd, your shoe untied, and everything about you demonstrating a careless desolation" (3.2.364–372). Rosalind offers this instruction to Orlando because she would not have him fall into such a stereotype. There are in fact warning symptoms, for he readily admits to being "love-shak'd." Rosalind notes with comic disapproval that Orlando "abuses our young plants with carving 'Rosalind' on their barks," hanging "odes upon hawthorns, and elegies on brambles" (ll. 352–354). Touchstone has no difficulty finding material for parody in Orlando's verses, and to Jaques Orlando is "Monsieur love."

Still, with Rosalind's curative instruction, Orlando learns to transcend the caricature of love melancholy represented in all its splendor in Silvius, whose many "actions most ridiculous" include sighing "upon a midnight pillow," "Wearing thy hearer in thy mistress' praise," and breaking from company abruptly, "as my passion now makes me." His is "the pale complexion of true love," and he follows Phebe "Like foggy south, puffing with wind and rain." He is "all made of sighs and tears."[28] Rosalind's amused impatience with such behavior, and her criticism of the scornful Phebe whose stereotypical feminine archness encourages such abasement in the male, are an essential perspective on the clichés of pastoralism.

Similar lessons are offered by Viola in *Twelfth Night* to the love-surfeited Orsino, who worships the unresponsive Olivia with "fertile tears, / With groans that thunder love, with sighs of fire" (1.5.250–251), and by Juliet to Romeo, whose exaggerated love symptoms learned in the service of Rosaline linger on in Romeo's mannered conceits and idolatrous vows (*Romeo and Juliet*, 2.2.109–110). Shakespeare's contrastive languages of gesture in love, one derived from the commonplaces of literary tradition and one iconoclastically forged from experience, are defined for us in good part by woman's wit. Comic success in these plays (and in this regard *Romeo and Juliet* begins as comedy) is measured by the triumph of the iconoclastic viewpoint, or, more precisely, by its ability as a liminal language to reform stereotype and render it socially useful in the reaggregated world of order with which Shakespeare's romantic comedy usually ends.

Servants, as outsiders and bystanders, are no less able to laugh at stereotypical love symptoms. The device is a venerable one in Tudor drama, in such diverse plays as John Medwall's *Fulgens and Lucrece* (ca. 1497) and John Lyly's *Endymion* (1588). Touchstone, already cited, provides an example in Shakespeare. Servants are in fact able to be more openly irreverent than women, in the holiday inversions of wisdom and simpleness that abound in Shakespeare's love comedies, and they are often paired with masters whose love symptoms are comically exaggerated. Speed, the witty servant in *The Two Gentlemen of Verona*, professes to know that his master is in love by the following stigmata:

> Marry, by these special marks: first, you have learn'd, like
> Sir Proteus, to wreathe your arms, like a malcontent; to
> relish a love-song, like a robin-redbreast; to walk alone, like
> one that had the pestilence; to sigh, like a schoolboy that
> had lost his A B C; to weep, like a young wench that had
> buried her grandam; to fast, like one that takes diet; to
> watch, like one that fears robbing; to speak puling, like a
> beggar at Hallowmas. (2.1.17–25)

When Valentine asks, "Are all these things perceiv'd in me?" Speed
punningly replies, "They are all perceiv'd without ye," that is, they
are outward signs. The contrast between Valentine's self-absorption in
what is for him a unique experience, and Speed's deft ability to see
what is so typical about his master's encounter with love, is essential
to our amusement at the scene.

Moth in *Love's Labor's Lost* is another servant whose comic irreverence
for his lovelorn master gives us an outsider's perspective on the conventional lore of Elizabethan psychology. Many of the particular symptoms suffered by Moth's master, the fantastical Don Armado, are those
also afflicting Valentine. The latter is said to "relish a love-song"; Don
Armado is satirically instructed by Moth "to jig off a tune at the tongue's
end, canary to it with your feet, humor it with turning up your eyelids,
sigh a note and sing a note, sometime through the throat, as if you
swallow'd love with singing love, sometime through the nose, as if you
snuff'd up love by smelling love" (*Love's Labor's Lost*, 3.1.11–16). Armado is also mockingly encouraged to pull his hat over his brows and
to fold his arms, like Valentine, in gestures that were conventionally
associated with love melancholy.[29] Moth urges Armado to stand "with
your hat penthouse-like o'er the shop of your eyes; with your arms
cross'd on your thin-bellied doublet like a rabbit on a spit; or your
hands in your pocket like a man after the old painting" (ll. 16-20). The
gesture of folded arms, moreover, visually links Armado with the lovesick young lords whose behavior he continually apes. Berowne speaks
of Cupid as "lord of folded arms, / Th' anointed sovereign of sighs and
groans, / Liege of all loiterers and malcontents" (ll. 179–181). The King
of Navarre, confronting Longaville with his hypocritical concealment
of love, chides him ironically: "You do not love Maria! Longaville /
Did never sonnet for her sake compile, / Nor never lay his wreathed
arms athwart / His loving bosom to keep down his heart!" (4.3.129–
132). Posturing, affectation, and hypocrisy deserve the comic exposure

they receive in this play, through servants' commentary as well as through the device of misdirected letters.

The language of conventional gesture in love is for Shakespeare, then, a language of comic exaggeration used chiefly by women, servants, bystanders, and others whose "outsiderhood" characterizes their satiric function in a world of inversion and holiday. What do we learn from their dialogue about the actual physical gestures used on Shakespeare's stage to depict love? Clearly, although stage directions are few, Shakespeare demands two contrastive acting styles: the overstated posturing of a Don Armado or Silvius, and the more subtle gesture of self-knowing young people in love such as Orlando (once he has gained some wisdom in love, at any rate), Rosalind, and Viola. One is a more "formal" style and the other more "natural," and the value of the polarity lies in the instructive contrast between the two.

The use of such a contrast is particularly evident in Benedick's skeptical journey toward falling in love in *Much Ado about Nothing*. To "look pale with love" is the symptom that Benedick is most anxious to avoid. "Prove that ever I lose more blood with love than I will get again with drinking," he insists, "pick out mine eyes with a ballad-maker's pen and hang me up at the door of a brothel-house for the sign of blind Cupid" (1.1.236–243). It is like him to refer to Elizabethan psychological lore in this way, at once familiar with the popular legend that each sigh costs the heart a drop of blood to be replenished by wine,[30] and tongue in cheek about the crude literalism of signs. In his view, a man's falling in love writes itself on the forehead "in an invisible baldrick." If he himself becomes so afflicted, Benedick vaunts, may the bull's horns be planted in his forehead, and "let me be vilely painted, and in such great letters as they write 'Here is good horse to hire,' let them signify under my sign 'Here you may see Benedick the married man' " (ll. 230–256). Benedick's cynicism about love's signs is moreover encouraged by what he sees in the conventional young Claudio, his fellow officer, for Claudio is all too ready to "be like a lover presently" and "tire the hearer with a book of words" in his mistress' praise (ll. 294–295).

When Benedick succumbs at last to love, his friends of course cannot resist scoffing at him in the visual terms that he has so vehemently rejected. The jokes about him are nearly all directed at his new and outwardly conventional appearance. He "brushes his hat o' mornings," his friends observe, and rubs himself with civet. His new clothes put

Don Pedro humorously in mind of "a Dutchman today, a Frenchman tomorrow, or in the shape of two countries at once, as, a German from the waist downward, all slops, and a Spaniard from the hip upward, no doublet." Most strikingly, he has shaved his beard and permitted the ornament of his cheeks to stuff tennis balls (3.2.32–44). Benedick's friends seek comic revenge for his hostility to love by labeling him as a type, an affected dandy, "Benedick the married man." Their language deals in reductive caricature, seeking humor in the face value of the sign. Yet their joking would have no point if Benedick were not in fact transformed in appearance. This most unconventional of men has discovered that he is like other men. There is something refreshing in Benedick's realization that he is susceptible to female charm, and his typicality manifests itself in a conventional adopting of costume suited to his new role as lover. At the same time, Benedick's achievement in love remains highly individual. Paradoxically he can now play a typical role without fear of its potentially reductive labels because of the self-knowledge he has attained. He has reconciled the apparent conflict between the two languages of gesture.

Shakespeare's women in love often succeed too in finding gestures that are typical and yet restrained and plausible. Rosalind in *As You Like It* certainly knows how a disdainful mistress is supposed to overact, for she observes in Phebe the "red glow of scorn and proud disdain" (3.4.52) of the stereotype. Rosalind herself professes expertise in the exaggerated signs of feminine behavior, recalling for Orlando how she, to cure a lovesick soul, would "grieve, be effeminate, changeable, longing and liking, proud, fantastical, apish, shallow, inconstant, full of tears, full of smiles; for every passion something and for no passion truly anything" (3.2.399–402). Yet left to herself, Rosalind is more apt to "go find a shadow and sigh till [Orlando] come" (4.1.208–209), or swoon at the sight of his blood on a handkerchief.

Sighs and tears, "womanish" signs in men, are for women themselves the natural tribulations of lovesickness, "poor fancy's followers" (*A Midsummer Night's Dream*, 1.1.155). Helena, in *All's Well That Ends Well*, cannot conceal from the Countess her being in love with Bertram, for her paleness and sorrow are eloquent signs to the sympathetic older woman: "thy cheeks / Confess it, th' one to th' other," the Countess tells Helena, "and thine eyes / See it so grossly shown in thy behaviors / That in their kind they speak it" (1.3.173–176). Viola (Cesario) in *Twelfth Night* knows that Olivia is in love by her languishing silences and moodiness: "methought her eyes had lost her tongue, / For she did speak in starts distractedly. / She loves me, sure!" (2.2.20–22). The sensitivity of such women to a delicate and suitable language of gesture renders them able to instruct men who, though given to flamboyant signs of love melancholy, to folded arms and hats pulled over brows, to wooing their mistresses with music, to neglect of dress or conversely to fastidiousness, and to excesses of tears, sighing, and paleness, are nonetheless sometimes able to overcome their penchant for theatrical stereotypes and learn nuance. Shakespeare's contrastive languages of gesture in depicting love reveal with a special clarity the inadequacy of Renaissance stereotypes as well as their usefulness in the theater.

The more distressing passions like sorrow, fear, and anger present Shakespeare with a more striking polarity, and hence a more intense challenge, in his use of contrastive languages of gesture. On the one hand, the strong passions lend themselves to disfiguring facial expressions and movement. Strong passions call for vivid acting, and Shakespeare wrote for spectators who were familiar with a universally comprehended lore of conventional signs through which Renaissance students of behavior cataloged the predictable physical manifestations of potent inner distress. On the other hand, the violence of such gestures would appear to invite the kind of overacting that Hamlet mistrusts when, for example, he admonishes the player of Lucianus in "The Murder of Gonzago" to "leave thy damnable faces, and begin" (*Hamlet*, 3.2.251). How are Shakespeare and his actors to depict strong emotion through an understood language of gesture without tearing a passion to tatters, and how are they to signal a more private distress that can find little comfort in stereotyped gestural response?

Shakespeare had to depend ultimately on the professional skills of his colleagues in the acting company not to make the judicious grieve by strutting and bellowing.[31] He considerably aids their task, nonetheless, by distinguishing occasions when strong gesture is dramatically appropriate from those when it is not. Strong gesture belongs to public and ceremonial occasions, as when momentous news is announced to a royal assembly, or when the community publicly mourns the death of a leader. Grief over the loss of a child, spouse, or parent requires demonstrative response, emphasizing the social role of those participating in a ritual. If an important figure has died, the ceremonial response is directly that of a rite of passage. Signs are meant to be interpreted at face value and to serve a symbolic, traditional function. Ceremonial gestures of sorrow and other strong emotions are rhetorical ornaments, appropriate garments put on for an occasion of grave social significance.

Conversely, strong gesture may be overstated and inappropriate. Grotesque distortions of the visage and histrionic gesture may betoken frenzy and destructive loss of control. In a comic context, exaggerated and stereotypical fear or anger not shared by the spectators may seem trite or ludicrous. The inadequacy of stereotypical gesture is especially marked in the liminal world of inversion, ambiguity, and disguise. Sometimes the gestures invoked, like pallor and hair standing on end, are so conventional and so unsuited for the theater that they are employed only in reported scenes of offstage event. We hear rhetorical set pieces verbally composed of Renaissance truisms about the physical signs of strong emotion, rather than seeing actors portraying the thing itself. Such devices offer a critical perspective on the conventional language of Elizabethan psychology by stressing its unsuitability, its ambiguity in context, its failure to record authentic experience. The interplay between stereotypical gesture and a more plausible language suited to stage action constantly tests the abuse and proper use of histrionic gesture on Shakespeare's stage.

Clarity of meaning is paramount in ceremonial demonstrations of grief. It is seen, for example, in the certainty with which characters onstage understand the portentous look of those who arrive with unwelcome news. "There's business in these faces," says Cymbeline, commenting on the approach of Doctor Cornelius and the Queen's ladies. "Why so sadly / Greet you our victory? You look like Romans, / And not o' th' court of Britain" (*Cymbeline*, 5.5.23–25). And in fact their visually eloquent soberness is occasioned by the death of Cymbeline's Queen. In moments of bad tidings such as these, Shakespeare underscores the reliability of visual signs by allowing them to "speak" first. The furrowed brow, trembling, shaking of the head, weeping or sorrowful look of the eye, and hand held on breast are given their theatrical moment to communicate directly to the audience and then be interpreted by onstage observers. The Earl of Northumberland, awaiting news from Shrewsbury field in the opening scene of *2 Henry IV*, sees disaster written in the expression and movement of Morton before that person has time to speak; the shaking of his head, the trembling, the furrowed brow, and the whiteness of his cheek are all "like to a title-leaf" foretelling "the nature of a tragic volume" whose contents are the death of Northumberland's son Hotspur (1.1.60–61). Archbishop Scroop, in *Richard II*, wordlessly conveys to the King his unwelcome news by his "sour" looks and his "dull and heavy eye" (3.2.193–196). Cleopatra knows from unwilling eye and face when messengers bring her vexing news of Antony's intended departure or marriage to Octavia.[32]

Shakespeare insists so strongly on the interrelation of gesture and meaning in such public utterances that he occasionally joins spectacle and speech in a prolonged theatrical moment. When the Earl of Salisbury in *King John* must deliver to Constance the sad news of a marriage that threatens her son's dynastic hopes, for example, her repeated questions call attention to the gestures of the actor portraying Salisbury and the equivalence of those gestures to verbal speech:

> What dost thou mean by shaking of thy head?
> . . . . .
> What means that hand upon that breast of thine?
> Why holds thine eye that lamentable rheum,
> Like a proud river peering o'er his bounds?
> Be these sad signs confirmers of thy words?   (3.1.19–24)[33]

Words and signs reinforce one another, using the conventional language of gesture and of sorrowful utterance to intensify an abrupt change of direction, a crisis, a moment of painful realization.

Public grief justifies histrionic gestures that can appear misplaced or exaggerated in a less solemn context. The wreathing or folding of arms, for instance, used (as we have seen) as a stereotypical token of love melancholy in *Love's Labor's Lost* to identify Don Armado as an affected poseur and in *The Two Gentlemen of Verona* as part of Speed's mocking inventory of Valentine's love symptoms,[34] is painfully eloquent on the occasion of Lucrece's ravishment in *The Rape of Lucrece*. Alone with her sorrow, the heroine laments that she has "no one to blush with me, / To cross their arms and hang their heads with mine" (ll. 792–793). Later, when she is joined by her husband and his associates, she shares her grief with them through gesture, accompanying her sad tale "With head declin'd, and voice damm'd up with woe, / With sad set eyes, and wreathed arms across" (ll. 1661–62). Sorrow like hers needs physical expression; conventionality of gesture in such an instance is not hackneyed but appropriate. Significantly, she sees the gesture as com-

83

munal, a ritual to be performed with those persons who will second her grief and support her cause. Lavinia's fate in *Titus Andronicus*, so like Lucrece's, calls forth from her grieving uncle Marcus a similar gesture of "sorrow-wreathen knot" (3.2.4), though in this instance the need for communal and family gesture ironically intensifies the inability of Lavinia herself and Titus, owing to their dismemberment, to complete the ceremonial forms of sorrow that the occasion demands.[35] The related communal gesture of pulling the hat over the brows, used in *Love's Labor's Lost* and elsewhere[36] to denote foolish love melancholy, seems appropriate for Macduff's grief over the slaughter of his wife and children (*Macbeth*, 4.3.208–210), though here too, as in *Titus*, the emphasis is on the dislocations under tyranny that deny the sufferer the public and ceremonial grief that his words and his gestures yearn to express.

Because public and ceremonial mourning is part of a rite of passage, it incorporates into its function transition as well as reincorporation. Highly conventional and formal in its signs, it must still express a liminal sense of powerlessness and equality in the presence of death before reaffirming order and hierarchy. Death, darkness, the womb, and invisibility are all metaphors for the liminal state.[37] Perhaps the transitional character of mourning helps explain the transcending and even reversing of sexual roles so commonly a part of ceremonial grief. Men, as we have seen, find themselves able to shed "womanish" tears of regret for civil slaughter or the failure of a great enterprise. Men bestow kisses of farewell on their fallen comrades in strife or battle as they would never do in other circumstances.[38] Men's role in ceremonial grief calls for tenderness, vulnerability, and a host of "feminine" values forbidden them in their normal sex-stereotyped roles.

Women are transformed in an opposite direction. No longer muted or restrained as in more private emotions, women take the initiative in ceremonial mourning. Their role becomes one of showing depth of feeling through marked physical manifestations of sorrow. They often act in concert, and speak for the community. They unbind and tear their hair, scratch their cheeks, beat their breasts, and utter lamenting cries. They do so on Shakespeare's stage as in many traditional societies that regularly enjoin ritual public grief. Loose or disheveled hair is a conventional sign in Tudor drama of distraction, grief, or madness, as for instance in W. Wager's *The Longer Thou Livest the More Fool Thou*

Art.[39] It is a commonplace in the emblem books, as in Alciati's Emblem 56 and Whitney's Emblem 30.[40]

Shakespeare's use of this highly conventionalized language of gesture is not without its irony, however. The many women who gather to beat their breasts and tear their hair in *Richard III* are widowed, forgotten, desperate women whose plight suggests that of *Respublica* herself. "Why do you weep so oft, and beat your breast?" (2.2.3), ask the Duke of Clarence's children of their grandmother, the Duchess of York. The answer is that Richard of Gloucester, her youngest son, has arranged the murder of his own brother Clarence. The Duchess assembles with other widowed women, powerful only in their curses and gestures of grief, to mourn the tragedy of England's civil conflict and thus perform a ceremonial of grief that must precede any restoration of order. In their function as bystanders, unable to prevent the catastrophe at hand, they remind critics of the traditional chorus in the Greek theater.[41]

The widow Constance in *King John*, similarly victimized by a power struggle among men, makes of her disordered hair a token of her affliction and her painful conviction that she will never see her child again. At one moment, she binds up her tresses as a reminder that "my poor child is a prisoner"; at another, she tears and unbinds her hair, saying, "I will not keep this form upon my head / When there is such disorder in my wit" (3.4.61–102). Her binding and unbinding of her hair express her powerlessness at the hands of the King of France and Cardinal Pandulph. The only authority such women enjoy is that of prophecy, like Cassandra in *Troilus and Cressida*, whose entrance "*raving*" (2.2.99) means that she has her hair about her ears in prophetic mourning for the fall of Troy.

What interests Shakespeare in ceremonial and traditional gesture, then, is its ability to express a personal experience of sorrow that transcends and even criticizes hierarchical social function. He can be more openly critical of formalized grief when its conventional expression exceeds the occasion for which it is intended. At such moments Shakespeare makes us aware through irony of the imprecision and crudeness to which physical signs are vulnerable. The wringing of hands, for example, seems appropriate enough in *The Two Gentlemen of Verona* when Silvia is distressed at the banishment of Valentine, "Wringing her hands, whose whiteness so became them / As if but now they waxed pale for woe" (3.1.227–228). In this comedy, however, painful separation easily collapses into parody, as when Launce tells us how his own departure from his family was marked by "My mother weeping, my father wailing, my sister crying, our maid howling, our cat wringing her hands" (2.3.6–7). The Nurse in *Romeo and Juliet* uses the same gesture as she returns to Juliet with the news of Tybalt's death and Romeo's banishment—"Ay me, what news?" Juliet asks, "Why dost thou wring thy hands?" (3.2.36)—but the gesture only ushers in an exchange of dialogue fraught with ambiguity and misunderstanding. The subsequent grief of Juliet's family over her apparent death, though earnestly felt, seems artificial to us because it is ironically misdirected. Gertrude, too, evokes an impatient response from Hamlet by her "wringing of [her] hands" at the slaying of Polonius. Her response is genuine enough, and appropriate to the desperation of her present situation, but she has not yet learned to express a sorrow for the deed that most concerns her grieving son. Hamlet does not want the wringing of hands for Polonius, just as he cannot be satisfied with the "trappings and the suits of woe" in which he is garbed; he wants to "wring [Gertrude's] heart" (*Hamlet*, 1.2.86, 3.4.35–36).

Shakespeare approaches the conventional language of grief, then, with a respect for its ability to channel potentially destructive emotion into forms that are consoling to the community. Even so, what he embraces most of all is the liberating process through which stereotypical social roles are enlarged and transformed into allowed patterns of male tenderness and female self-assertion. He chafes at empty forms of grief as inexpressive of felt need, and searches for private expressions of grief in situations that public mourning cannot reach because an unfeeling social order has lost contact with those who would honestly know themselves. In the theater Shakespeare's dual view of gestural language accounts for both his extensive use of formal grieving gesture and his ironic contexts that so often define the limits of stereotypical action.

In depicting fear and anger on his stage, Shakespeare encounters a particularly sharp confrontation between two languages of gesture, one plausible and one stereotypical. Fear and anger call for riveting effects that can prove difficult to carry off in the theater, or are too easily overdone. Elizabethan treatises on fear, for example, spoke of hair standing on end, gooseflesh, rapid beating of the heart, weakness of limb, knocking of the knees, inability to speak, starting or widening of the eyes, and pallor. These symptoms accord with Renaissance medical theory, which asserted that in fear the heart contracts, withdrawing heat from the body in order to comfort the heart; the skin not only loses its color but shrivels, producing gooseflesh and hair standing on end.[42] Some of these symptoms are not really visual or theatrically feasible, however, and an important question remains as to what Shakespeare's spectators actually saw on stage.

We do catch glimpses from time to time, to be sure, of the real action of fear, as when the young Rutland faces the imminent prospect of slaughter in *3 Henry VI*. "How now, is he dead already?" mocks his cruel executioner, Clifford, "Or is it fear / That makes him close his eyes?" (1.3.10–11). The gestures called for are understated and plausible. When Horatio and the soldiers on guard encounter the Ghost of Hamlet's father, the reaction is no less suited to the terror of the occasion: Horatio admits that the apparition "harrows me with fear and wonder," and Bernardo comments to Horatio after the Ghost's first disappearance that "You tremble and look pale" (*Hamlet*, 1.1.44–54). Even here, the mood of fear is created to a significant extent by descriptive evocation after the event. Horatio, in reporting the encounter to Hamlet, says of Bernardo and Marcellus that the figure of Hamlet's father walked "By their oppress'd and fear-surprised eyes," while they, "distill'd / Almost to jelly with the act of fear, / Stand dumb and speak not to him" (1.2.203–206). The nameless terror of such an experience is communicated in the first scene by the actor's frightened gesture and then in the second by the more atmospheric language of narrative account. The former is limited by necessity to the concrete language of acting; the latter permits unrestrained use of the exaggerated terms of Renaissance medical theory.

Some of Shakespeare's most heightened evocations of terror are not staged before our eyes at all. Imagined offstage action allows him to use the standard Elizabethan depictions of fear as set pieces of description rather than as guides to plausible stage action. When the Ghost in *Hamlet* tells his son of the horrors of his current torment in which his sins are being "burnt and purg'd away," he chooses images that by their very overstatement go beyond the bounds of plausible acting. Every word of his untold tale, he says to Hamlet, would "freeze thy young blood, / Make thy two eyes, like stars, start from their spheres, / Thy knotted and combined locks to part, / And each particular hair to stand an end, / Like quills upon the fearful porpentine" (1.5.14–21). Hamlet, in turn, is described as using overstated gesture in his encounter with Ophelia in her private chambers, "Pale as his shirt, his knees knocking each other, / And with a look so piteous in purport / As if he had been loosed out of hell / To speak of horrors" (2.1.78–81). Ferdinand, in *The Tempest*, is reported to have leaped from the seemingly wrecked vessel, its rigging aflame with St. Elmo's fire, into the foaming sea, "With hair up-staring—then like reeds, not hair" (1.2.213).

Even when characters respond on stage to some terrifying event, the language they use to describe their own gestures can rely heavily on standard medical parlance. They speak of their hair standing on end, for example, even though the actors do not literally suit the action to the word; the many costume inventories of the period are notably lacking in the so-called fright wigs that the actors of later centuries sometimes employed to mimic the rising of hair from the scalp.[43] Shakespeare's actors seem instead to have used his words to suggest what then need not be literally seen. Macbeth is deeply troubled, when the witches' first prophecy has proved true, by an evil suggestion "Whose horrid image doth unfix my hair / And make my seated heart knock at my ribs, / Against the use of nature" (*Macbeth*, 1.3.135–137). Brutus, encountering the ghost of Julius Caesar at Philippi, asks what it is "That mak'st my blood cold and my hair to stare?" (*Julius Caesar*, 4.3.280). When Queen Margaret curses her many enemies in *Richard III*, causing them to "tremble" and "quake like rebels," Buckingham remarks that "My hair doth stand an end to hear her curses" (1.3.159–161, 303). The exaggerated gesture of the hair, drawn from commonplace Renaissance accounts of fear, is more suited to verbal suggestion than to theatrical mimesis.

Pallor too is a reaction more easily described in words than physiologically induced by the actor; accordingly, its effect is sometimes created by evoking in words a psychological truism that complements what the actor actually does with his expression. The standard theory invoked in such verbal descriptions was that the blood retires to the inner regions of the body in a reaction to fright, leaving the features bloodless and pale. We can see this theory reflected, for example, in Macbeth's derisive rebuke to a frightened servent for his "goose look," "linen cheeks," and "whey-face." "Go prick thy face, and over-red thy fear, / Thou lily-liver'd boy," Macbeth jeeringly commands (*Macbeth*,

5.3.12–17). The actor playing the servant need not actually go pale, for Macbeth's words provide this effect while the actor presumably simulates the experience of fear by cowering before Macbeth, hesitating, and the like. For serious representations of fear Shakespeare consistently relies on his actors to portray the emotion in plausible and even subdued gesture, while they speak verbal set pieces that invoke the more stereotypical effects found in Renaissance medical theory.

Shakespeare also finds use for the stereotypical symptoms of fear in comedy, since comic cowardice thrives on overstated and stock response. Amused reports of cowardly behavior seem to correspond with the outlandish behavior we see on stage. In *1 Henry IV*, for example, the thieves who run away from the disguised Hal and Poins after the Gads' Hill robbery put on a fine display of abject retreat. Hal laughs to see them "all scattered and possess'd with fear / So strongly that they dare not meet each other; / Each takes his fellow for an officer" (2.2.104–106). Later, at the tavern, Hal chides Falstaff for having "carried your guts away as nimbly, with as quick dexterity, and roar'd for mercy, and still run and roar'd, as ever I heard bullcalf" (2.4.256–258). However much Falstaff may have played the lion in instinctive cowardice, the account seems a fair estimate of the thieves' broad gestures of comic fear. As Bardolph concedes with the faultless logic of a truebred coward, "Faith, I ran when I saw others run" (l. 299). The terror of the Clowns in *The Winter's Tale* at being held responsible for Perdita's elopement produces comic gestures that are no less exaggerated. "Never saw I / Wretches so quake," relates a lord. "They kneel, they kiss the earth, / Forswear themselves as often as they speak" (5.1.198–200). We trust the reliability of this report because we have already seen the Clowns reacting to Autolycus' colorful account of the tortures that Florizel's accomplices are to suffer. Puck, in *A Midsummer Night's Dream*, frightens the Athenian tradesmen at their rehearsal and then regales Oberon with an account of their panic. We share the laughter because we too have seen them scatter like wild fowl, fall over one another, cry "Help!" and "Murder!", lose the strength in their legs, and so on (3.2.19–30). The comic portrayal of fear is instructive because it is able to use uninhibitedly the standard Elizabethan signs of fear that Shakespeare elsewhere finds too stereotyped for serious expression.

Anger, even more than fear, seems to invite overacting in the theater. Furious bluster is, after all, the trademark in the medieval religious drama of King Herod and Termagent, those ludicrous villains whose howls and overstated gestures are cited by Hamlet to warn the traveling players against sawing the air too much with their hands "in the very torrent, tempest, and, as I may say, whirlwind of your passion" (*Hamlet*, 3.2.4–7). Renaissance medical theory too reflects a widespread attitude toward anger as extravagantly violent. According to the handbooks, anger is a mixed emotion and hence inherently unstable. Being compounded of grief at a discomfiture and desire for vengeance, it can lead to opposite effects: pallor can be induced by the migration of the blood to the heart, as in grief, whereas choleric anger can puff up the heart and send "burning flames and kindled spirits" ascending into the head where they produce reddened countenance, fiery eyes, and a host of terrible effects. "From hence," writes La Primaudaye, "commeth change of countenance, shaking of the lippes and of the whole visage, stopping of speech and such other terrible lookes to beholde, more meete for a beaste then for a man."[44] The sufferer's eyes, "full of fire and flame which this *Passion* doth kindle, seeme fiery and sparckling; his face is wonderfully inflamed as by a certaine refluxe of blood which ascends from the heart: his haire stands vpright and staring with horror, his mouth cannot deliuer his words: his tongue falters, his feete and hands are in perpetuall motion."[45]

Shakespeare's characters are well aware of these Elizabethan commonplaces about anger and its ability to induce intense physical distortions in the face and body. His characters use this familiar language of signs as they describe in one another's behavior the gnawing of lips, choking, humming, sourness of demeanor, glaring or staring of the eye, foaming at the mouth, setting the teeth, stretching the nostrils, kicking the rushes beneath one's feet,[46] showing an angry spot of red in the brow or in the eyes, trembling, sweating, and showing pallor. Yet they do so in images that make plain the stereotypical nature of this language and its unsuitability at times for direct action in the theater. Set pieces describing offstage action are common, as when Menenius and others visit Coriolanus at his camp outside Rome. Coriolanus is reported to "bite his lip / And hum at good Cominius" (*Coriolanus*, 5.1.51–52), and his anger grows to godlike proportions in Menenius' hyperbolic account:

> The tartness of his face sours ripe grapes. When he walks,
> he moves like an engine, and the ground shrinks before his
> treading. He is able to pierce a corslet with his eye; talks
> like a knell, and his hum is a battery.   (5.4.17–21)

On stage, to be sure, Coriolanus does display real anger toward the plebeians. The effect of the reported speeches in Act 5, on the other hand, is to evoke through the deliberately exaggerated language of Renaissance medical theory the image of an angry Mars. Coriolanus cannot effectively continue to play the role assigned to him, for he is, as he freely confesses, no actor. The language of wrathful gesture mocks him because its heightened terms do not describe the complex man we see on stage yielding to his mother's entreaties.

Reports of the visible signs of anger can also be used to describe characters who are on stage, thereby providing the audience with visual detail about changes in countenance which the audience might not be expected to see or which the actors might find difficult to simulate. As Caesar and his train pass by Brutus and Cassius in *Julius Caesar*, Brutus expresses his conclusion that things have not gone well for Caesar by observing, "The angry spot doth glow on Caesar's brow, / And all the rest look like a chidden train." Calpurnia is pale, notes Brutus, but Cicero too is reddened; he "Looks with such ferret and such fiery eyes / As we have seen him in the Capitol, / Being cross'd in conference by some senators" (1.2.183–188). These speeches assuredly contain hints to the actors of Caesar's entourage about how they are to behave on stage, but the details of angry reddening and fiery eyes are supplied from Renaissance medical theory and convey to the audience in a universally understood language what would be visually appropriate for such an event. Cardinal Beaufort's "red sparkling eyes" in *2 Henry VI* are similarly described for us by the Duke of Gloucester as a token of malice (3.1.154). When the Duke of Suffolk, in the next scene, falls from favor because of his enemies' machinations, he proclaims his hatred for them in a set speech telling how he would act if curses could kill. He would pronounce curses, he says,

> Deliver'd strongly through my fixed teeth,
> With full as many signs of deadly hate,
> As lean-fac'd Envy in her loathsome cave.
> My tongue should stumble in mine earnest words,
> Mine eyes should sparkle like the beaten flint,
> Mine hair be fix'd an end, as one distract. (3.2.313–318)

His own anger, evident on stage, is fortified by this descriptive catalog.

These descriptions all refer to the traditionally reddening effects of rage, but the same dramatic means can be used to invoke the pallor that alternatively results from the mixed nature of rage, from its grieving rather than its vengeful aspect. Benedick's erstwhile companions in *Much Ado about Nothing*, Claudio and Don Pedro, note that Benedick "looks pale" as he quarrels with them, prompting Don Pedro to ask, "Art thou sick, or angry?" When Benedick thereupon "changes more and more," Don Pedro concludes, "I think he be angry indeed" (5.1.131–141). This extreme change of color, like reddening, is more a commonplace symptom from medical lore than a cue for the actor.

The extreme signs of rage are sometimes directly employed on Shakespeare's stage, but only as a way of depicting a terrible madness that can account for such extravagant behavior. The association between rage and madness is a commonplace of medical treatises; anger is viewed as a disease of the spirit and body that might well prove "grievous to suffer, and dangerous to life.[47] As John Davies of Hereford expresses it,

> No *Beast* is halfe so fell, in maddest moode,
> As *Man*, when *Furie* sets on fire his *bloud*.
>
> From which *fire* flie out *Sparkles* through his *eies*,
> Who stare, as if they would their *holdes* inlarge,
> The *Cheekes* with boiling *Choler* burning rise,
> The *mouth* doth thundring (*Canon*-like) discharge
> The *fire* which doth the *Stomacke* overcharge:
> The *teeth* doe (grating) one another grind;
> The *fists* are fast, in motion to giue *charge*,
> The *Limbes* doe tremble, *feete* no footing find
> But stampe, or stand vnconstant as the *Winde*.[48]

Shakespeare's characters who act in this fashion are regarded as suffering a kind of madness, not of a despondent and suicidal sort as in melancholia, but of uncontrolled fury. When Othello rolls his eyes and gnaws his nether lip as he prepares to kill Desdemona, she perceives these signs as "portents" that "Some bloody passion shakes your very frame" (*Othello*, 5.2.45–47). The symptoms are all the more remarkable in one whose nature has been reported to be such as "passion could not shake" (4.1.267). Tybalt similarly shakes and trembles in *Romeo and Juliet* as he withdraws reluctantly from an encounter with Romeo at Capulet's ball, saying, "Patience perforce with willful choler meeting / Makes my flesh tremble in their different greeting" (1.5.90–91). Staring of the eyes is a part of Cassius' passionate demeanor during his quarrel with Brutus in *Julius Caesar*; Brutus interjects, "Must I give way and room to your rash choler? / Shall I be frighted when a madman stares? . . . Go show your slaves how choleric you are, / And make your bondmen tremble" (4.3.39–44). The repeated emphasis on staring, trembling, and rolling the eyes suggests the kind of stage action that an Elizabethan audience would recognize as a conventional sign of furious distress.

Shakespeare does acknowledge that "hard-favor'd rage" can be an admirable sign of manly zeal in time of war, as when Henry V at Harfleur challenges his soldiers to "Stiffen the sinews," "lend the eye a terrible aspect," "set the teeth and stretch the nostril wide," and so on (*Henry V*, 3.1.7–15). For the most part, though, Shakespeare uses the gestural language of wrath to describe a physical condition that is debilitating and suffocating. The Duke of York is so dismayed at the loss of many French territories in *1 Henry VI* that he can scarcely utter a sound: "Speak, Winchester," he says, "for boiling choler chokes / The hollow passage of my poison'd voice" (5.4.120–121). The Duke of Buckingham, according to firsthand reports of his trial for treason in *Henry VIII*, "was stirr'd / With such an agony he sweat extremely, / And something spoke in choler, ill and hasty" (2.1.32–34). We are told that mighty Ajax, stung to vengeful anger in *Troilus and Cressida*, "foams at mouth" (5.5.36). Choler can be accompanied by melancholy silence and trembling, as in the case of Parson Evans awaiting a duel with Dr. Caius in *The Merry Wives of Windsor* ("Pless my soul, how full of chollors I am, and trempling of mind! . . . How melancholies I am!" 3.1.11–13), or of Aaron the Moor in *Titus Andronicus* contemplating revenge with "my deadly-standing eye, / My silence, and my cloudy melancholy" (2.3.32–33). Most of these effects are offstage or provide details the audience would not easily see in the actor's countenance, so that the stock images of rage are used as a verbal means of offsetting and complementing what the audience does see on stage.

In the depictions of love, sorrow, fear, and anger that we have examined so far, Shakespeare reveals a continuing interest in the problem of interpretation. What is Polonius to make of Hamlet's appearance in Ophelia's chamber with his doublet all unbraced, his stockings fouled, and no hat upon his head? Diagnosis seems simple enough, but Polonius is misled; conventional signs by their very nature lend themselves to superficial judgments. Yet an ability to read the ordinary meaning of signs is essential to many interpretations on stage, as when the Earl of Northumberland in *2 Henry IV* sees disaster in the furrowed brow and trembling of the newsbearer from Shrewsbury field. Scenes of visual interpretation often coincide with a turning in the plot, with the arrival of momentous news or some other significant revelation. How are spectators, both onstage and in the theater auditorium, to judge correctly the significance of the visual signals presented to them?

Shakespeare seems particularly concerned with questions of interpretation in a group of emotions that include amazement, distraction, and shame. These emotions arise at times of crisis in the lives of protagonists and are usually witnessed by onstage spectators who describe and interpret what they behold. We in turn are witnesses to both the gestures and the response. This witnessing produces an interplay between stage action and verbal description that centers on the problem of meaning in visual language.

A number of stage directions in Shakespeare seem to recognize amazement or stupefaction as identifiable by a clearly defined set of theatrical signs. "*Enter Cromwell, standing amazed*," reads a stage direction in *Henry VIII*, as the loyal follower of Wolsey comes to his fallen lord after having heard the news of Wolsey's reversal of fortune. The stage direction implies that an actor would know what to do and the audience how to interpret. The gesture is marked by a frozen posture and an inability to speak. Certainly Wolsey is not at a loss to understand the meaning of Cromwell's gesture. Though Cromwell professes "I have no power to speak, sir," Wolsey knows what he is thinking. "What, amaz'd / At my misfortunes?" (3.2.372–374). In *Richard II*, similarly, the stage direction specifies "*Enter Aumerle, amazed*," when this young supporter of King Richard breaks in upon the new King Henry IV in hopes of obtaining pardon before his father, the Duke of York, can arrive. "What means our cousin, that he stares and looks / So wildly?" asks King Henry, reading the look of Aumerle in a glance (5.3.23–25).

Sudden amazement is plainly written on the faces of the courtiers in *Richard III* who hear Richard of Gloucester's abrupt announcement of the death of the Duke of Clarence, whom they all thought pardoned: "*They all start*" (2.1.80). The visible effect on them is pallor. "Look I so pale, Lord Dorset, as the rest?" asks Buckingham, to which Dorset replies, "Ay, my good lord; and no man in this presence / But his red color hath forsook his cheeks" (ll. 84–86). Speechlessness, staring, starting, and turning pale are thus the chief signs of amazement. The turning pale is not easily simulated or perceived in an Elizabethan theater and therefore is supplied verbally, but the other signals are straightforward and intelligible.

Distraction or preoccupation is a state of mind that particularly calls for interpretation, since the person who behaves thus is withdrawn into himself and must be understood chiefly through gestures. We find in Shakespeare, accordingly, a number of speeches that spell out in some detail how a character behaves in a state of preoccupation, as seen from the observer's point of view. When Wolsey, in *Henry VIII*, discovers to his horror that he has permitted a letter meant for the Pope to come to the eyes of King Henry, thereby betraying Wolsey in his attempt to stay the divorce of Queen Katharine, Wolsey is minutely observed in his "moody" and "vex'd" state of mind by the Duke of Norfolk:

> Some strange commotion
> Is in his brain. He bites his lip, and starts,
> Stops on a sudden, looks upon the ground,
> Then lays his finger on his temple; straight
> Springs out into fast gait, then stops again,
> Strikes his breast hard, and anon he casts
> His eye against the moon. (3.2.112–118)

Well may the King conclude, "There is a mutiny in 's mind." Norfolk's account is conventionalized, and presumably in the theater we are given the opportunity to compare this finite repertory of appropriate movements with the free range of gesture to which the actor has access.[49] Even so, Wolsey's actions on stage must correspond to the particularized description of his lips, eyes, fingers, arms, and gait, for we see him the entire time that Norfolk is talking quietly to Surrey and Suffolk. Interpretation depends on the fixed relationship between gesture and meaning. Wolsey, unaware that he is observed, cannot conceal his state of mind from the discerning viewer because preoccupation declares itself in almost involuntary telltale actions.

Distracted persons are thus especially good subjects for interpretation of visual signs; their preoccupation renders them oblivious of observation, while the strength of the emotion produces a markedly physical response. Brutus' preoccupation on the eve of the assassination of Caesar, in *Julius Caesar*, conveys itself through gestures that Portia finds unmistakable in meaning. She recalls to Brutus how "yesternight, at

95

supper, / You suddenly arose, and walk'd about, / Musing and sighing, with your arms across . . . you scratch'd your head, / And too impatiently stamp'd with your foot," and "with an angry wafture of your hand, / Gave sign for me to leave you" (2.1.238–247). Although these actions are described as having taken place offstage, they appear to be an honest expression of the relationship we see on stage. So too with Hotspur, who on the eve of another desperate adventure is observed by his wife to be preoccupied in many of the same ways:

> Why dost thou bend thine eyes upon the earth,
> And start so often when thou sit'st alone?
> Why hast thou lost the fresh blood in thy cheeks,
> And given my treasures and my rights of thee
> To thick-ey'd musing and curs'd melancholy?
>
> (*1 Henry IV*, 2.3.42–46)

We learn further that Hotspur murmurs in his sleep and is so bestirred by his visions that "beads of sweat have stood upon thy brow / Like bubbles in a late-disturbed stream, / And in thy face strange motions have appear'd, / Such as we see when men restrain their breath / On some great sudden hest" (ll. 58–62). Clearly these mannerisms are consistent with Hotspur's onstage behavior and help provide ready identification of his "humour" for the audience, as for his wife.

Even if amazement and preoccupation declare themselves in gestures that are reassuringly interpretable on Shakespeare's stage, however, the potential for ambiguity or deception remains strong. The emotion of shame is especially hard to diagnose from its outward symptoms. The shameful blush may represent one of two opposite responses: dismay and confusion at an undeserved accusation, or admission of guilt. The choice between the two is difficult for the viewer who must draw conclusions from signs that are visually indistinguishable. The choice is also one of moral judgment, deciding innocence or guilt. Shakespeare underscores the complexity of the interpretive task by presenting us with not one onstage audience (as usually with amazement or preoccupation) but with two, or even more, divided among themselves about the meaning of what they and we presumably behold. The fact that the blush itself is not really visible in the Elizabethan theater intensifies the focus of the scene on contrasting interpretive statement and on the illusory potential of gesture. We as theater audience possess an omniscient knowledge of the issue being judged and hence are in a position

to evaluate the responses of those who offer an opinion, but that om-
niscience paradoxically increases our awareness of the relativity of visual
signs.

The public accusation of Hero in *Much Ado about Nothing* builds the
scene at church around Hero's blushing response to Claudio's wrongful
but earnestly intended accusations. Hero says nothing; her lover, her
father, her priest, and her friends must judge her from the way she
acts. Claudio is convinced that her blushes are "but the sign and sem-
blance of her honor" when he accuses her of infidelity:

> Behold how like a maid she blushes here!
> O, what authority and show of truth
> Can cunning sin cover itself withal! (4.1.33–35)

He concludes, "her blush is guiltiness, not modesty" (l. 41). Leonato,
Hero's father, is even more strongly convinced that her blushes are
affirmations of guilt: "Could she here deny / The story that is printed
in her blood?" (ll. 120–121). Friar Francis, on the other hand, who has
noted "A thousand blushing apparitions / To start into her face, a
thousand innocent shames / In angel whiteness beat away those blushes"
(ll. 158–160), knows from his experience in observation that Hero is
innocent. We are thus presented dramatically with three competing
readings of her outward responses: that they are false signs of innocence,
or the signs of guilt, or true signs of innocence. Our knowledge of her
innocence enables us to know which interpretation is true, so that a
correlation exists for us between gesture and meaning, but the dramatic
emphasis in the scene itself is on error. We are similarly invited to
examine the causes of misinterpretation when the wrongly accused
Hermione in *The Winter's Tale* declares her belief that in the eyes of
the gods "innocence shall make / False accusation blush" (3.2.30–31),
or when the innocent Humphrey of Gloucester in *2 Henry VI* vows to
his false accusers that "thou shalt not see me blush / Nor change my
countenance for this arrest" (3.1.98–99). Wolsey, confronted with evidence of dealing behind the King's back in *Henry VIII*, is taunted by
his political enemies to "blush and cry 'guilty' " and thereby "show a
little honesty," but his retort offers an opposite construction on his
gesture: "If I blush, / It is to see a nobleman want manners" (3.2.305–
308).

The blush thus illustrates several aspects of the visual signaling we
have been examining in this chapter: Shakespeare's ready acquaintance

with conventional associations of stock gestures or expressions, his reliance on those gestures as a language for the communication of inner feeling, and at the same time his perception that they are inherently limited by their conventional nature and hence prone to exaggeration and distortion. His attractive characters discover that they need to be wary of appearances, for the language of gesture seems all too well suited to exaggerated self-indulgence. The folded arms, tears, sighs, paleness, and eccentric dress of the lover are a form of self-parody, expressed in the stereotypes of Renaissance psychology. Distressful passions like sorrow, fear, and anger are apt to produce tearing of hair, trembling, wringing of hands, rolling of eyes, gnawing of lips, foaming at mouth, and the like, that are justified only by the most intense misfortune or by communal grieving; for these gestures can bespeak a kind of madness. Especially when such symptoms as blushing, pallor, gooseflesh, and hair standing on end are invoked, the language of gesture is best suited to description of offstage action or to asserting in psychological parlance what the audience cannot in fact see on stage.

Despite all these tendencies toward overstatement, and the attendant danger of misinterpretation that is demonstrable in scenes with two or more onstage audiences disagreeing among themselves on the meaning of visual symptoms, Shakespeare's characters do find something invaluably normative in the gestural language of emotion. The wearing of gesture is in the final analysis a function of role; the gesture must be appropriate and typical because the emotion itself is typical. In love, one acts out the experience of lovers everywhere; in grief, one shares communally with others not only the feelings of sorrow but the gestures through which it is expressed and relieved. To come fully to terms with one's humanity is neither to deny one's feelings nor to luxuriate in them, but rather to respond as others have done to fear, sorrow, or anger, and thus to grow more wholly aware of one's participation in the natural and social order.

ᙋIV
The Language of
Theatrical Space

> May we cram
> Within this wooden O the very casques
> That did affright the air at Agincourt?
>
> —*Henry V*

THE ABSENCE of scenery on the Elizabethan stage had the effect, as we saw in Chapter I, of encouraging a visually symbolic use of the stage façade and of the actors grouped in front of it. Actors used the stage as a platform from which to project a story, relying on spatial relationships of above, below, opposite, and the like, to define stage locations and hierarchical social patterns. Placements above and within, on the gallery walls and in the "discovery space" backstage, provided acting stations not for separate scenes but for brief appearances spatially defined in relation to the main stage. Large stage properties, sparingly employed, could become the physical and expressive center of a throne room or a deathbed scene. With painted heavens above and trapdoor (or doors) leading to the underworld below, the main stage could suggest the earth itself, the realm of human activity, set in the midst of a cosmic *theatrum mundi*. Rich architectural detail and the framing of the stage pillars provided, in George Kernodle's opinion at least, a picture with affinities for medieval art, royal entries, masques, and other pageantry in which Tudor spectators had learned to read allegorical and emblematic meaning.[1]

As with the symbolic costuming and conventional gesture that were so integrally a part of stage spectacle in Tudor dramatic entertainment, the symbolic stage façade and formalized spatial relationships of actors were essential features of Shakespeare's received tradition. He found in them a well-understood language of theatrical space, one through which he could invoke a structured world of status and meaningful differentiation. Vertical distinctions and proximity or distance on stage could suggest systems of rank, degrees of complexity, and entitlement to obedience. His extensive use of pageantry indicates how often he turned to such a visual language. Its correspondences seemed to offer reassurance both of reliably perceived meaning in the theater and of a larger fixity in the social and moral order.

Yet this conventional language of theatrical space presented Shakespeare with limits, as did the language of costuming and gesture. However much he learned from the symbolic staging practices of Tudor popular drama and civic or royal entertainment, he was also acquainted with neoclassic staging and its liminal suggestions of illusion and ambiguity. His early comedies employ neoclassic methods of illusion in staging that visibly enhance the holiday inversions of costuming and gesture we have already examined. In *The Comedy of Errors* he apparently adheres throughout to the illusion of two houses facing on a street; and, although he subsequently abandons this scheme for the duration of an entire play, he does retain its essential features in many individual comic scenes of mistaken identity and saturnalian escape.

Shakespeare's access to two stage languages in his dramatic heritage, one embodying a symbolic pageantry of moral example and the other an illusory mirroring of social manners, invites two contrasting ways of interpreting the theatrical façade and spatial arrangements through which dramatic actions are realized. The dialectic encourages at once a formal view of the symbolic stage façade and a more liberated, even ironic, perception of it. The façade's imposing structures and fixed spatial relationships invoke order and degree, but at times those values appear so illusory as to call in question the very certitude of symbolic meaning. In dramas of political conflict, such as the history plays, verticality becomes inverted; kings are brought low by a literal descent in the theater, while those of lower rank enact the status elevation and reversal so characteristic of liminality in rites of passage.[2] The structures these characters occupy in the theater visually simulate royal fortresses or cities under attack. Figures of public greatness appear on stage in scenes of privacy, informality, and nighttime that invert or undercut distinctions in rank. In dramas of private and domestic conflict, including the comedies and love tragedies, the stage façade is made to represent the dwelling of a parent or other figure of authority against whom youth and love are in rebellion. Dramas of public conflict tend to emphasize symbolic meaning that is threatened, whereas dramas of domestic conflict tend to emphasize the holiday experience that seeks to free itself from restraints. We are presented in either case with a spatial language of symbolic order rooted in the past and extending its promise of legal custom into the future, in conflict with an illusory theatrical world of present time and place where anything can happen.

Shakespeare, in his early history plays, begins with the theatrical façade as a sign of hierarchical order, but insists on its vulnerability to conflict and dissension. One of his earliest spatial discoveries about his theater was that it is admirably suited to military action before the walls of a place under siege. The building could hardly provide him a better spatial metaphor for civil strife in England's internecine wars of the fifteenth century. Here Shakespeare turns naturally to medieval and Tudor popular staging traditions of siege warfare, as practiced in *The Castle of Perseverance* (ca. 1425) and continued in Tudor moralities like *Horestes* (1567). James Burbage's Theatre, erected in 1576, and the other commercial theatrical buildings that followed, must have provided impetus for acting companies eager to exploit the spatial dimensions of their new home. The notable success of *1 Henry VI*, as evidenced by Thomas Nashe's tribute,[3] suggests a fundamental compatibility at the start of Shakespeare's career between the vast subject of England's civil wars and the theatrical arena in which those wars are refought.

The space positively encourages scaling operations, breaking through gates, appearances aloft, and other stirring effects, rendering them at once visually plausible and symbolic. Without scenery, indeed without any changes in appearance, the main stage can become for an extended period of action the ground before some town or castle under siege, with the town or castle lying behind the tiring-house façade and presenting its exterior to the attackers. Appearances in the gallery become, with a visual literalness, appearances "on the walls," allowing the defenders to hurl insults on their attackers below or negotiate terms of a surrender. A main door in the façade gives a plausible impression of town gates and makes possible real incursions or excursions through that aperture. This visual tour de force (which, owing to the flexibility of the nonscenic stage, can be interspersed with other less visualized locations) is extensively pictorial, exploiting virtually every part of the theater for its physical shape and above all for the spatial relationship of parts of the building to one another. The hierarchical implications are evident in vertical structures and stout walls offering a haven against attackers for persons of rank. The theater becomes a visual metaphor and embodiment of a medieval fortress.

As a background for civil strife, on the other hand, this military environment in which the spectators are assaulted by the sights and sounds of conflict is perceived to be a world of confrontation and sudden reversal. Gates and walls in these sieges never seem to hold against the enemy. An inner weakness vitiates what appears to our visual sense to be so strong. The chaotic violence of war contrasts visually with the assurances of harmony and order to which the "heavens" literally over-head would seem to attest. The theatrical building gives the impression of being at war with itself.

From the start of *1 Henry VI*, visual parallels in the theater call attention to an ominous circumstance: the fates of England and France are intertwined. Both internecine strife in England and military ad-venturing in France are represented to us visually as conflict before walls under siege, and the parallelism in method of staging helps to reinforce a dismal resemblance between civil conflict at home and mil-itary indecisiveness abroad. First we see Humphrey of Gloucester's blue-coated servants and the tawny-coated followers of the Bishop of Winchester clash before the gates of the Tower of London, with Wood-ville the Lieutenant of the Tower speaking "*within*" the tiring-house as though from inside the fortress (*1 Henry VI*, 1.3.14). Immediately there-after, in a sequence of scenes, the tiring-house façade represents the walls of Orleans. Joan la Pucelle and her French cohorts "*enter the town with Soldiers*," capture the city, and appear shortly afterward "*on the walls*" to hurl mocks at the ousted English on the main stage below. Their victory tableau is visually and ironically similar to those actually mounted on city gates in Elizabethan victory celebrations.[4] Thereafter, in a scene represented as taking place that very night, Talbot and his forces assault the tiring-house walls "*with scaling ladders*," ascending into the gallery and occupying the tiring-house while the French are ig-nominiously obliged to "*leap o'er the walls in their shirts . . . half ready, and half unready*," jumping down onto the main stage as though by way of escape (1.4–2.1). The seesaw struggle for Orleans seems to grow out of the factional feuding at home. The sieges of Rouen and Bordeaux, occupying a major portion of Acts 3 and 4, are visualized by means of assaults through city gates and appearances "*aloft*," "*on the walls*," and even "*on the top*" in some upper vantage point of the theater (3.2.17–

74, 4.2.2–5).⁵ The last use of "walls" in this play is to stage an ironic surrender: it is Reignier who descends from his appearance "*on the walls*" at Angiers to negotiate with Suffolk a marriage treaty (5.3.130) that to all loyal Englishmen is mere capitulation.

Civil war at home, in *2* and *3 Henry VI*, makes use of the same iconoclastic disparity between a visually noble fortress representing beleaguered England and the ignoble vacillation taking place in her midst. Appearances aloft of Lord Scales "*upon the Tower, walking,*" to citizens who enter "*below,*" and of King Henry "*on the terrace*" receiving the submission of Jack Cade's rebels on the main stage "*with halters about their necks*" (*2 Henry VI*, 4.5, 4.9), stress hierarchical patterns at a time when Cade's outrages savagely mimic the bickering among England's purported leaders. Henry's physical elevation in the theater can only mock his indecisiveness and impotence as a ruler; a fitter physical symbol for him is the molehill to which he retires during the fighting in Yorkshire (*3 Henry VI*, 2.5). The struggle between Yorkists and Lancastrians to control the tiring-house and its gallery, or walls, at York and Coventry, the admittance through the city gates and hurling of defiances down onto the main stage (4.7, 5.1), all subject the fortress to pressures of wavering loyalties and the uncertain chance of internecine conflict.

It is thus spatially fitting that Richard of Gloucester should murder King Henry "*on the walls*" of the Tower of London at the end of *3 Henry VI* (5.6), in a scene that figuratively reveals once more the breach of England's royal fortress by homebred treachery. The reversal of legitimacy dramatized in this scene finds it sad confirmation in *Richard III*, when Richard appears "*aloft*" to the commoners who have come to ask him to accept the throne (3.7.94). The fortress is no longer under siege, but we know that its duplicitous master has achieved his ascendancy through England's division against herself—through the reversals of fortune, hollow triumphs, and dismal capitulations that have characterized the struggle for possession of the tiring-house and its façade. The traditional iconography of Richard's visual ascendancy to the gallery is all the more ironic because it is a tableau familiar to audiences of street shows and royal entries, in which the royal figure receives petitions from his subjects.⁶ The theater building thus embodies, in its vertically related playing areas, the inconclusive battleground that England and her French territories have become during the Wars of the Roses. The siege of Angiers in *King John*, with its

English and French armies meeting before the gates and walls of the contested city (2.1), similarly explores a visual metaphor of impasse that well expresses the ambiguity of King John's irregular dynastic title.

The splendid pageantry of *Richard II*, as exemplified in the trial before Richard at Coventry wherein Richard is seated visually at the apex of a hierarchical pyramid, establishes its vertical patterns of differentiation only to reverse them in presentational images of descent and deposition. Shakespeare carefully stages the moment of reversal, the capitulation of Richard to Bolingbroke at Flint Castle, in terms of vertical stage movement and relationships. He devises a visual language of the fall of princes, finding a graphic theatrical counterpart for the poetic image patterns of rising and falling and the mythological references to the fall of Phaethon long noted by the New Criticism.[7] Shakespeare took a hint for the vertical presentation of this scene from Holinshed, who describes how Bolingbroke "mustered his armie before the kings presence, which vndoubtedlie made a passing faire shew," while King Richard "was walking aloft on the braies of the wals, to behold the coming of the duke a farre off."[8] The metaphoric import of Richard's actual descent, on the other hand, is Shakespeare's own, and it underscores his iconoclastic view of the theatrical façade as a beautifully ordered structure vitiated by political division and irresponsibility. Once more the *theatrum mundi* of the Elizabethan stage is a fortress under siege, and once more the fortress will not hold.

The main stage provides the location for the mustering of Bolingbroke's army to which Holinshed refers, within view of the Welsh castle. As in *King John*, Act 2, set before Angiers, the speeches of the characters invoke the presence of castle walls, represented by the tiring-house façade. Young Percy, or Hotspur, approaches his allies with the news that "The castle royally is mann'd" and that Richard lies "Within the limits of yon lime and stone" (3.3.21–26). The castle is symbolically suggestive of Richard himself, beleaguered and yet impressively royal. The distance and vertical separation between Bolingbroke's forces and Richard's castle walls give a visual immediacy to the delicate negotiations that must be conducted between the two men. Stage movement indicates with precision each step in the process. Bolingbroke orders some of his noble associates to "Go to the rude ribs of that ancient castle" and "Through brazen trumpet send the breath of parley / Into his ruin'd ears" (ll. 32–34). Northumberland is to head this parley, laying forth Bolingbroke's proposal to the royal inmate of the castle while Bolingbroke and his forces march "here . . . Upon the grassy carpet of this plain" (ll. 49–50). This march is so placed "That from this castle's tottered battlements / Our fair appointments may be well perus'd"; that is, the warriors and their might are plainly visible from the walls. The negotiating team meanwhile advances to the walls; the trumpets sound a parley from below and are answered within.

Richard's appearance *"on the walls"* at this juncture (l. 61), accompanied by Carlisle, Aumerle, Scroop, and others, bestows upon him the kind of vertical and central placement to which he has been accustomed at tournaments or in throne scenes. Still literally above the heads of his subjects, he acts the role of one who is unattainably distant from them. He deigns to notice Bolingbroke at a distance—"yon methinks he stands"—but, according to the formalities that are followed even in this highly irregular political situation, he addresses himself only to Northumberland. These visual conventions of hierarchy are invoked, as is often the case in Shakespeare, only to be devastatingly undercut; for Northumberland's message is that Richard is to signify his acceptance of Bolingbroke's return to England on behalf of his dukedom by coming down where he and Bolingbroke may be on equal terms. What is required is that Richard descend into the "base court," exiting from above and reentering onto the main stage—now imaginatively transformed from the "grassy carpet" in front of the castle to the outer and lower courtyard within its walls.[9] Only when this descent is complete will Bolingbroke, having received the implicit submission he has demanded, undertake to show his duty to Richard as his feudal superior. Throughout this scene the spatial implications of a defended fortress, a negotiated surrender, a descent, and a show of submission to royal authority eloquently direct our attention to a profound reversal in English political history.[10] This reversal fittingly coincides with the *peripeteia* of the play itself, the structural moment when the vertical distinctions upon which Richard has depended begin to work against him.

Although Shakespeare uses the visual stage metaphor of a fortress under siege most prolifically in his early historical plays, he does not abandon it later. He invokes it again at "girded Harfleur" in *Henry V*, and with the same theatrical immediacy that is at once iconic and iconoclastic. The presentational effects quite overwhelm the senses. We are asked by the Chorus to "work" our thoughts "and therein see a siege" with ordnance pointed at Harfleur, whereupon the "nimble gunner" touches the "devilish cannon," a stage direction specifies "*Alarum, and chambers go off*" (presumably offstage), and suddenly we are before the walls of Harfleur, our imagination considerably bolstered by the spatially plausible use of the tiring-house façade. A scaling operation involving real ladders is before our eyes,[11] the sound of cannon is in our ears, and the smell of gunpowder and smoke is in our nostrils (3 Chorus 25–33). Nonetheless, we are insistently reminded as well that such devices are illusory, even woefully inadequate, and that Shakespeare's company cannot in fact "cram / Within this wooden O the very casques / That did affright the air at Agincourt" (1 Chorus 12–14). The immensity of the enterprise mocks the images that presume to conjure it. And the great event itself is mocked, or at least qualified, by the harsh realities of war, by Henry's candid talk of uncontrolled plunder and ravishment at the hands of the soldiers he now musters "*before the gates*" of Harfleur (3.3.1–27). The fortress under siege must fall in the cruel chance of war.

So too in *Coriolanus*, where the protagonist's laying siege "*as before the city Corioles*," his summoning of its citizens to the "*walls*" before being driven back to the "*trenches*,"[12] and his being "*shut in*" the city gates for a time with no Roman assistance (1.4)[13] are unforgettable visual images of both the intrepidity and the haughty isolation that earn Caius Marcius first the accolade of "Coriolanus" and then the hatred of Rome's citizens. Timon's similar misanthropy in *Timon of Athens*, provoking him to turn his back on Athens' walls in self-imposed exile, is visually contrasted with Alcibiades' more successful confrontation with the citizens of Athens; Alcibiades' besieging forces demand and receive admittance from the city senators who appear to him "*on the walls*," thus finding an accommodation that for Timon proves impossible (4.1.1, 5.4.2, 81). Athens' walls close in a complacent and worldly self-interest that Timon can only reject with disgust.

Metaphorical applications of the Elizabethan stage façade to images of subverted hierarchy are not limited in Shakespeare to the fortress under siege. What Francis Fergusson calls the "idea" of the Elizabethan theater,[14] with its painted heavens above and trapdoor or doors opening below, serves as an ironical framework for the opening of *Titus Andronicus*. Once again, in a play at the start of Shakespeare's career, we see in the theater a vertically oriented Boethian universe, with divine authority above and the nether world below, invoked not alone for its conventional values, but as an impassive witness to factionalism, brutality, and treachery.

G. K. Hunter has shown how a tripartite universe, spatially depicted at the start of *Titus Andronicus* by three levels of action, represents a polarization of authority in the struggle for Rome. The upper acting area, the gallery "aloft" peopled by the tribunes and senators as in the Senate House, denotes "the seat of Roman political power, whether Imperial or Republican." The space beneath the stage, into which a "Tomb" is presumably opened as into the lower world, locates "the metaphysical commitment of the traditional Roman to stern self-sacrifice in the interests of the state, to warrior citizenship based on family piety." The space between these two realms, the main stage where Titus and others enter as though before the Capitol, gives to Titus and Lavinia as principal characters "a field appropriate to their endeavour throughout the play to bridge the gap between the world of Power and the world of Right."[15] Though pagan in its assumptions, the scheme has affinities to the medieval conception of *theatrum mundi* embodied in the theater façade itself. The visual summing up of such an ostensibly ordered universe is, however, anything but reassuring. Every level of action is invaded by conflict: the choosing of a new emperor to assume the pinnacle of authority does not go as planned and yields power to a tyrant, a ritual sacrifice for the shades below assumes the character of vengeful slaughter, and on middle earth the issue of Lavinia's marriage leads to violent abduction and the execution by Titus of his own son. The "visual diagram of meaning"[16] in which the characters must discover their proper places is one that highlights moral enervation and self-blindness. A splendid tripartite universe mocks those in its midst and steadfastly refuses to reveal the will of the gods.

Similar ironies of visual hierarchy can be found in the monument scene of *Antony and Cleopatra* (4.15), where the lifting up of the dying Antony to Cleopatra and her women simultaneously emphasizes his tragic failure (expressed in the heaviness of his body and the cumbersomeness of lifting him aloft right before the spectators' eyes) and his elevation to mythic greatness as the immortal lover of the Egyptian queen.[17] Vertical ascent and descent in *Julius Caesar* call up a sense of ceaseless rise and fall as Caesar is cut down "Even at the base of Pompey's statue" (3.2.187), as Brutus and then Antony ascend into the public pulpit, and as Antony descends to the level of his auditors to make a ring around the corpse of Caesar and thereby reenact for his own purposes the central violent action of the play.

Thus far we have focused on Shakespeare's use of the theatrical façade to invoke public structures such as the Tower of London, walls under siege, the Senate House, or a monument—structures against which he can then reveal inversions of order in the rise and fall of great men. Shakespeare calls upon a traditional language of theatrical space, available to him in Tudor plays like *Horestes*, to summon up a world of hierarchy and cosmic pattern that is often under assault. If we turn to neoclassic tradition, on the other hand, with its emphasis on ambiguity and surprise, we find Shakespeare using the stage façade to frame a world of illusion, escape, and rebellion against authority. The two modes of locating stage space are to be found side by side in Shakespeare from his earliest years; his early experiments with *Henry VI* and *Titus Andronicus* are paralleled by his fascination with illusory staging in *The Comedy of Errors* and *The Taming of the Shrew*.

The Elizabethan stage lends itself with equal facility to these two modes of spatial representation, for in both cases the significant element is not scenic verisimilitude but spatial relationship. The walls of a town or a Senate House look down, from the vantage of the gallery, onto the main stage below as onto a plain flat place before those walls. Similarly, in Shakespeare's adaptation of neoclassic staging, the house of Shylock or Brabantio or Antipholus of Ephesus looks out upon a street lying before it, or the house of the Capulets faces its orchard garden below. No scenic alteration is required to differentiate stone walls and town gates from windows and doors. The stage façade is able to simulate both locations in that parapets and windows are *above*, while doors or gates open from the plain or street lying *before* a structure into the town or house lying *within*, its interior unseen. A visual way of thinking about the theatrical building insists in both cases on the primacy of interplay between gallery, main stage, and doors, whether the façade is understood to represent a besieged town or a dwelling. In both modes of staging visual separation lends itself to metaphoric interpretation. Yet because a house is more private than city walls or Senate House, it better suits a world of disguise and holiday.

If, as seems likely, Shakespeare began his exploration of such liminal spatial relationships in *The Comedy of Errors*, his indebtedness to neoclassic theater is clear enough. In modified form he seems to have adopted the model set forth in *Ralph Roister Doister* and *Gammer Gurton's Needle*, for example, where two or more houses face on a street scene throughout the play. Shakespeare evidently intends one stage door to represent the dwelling of Antipholus of Ephesus throughout, with the Abbey near at hand and represented by another door.[18] What attracts Shakespeare to such a setting is not the verisimilar scenic effect—there is no indication that scenery or stage housing was used in the original production—but rather the spatial interconnection of the main stage and the space lying within. The stage façade becomes a part of Shakespeare's comedy of illusion and misunderstanding, much as it must have done on Plautus' and Terence's stage before him. Antipholus of Ephesus arrives at one point to find his house door—presumably a door in the tiring-house façade—locked against him. He and his servant Dromio call in vain to those in the house, who speak apparently from within. When Luce and then Adriana "enter" and yet are presumed to be still inside the house, they may be visible to the audience as they stand in the gallery or some such acting area, out of sight of the frustrated master and his servant on the main stage (3.1.47–60).[19] The façade thus expresses misunderstanding and inversion between husband and wife and between servant and servant; it is a device of complication.

Later in the play, on the other hand, this same façade becomes the means of revelation and discovery. It is through the stage door representing the Abbey that the Abbess emerges with Antipholus and Dromio of Syracusa to undeceive all those who have begun to question their own sanity. The actors' tiring-house contains all secrets and eventually explains all mysteries; with its two or more doors, it is at once the source of comic confusion and eventual clarification. The apertures into the façade are not, on Shakespeare's illusionistic stage, simply a means of allowing characters to appear from and disappear into an understood offstage location; they stress a duality between what is seen and unseen, between what a character supposes to be within and what in fact is to be found there. The stage façade is an essential source of illusion in the liminal world of Shakespeare's first comedy of mistaken identities.

In subsequent plays that use the theater façade to picture a private house looking out on a street or garden, Shakespeare abandons the neoclassic convention in *The Comedy of Errors* of assigning one stage door to a fixed domicile throughout the play, but he does not abandon the spatial metaphor of walls, doors, and windows as an illusory barrier separating those who are within from those who are without. In the absence of scenery the visual metaphor can be conjured up at will, as in *The Taming of the Shrew*, when Petruchio declares, "I trow this is [Hortensio's] house," and bids his servant Grumio knock "at this gate" (1.2.4–11), or in Act 5 of the same play when Vincentio is told, "Sir, here's the door, this is Lucentio's house," and proceeds to "*knock*" (5.1.8–13). The gallery or similar space above is no less readily pressed into service as a window, as when the Pedant "*looks out of the window*" at Vincentio and bids him be packing, then exits from above and reenters below to confront Vincentio about the beating of Biondello (ll. 15–58). Once again the façade is integral to the comedy of visual misunderstanding, though the illusion is flexibly applied to particular scenes rather than the entire play and allows the façade to represent different houses in succession or alternation. Windows, doors, and the area before the "house" are meaningfully related in space, their illusory function considerably enhanced by suitable architecture.

A common feature of many such houses in Shakespeare is that they are parental, thereby defining through the visual structure an authority from which escape is necessary. The enclosed space within is associated with darkness, misunderstanding, and age. In *The Merchant of Venice* Jessica appear "*above*," apparently at a window of Shylock's house, when Lorenzo comes to assist in her elopement. "Here dwells my father Jew," Lorenzo tells his companions (2.6.26). Jessica throws down a casket and, being bidden to "descend," says she will gather more wealth from the house; she exits above and reenters below soon after.[20] The seeming window at which we have seen her is one of those "casements" which the mistrustful Shylock shuts up against the sights and sounds of the Venetian, Christian world (2.5.35). (Jonson's *Volpone* achieves a similar effect when Celia appears at "that windore" of Corvino's house and is addressed by Volpone below disguised as Scoto of Mantua, on a scaffold beneath her window, 2.2.1.) Silvia appears above in *The Two Gentlemen of Verona*, at what we take to be her window in the palace of the Duke of Milan, when Proteus comes to call on her with a musical serenade and is overheard in his perjuries by his devoted Julia. "Now must we to her window, / And give some evening music to her ear," says Proteus (4.2.16–17). This is presumably the same window from which Valentine had hoped to rescue her by means of a "ladder made of cords" (2.4.179), before he was intercepted by the Duke. Later, the good Eglamour assists in her elopement (5.1). In these plays youth and freedom are associated with the street lying before the house, with windows opening onto the world outside its confining walls, with descent and release.

The father's house can be juxtaposed with another imagined dwelling in order to dramatize conflict for those whom the parent's house seeks to confine. The tiring-house façade in *Othello* is first used in such a way as to suggest Brabantio's house, from which Desdemona has eloped. Iago and Roderigo call aloud "Here," at "her father's house," to inform him of the escape, and Brabantio appears "*above*," evidently at the window of his house (1.1.75–82). Asked if all his family is "within," he disappears from the "window" into the tiring-house, as though into his dwelling. Moments later he appears below, on the main stage, "*with Servants and torches*," to undertake the search for Desdemona and Othello. In the next scene Othello too appears with Iago and "*Attendants with torches*," in a scene that is visually parallel; yet the tiring-house now represents the inn called the Sagittary where Othello stays with Desdemona. He says that he will "spend a word here in the house" (1.2.48), exits as though into the interior, and returns to confront Brabantio and the watch. The striking visual repetition underscores the seriousness of Desdemona's choice as she moves from her father's world to that of Othello. In a neoclassic stage setting, with two houses facing on a street scene, the two dwellings of Brabantio and Othello would be simultaneously visible. Shakespeare's spatial method is more one of superimposition, allowing the whole façade, with its plausible rendition of a house exterior, to stand first for one and then the other. The spectators' participation in completing this image requires imagination, but it is aided by recurrent visual reminders.

Shakespeare's fullest expression of the stage façade as a parental house forcing the separation of lovers is to be found in the love scenes of *Romeo and Juliet*. The vertical separation between Juliet's window and the orchard or garden below lends itself to recurrent visual images of ascent and descent, aspiration and despondency. The setting is not a house on a street, as derived from neoclassic staging, but a plausible variation of it; the main stage is as well suited to represent a garden as a street. No scenery is needed to establish the main stage as the garden before Juliet's window; Romeo is said to have "leapt this orchard wall" in order to hide from Benvolio and Mercutio (2.1.6), but his concealment almost surely makes use of a pillar or similar structure rather than a special property.[21] Juliet's window, on the other hand, is pointedly above—"o'er my head," as Romeo says. A light breaks through "yonder window" (1.2.2–27). No one speaks of Juliet's location as on a "balcony," as in later stage tradition; it is always a window. As such it stresses the distance that separates Juliet from Romeo, the privacy of her heretofore sheltered life, the difficulty of their union. They cannot come to each other to kiss and touch as they have done briefly at the masked ball.

Vertical ascent is therefore the means by which Romeo must attain Juliet, and it becomes the dominant image of his aspiring hopes. He is to use "cords made like a tackled stair, / Which to the high top-gallant of my joy / Must be my convoy in the secret night" (2.4.185–187). The Nurse, in speaking to Juliet of this ladder, bawdily glosses it as a means "by the which your love / Must climb a bird's nest soon when it is dark" (2.5.73–74). In anticipation of consummating their marriage, Romeo's thought is of mounting to her. These are verbal images only (though the cords are real enough), for we do not see Romeo "Ascend her chamber" as the Friar instructs him (3.3.147). The visual emphasis in the lovers' last living moments together is instead on descent. They enter "*aloft*," speaking of the imminent separation, and, having been warned by the Nurse of the approach of Juliet's mother, reluctantly part at the window. "Then window, let day in, and let life out," says Juliet, and Romeo answers, "Farewell, farewell! One kiss, and I'll descend" (3.5.41–42). If there were any doubt that Romeo actually climbs down by means of the rope ladder from the gallery to the main stage, coming down in front of the tiring-house façade, the ensuing dialogue would seem to resolve such a question. Juliet, perceiving her husband below her, exclaims, "Methinks I see thee, now thou art so low, / As one dead in the bottom of a tomb" (ll. 55–56). The vertical metaphor of fallen fortune and separation is thus related to the metaphoric use of space at the play's end in Juliet's tomb, where Romeo undertakes to "descend into this bed of death" (5.3.28).[22]

By contrast, Juliet's quarrel with her father is presented on the main stage, even though it presumably occurs in her chamber and follows immediately after Romeo's departure. Juliet "*goeth down from the window*" (3.5.67), in the usually reliable visual testimonial of the 1597 "bad" quarto, and reenters on the main stage to act out the stormy remainder of the scene.[23] We see again the care with which Shakespeare uses the upper acting area only for brief uncrowded appearances and for action that derives its metaphoric significance from its spatial elevation above the main stage. To continue Juliet's scene "above" once Romeo has left might seem to us logically verisimilar, but the acting space is too confined for many actors and, perhaps even more tellingly, the action of the quarrel bears no relation to persons appearing on a lower level of staging.

Romeo and Juliet thus illustrates with special clarity a recurrent use of the stage façade in Shakespeare's language of theatrical space: it is a parental dwelling from which the lovers must elope or where they must separate. Its walls are "high and hard to climb," as Juliet insists (2.2.63), its windows accessible only by ladders, its exterior forbidding.[24] As such it represents the structured world of authority, of traditional insistence on kinship obligations, obedience, and concern for appearances. The world lying before it is often seen at night, is sometimes associated with death, and is a place of secrecy and private aspiration. Its liminal status enhances the transitional, erotic, and unstable quality of the action taking place in its midst.

This framing of uncertain event by the structured façade of the theater building is not unlike the framing of city walls under siege or of Senate House in turmoil, except that the private house facing on street or garden, drawn from neoclassic tradition, is more readily attuned to the world of ambiguity and metamorphosis. In both uses of the façade vertical movement from one acting level to another may actually take place in full view of the spectators, in front of the façade, with insistent suggestions of separation, military disaster, or death. Romeo's descent by rope ladder from Juliet's window in the Capulets' house bears this kind of visual affinity with Antony's being heaved aloft to Cleopatra in her monument (*Antony and Cleopatra*, 4.15.8–38) or the French retreat from Orleans "*o'er the walls*" in *1 Henry VI* (2.1.38). Young Arthur, in *King John*, enters "*on the walls*" with the intention of leaping down as from the battlements of John's castle. "The wall is high, and yet will I leap down," he says, and leaps to his death, blaming his uncle's spirit for being in "these stones" (4.3.1–9).[25] Arthur urges us, in other words, to consider the structural edifice of the façade as a sign of the unfeeling political order from which he longs to escape. His leap is a kind of abortive elopement into the arms of death, reinforcing the visual similarity between an austere wall of stone and a parental structure denying sustenance to lovers or innocents. A dialectic in

Shakespeare's theater between structure and antistructure is powerfully enhanced by the architectural framing of the edifice and the vertical movements occurring in its midst.

The insistence on ironic vertical relationships between upper and lower areas applies not only to the gallery and main stage but to main stage and underworld beneath, and to main stage and "heavens" above. The world under the platform is of course not seen, but movement or sound there is always related to the main stage in such a way as to accentuate a contrast between human striving on earth and spectral mystery beneath. Liminal associations of death and the underworld give to the trapdoor and space below an aura of frightening transition, of ambiguity, of riddling inversion. Ghosts do not necessarily appear and disappear through the trap—in *Hamlet* the Ghost enters and exits on at least one occasion by regular stage doors[26]—but the Ghost's crying *"under the stage"* as he moves about in the "cellerage" comes distinctly from below (1.5.149–152), and its main effect is to persuade Hamlet's companions that something "wondrous strange" (l. 165) afflicts the state of Denmark. So too with the *"music of the hoboys"* heard *"under the stage"* in *Antony and Cleopatra* before the battle of Alexandria (4.3.12); the audience hears the sound effect for itself, but has its attention chiefly directed to the common soldiers who seek to interpret what such an omen must mean. Graves open into the underworld, as in Ophelia's burial scene in *Hamlet* or the burial of Titus' son in *Titus Andronicus*. The latter grave, perhaps rendered with the aid of a stage property in the form of a monument like one of the three "tombs" mentioned in Henslowe's *Diary*, anticipates a pit cunningly prepared to receive Bassianus, Martius, and Quintus.[27] Aaron buries gold "under a tree" near this pit (2.3.2), much as Timon discovers and reburies treasure in *Timon of Athens* (4.3.23–48).[28] From the underworld diabolic apparitions appear in riddling prophecy, like the spirit that *"riseth"* from the trap in *2 Henry VI* and then descends in *"Thunder and lightning"* while the Duchess of Gloucester watches the conjuration from *"aloft"* (1.4.13–41), or the apparitions in *Macbeth* that rise and *"descend"* in thunder (4.1.72–87). Movement between the main stage and the trap emphasizes falling, entrapment, victimization. Conversations with the lower world contrast the greed, ambition, and lack of self-knowledge of humankind with an inscrutable and all-foreseeing dark power that lies beyond—and beneath—the grave.

In his visual use of the decorated heavens, too, Shakespeare employs the spatial relationship of man on earth to the sky under which he dwells. The juxtaposition reveals man's smallness and uncertain happiness, as in Hamlet's evocation, already noted, of the "brave o'er-hanging firmament" and "majestical roof fretted with golden fire" so unlike the "quintessence of dust" that is man (*Hamlet*, 2.2.301–309). The heavens, hung "with black" for the funeral of Henry V in the opening of *1 Henry VI* as they evidently were for the performance of tragedies on the Elizabethan stage,[29] mock the political and military disarray with which Henry V's son will soon be unable to cope. Men look to the heavens "over our heads" (*Richard II*, 3.3.17) in Shakespeare for omens, taking warning at signs of planetary irregularity and tumult, and conversely finding comfort in signs of "degree, priority, and place."[30] The heavens in the theater do not physically change at such moments, but the deictic gestures demanded of the actor call into witness the impassively serene cosmos from which mankind seeks to know its fate. Only in the late plays like *Cymbeline* and *The Tempest* does Shakespeare turn to actual ascents and descents from the heavens, prompted no doubt by improved machinery and by the example of court masques; but even in some early plays the heavens are visually a part of the cosmos that the theater represents. Visually and metaphorically they are distant, patterned, beautiful, and unaffected by the human disorder and misunderstanding to which they bear mute witness.

In the heavens, then, as in the underworld, Shakespeare finds a traditional theatrical language fraught with Boethian connotations of cosmic hierarchy that he can use as a framework, sometimes ironic, for the ambiguous and transitional world of human endeavor where interpretation is often uncertain. Spatial meaning of above and below is defined always in relation to the main stage, the realm of human action.

The curtained recess or "discovery space" affords Shakespeare similar opportunities of juxtaposition. Used sparingly in the early plays,[31] it is for some time in Shakespeare little more than an arras or curtained doorway to facilitate entrance or exit, concealment, and perhaps the introduction of properties.[32] Falstaff hides from Mistress Page in *The Merry Wives of Windsor* (3.3.82) or goes to sleep behind the arras in the tavern scene of *1 Henry IV* (2.4.499–546). Claudius and Polonius spy on Hamlet; Polonius is slain behind the arras in the Queen's chamber. Not all concealments demand a curtain, to be sure, but Falstaff's position behind the arras at the scene's end in *1 Henry IV* seems to require a doorway through which the actor can get backstage without reappearing to the audience. The connotation of this space is at any rate negative: it assists in concealment for underhanded purposes, or is a dark prison for the likes of Malvolio in *Twelfth Night* (4.2).

Yet concealment is inversely related to discovery, and especially in the late plays we find Shakespeare using the "discovery space" to achieve the kind of revelation for which an enclosure is especially well suited. As a cave or hiding place, the discovery space looks out on the main stage and is spatially dependent on it. That which is hidden, lying within, exists only in contrast to that which is visible; having no separate reality, it is metaphorically as well as physically unsuited for whole scenes. The discovery space becomes a place of refuge, secrecy, and mystery, opening out upon the world of human conflict and offering a perspective on its failures. Timon's primitive cave in the wilderness provides him at once with a place of hiding and an observation post for anatomizing human greed. Standing in its entrance, he is able to overhear the flattering Poet and Painter before reentering *"from his cave"* (*Timon of Athens*, 5.1.28) to accost them with satiric wrath. The cave of Belarius in *Cymbeline*, though more hospitable than Timon's, offers too a radical perspective on the courtly world of Cloten and his mother. The "hovel" of poor Tom in *King Lear* is not only a place of concealment for the disguised Edgar but is visually juxtaposed with the Earl of Gloucester's "doors" that are shut against King Lear in the storm (2.4.308, 3.2.61–71).

Through a logical transition from concealment to revelation, the discovery space in the late plays becomes a place of *anagnorisis*, of the kind of visual "discovery" Shakespeare had earlier accomplished through unveilings, unmaskings, and other forms of reaffirmation of identity. A curtained space, representing a pavilion on board ship, allows Pericles to be unseen by the spectators and by those around him until he is discovered ("Behold him," *Pericles*, 5.1.37) and reunited with his daughter.[33] The drawing back of the curtain before the statue of Hermione in *The Winter's Tale* is a recognition that brings with it grace, wonder, and forgiveness. As in *The Tempest*, the proprietor of this discovery space is a controller of theatrical magic, one who gives us a glimpse through stage business into a mysterious world of illusion.[34] King Henry VIII is revealed when he *"draws the curtain and sits reading pensively"* (*Henry VIII*, 2.2.61), and later he watches over the deliberations of his Privy Council from a curtained position above (5.2.34). Discovery here suggests the realization that the eye of royalty, like the eye of God, knows more of human action than ordinary men suppose; at the last, all stands revealed and justice prevails in the triumph of Protestantism.

The revelation to Alonso and his party of Ferdinand and Miranda playing at chess in Act 5 of *The Tempest* shows the culmination of Shakespeare's growing interest in the curtained recess as a place of concealment and then revelation, where he presents not self-contained actions but dramatic epiphanies that necessarily open out onto the main stage. The use of the word "discovers" in what may well be an authorial stage direction,[35] "*Here Prospero discovers Ferdinand and Miranda, playing at chess*" (5.1.172), gives substance to the idea that Shakespeare intended the stage business of uncurtaining to coincide with the structural event of *anagnorisis*. When Prospero bids Alonso and the others to "look in" at his "cell" (ll. 167–168), he sets in motion the recovery of a seemingly lost son and the marriage that will atone for the errors of the past.

This discovery space is strongly associated with Prospero and his magic. Throughout much of the play it is evident backstage as Prospero's cell. Here lie the sources of his extraordinary power, the books that Caliban intends to seize and burn. Here too are the ducal garments, to be fetched by Ariel, in which Prospero will resume his authority as Duke of Milan (ll. 84–86). To this "poor cell" Prospero invites his guests at the play's end in a processional exit, for it has long been both his place of confinement and the center of his artist's world. The "discovery" of Miranda and Ferdinand is his last scene of theatrical illusion, his masterpiece as dramatist of *anagnorisis* and resolution. The discovery space is thus an essential part of Prospero's magic, as it is of Shakespeare's, in creating illusion. By means of this magical space both artists permit their spectators to know something of the mystery that lies behind the façade of the theater.

The physical stage thus offers Shakespeare two contrasting worlds of spatial gesture. One suggests, by its vertical ordering of heavens, earth, and underworld, a place of status and degree, where we encounter the imposing façade of city walls and fortifications or the private dwelling of authoritarian parents. The other world is a place of iconoclasm and illusion, of fall from high places, reversals of fortune, escape, and elopement, all signaled in visual gestures of descent and falling that are juxtaposed with the fixed structures around them. This other world is also, through the artist's magic, a place of discovery. By such means Shakespeare's theater of the world encompasses a mystery where truth lies concealed until it is at last revealed. Especially in the late plays this space opening into the unknowable inner world of the theater building becomes the artist's place of illusion, to which he invites us as spectators to share in the liminal experience of theatergoing.

Shakespeare may well have had practical reasons for not staging whole scenes in the gallery above or discovery space within the façade—reasons having to do with sight lines, audibility, limited spatial capacity, and the like—but the argument of this chapter thus far has been that he responded also to artistic and dramaturgical factors. The distinctive areas of Shakespeare's theater "work" in spatial relationship to his main stage, defining through juxtaposition the contrast between a wall and the plain lying before it, a house and its street or orchard, a grave and the surrounding graveyard, heaven and earth, a cave or cell and its environs. What of the more numerous occasions when these special areas are not occupied by the actors? The main stage, visually less distinctive than the areas above, behind, and below it, is hence less marked for specific locales. It can be used for any place at all, even for no place in particular, in ways that are impossible for the more visually particularized gallery and discovery space. What sort of spatial vocabulary can Shakespeare devise for the seemingly neutral space of the main stage when it is not defined, through visible juxtaposition, as the street or garden below a window or the ground in front of a wall or a cave?

At times, spatial visualization on the main stage can indeed be quite neutral, as in choric scenes when anonymous citizens discuss the state of the commonwealth; we need know only that they are somewhere in England or Scotland or Rome.[36] Characters can simply tell us where they are ("Well, this is the forest of Arden," *As You Like It*, 2.4.13) or indicate by their presence that we see them in an expected place—a countess in her palace, Venetian gentlemen somewhere in Venice.[37] Even in such instances, however, when the gallery and discovery space remain unoccupied, we realize that the theater façade may not be as neutral as we first supposed. The façade is still visible, even if the actors do not speak from its gallery. Stage doors opening into an imagined interior location help define a room, with other chambers or the outside world lying beyond those barriers. The gallery is well suited to the decor of a great hall. Kernodle's argument that the theater façade is equally adaptable to exterior and interior locations, as in medieval and

Renaissance art, enables us to see the capacity of this stage for visual contrast and juxtaposition.

Especially when Shakespeare changes locale within a single scene from outside to inside, we become aware of the presentational theater's protean ability to alter its sense of place. Such change, like that of garments worn by the actors, signifies a shift in the status of the characters. Visual change of location within a scene is, in other words, a signal of *peripeteia*, or reversal of fortune. As with *anagnorisis* in the "discovery space," reversal is at once a structural concept and a device of illusion in the Elizabethan theater. Changes of locale within a scene occur at a turning point in a conspiracy, a courtship, a change of government, a battle. The reversal juxtaposes an exterior or public view with a private one,. formality with intimacy.

The theater façade forms a part of both worlds, exterior and interior. In changes occurring within a single scene we can observe how this barrier, retaining its identity as a wall, is imaginatively altered from the exterior to the interior face of the partition. A particularly revealing instance occurs in *Henry VIII*. Archbishop Cranmer, summoned by his conservative enemies to the council chamber in London, where he is to answer charges of heresy, finds the doors of the council chamber "all fast" against him, and must wait "at the door"—presumably a door leading offstage into the tiring-house—until called (5.2.3–32). Thereupon, in what traditional editorial practice marks as scene 3 of Act 5, but which is really a continuous scene, a "*council table*" is "*brought in with chairs and stools*" and is placed under the "*state*" or canopy with seating for members of the Council. The stage is now the council room itself. The Chancellor, informed that Cranmer waits "Without," orders that he be admitted, and the doorkeeper informs Cranmer, "Your Grace may enter now." According to the Folio stage direction, "*Cranmer approaches the council table*" (5.3.5–7). Clearly he has never exited. He steps forward as though entering the room, though he has never left the stage.[38] The door at which he was standing has been imaginatively reversed, leaving him within the room he was waiting to enter. The continuity of this scene is made evident by the King's secret presence throughout, for he has watched this plot against his archbishop from a curtained "window," "above" in the gallery, until it is time for him to descend and intervene. "Above" remains "above" while outside is transferred to inside. The metaphoric signification seems clear: the transformation of stage from antechamber to council chamber coincides with the play's climactic *peripeteia*, the saving of Cranmer, which assures the triumph of Protestantism and the future reign of the infant Elizabeth. We are given a glimpse of the paradoxical ways of Providence in this play, working indirectly through factionalism and human failure toward the grand design of English Tudor history.

The change of orientation from exterior to interior within a scene can direct our attention to an arrival at a moment of destiny, a literal stage movement of reversal. Romeo and his friends, arriving at the Capulets' ball at the end of what is conventionally marked as Act 1 scene 4 of *Romeo and Juliet*, "*march about the stage*" to signify their going forward and then presumably retire to one side while "*Servingmen come forth with napkins*" (1.5.0 S.D.) to set up the stage for the Capulets' feast. The stage façade, used in a number of scenes in the play to represent the exterior of the Capulets' house, now looks inward upon a hall. Thus is set in motion the fateful meeting of the lovers. Richard II's capitulation to Bolingbroke in *Richard II* coincides with a reversal of the stage from the grassy plain in front of Flint Castle to a courtyard within its walls (3.3). The assassination of Julius Caesar begins with an assembly in front of the Capitol, but moves in procession to the Capitol itself after line 12, when Cassius instructs those present, "What, urge you your petitions in the street? Come to the Capitol" (*Julius Caesar*, 3.1.11–12). The stage façade, architecturally suited first to the front of the building and then to its interior, bears impassive witness to the fall of one who has boasted himself as constant as the Northern Star.

Political transitions in death and war sometimes make use of similar visual movements within a scene from one location to another, movements from fixed status to uncertain transition as in funereal rites of passage. The deathbed conference of Henry IV with his son, and the momentous transfer of royal authority that it entails, take place not in the Jerusalem Chamber where the scene is envisaged to begin but in some inner room, "some other chamber" (*2 Henry IV*, 4.4.132), to which the King is borne in full view of the spectators (4.5.1). The traditional marking of a new scene is inappropriate; almost surely Henry is not taken to the discovery space rearstage, but is carried in an invalid's chair or is conveyed to a curtained bed like that in *The Famous Victories of Henry the Fifth* (ca. 1587).[39] When Sir William Lucy in *1 Henry VI* encounters in succession the Dukes of York and Somerset on the plains of Gascony, and is refused aid for the beleaguered Lord Talbot, Lucy does not leave the stage even though the encounters must be imagined as taking place in separate locations (4. 3–4). These juxtapositions ensure us of the imminence of Talbot's overthrow. Reversals in the fortunes of war are not infrequently signaled by an imaginative transfer from the outside to the inside of a fortress, as in *1 Henry VI*, *Coriolanus*, and *Macbeth*,[40] in a series of alarums and excursions that are essentially continuous even though the stage may be momentarily cleared.

Shakespeare occasionally uses another kind of visual juxtaposition through which sudden reversals of fortune are viewed in an ironic light: the simultaneous presentation of two locations on stage, one offering mute comment on the other.[41] The device is commonly employed in medieval religious drama to create visual ironies, as when the throne of Herod and the manger of Christ, simultaneously visible in a Christ-mas play, enable spectators to measure both the immense contrast between these two kings and the paradoxical futility of Herod's asser-tions of worldly might.[42] Although Shakespeare's use of the device is relatively uncommon, it does reveal the capacity of his theater for a kind of metaphoric statement not possible on a more verisimilar stage.

In *Richard III*, for example, Richard and the Earl of Richmond sleep in their respective tents, presumably in widely separated camps at Bosworth Field, and are visited in turn by the ghosts of Richard's victims whose curses and blessings accentuate the contrast between these two contenders for England's throne (5.3).[43] The Earl of Kent, left in the stocks at Gloucester's house from Act 2 scene 2 of *King Lear* until he is discovered in scene 4 by the arriving Lear, sleeps out the intervening scene 3 on stage while Edgar makes his furtive appearance in soliloquy, seeking a place to hide from his father's wrath.[44] The simultaneous staging allows us to see them both at once, although they remain unaware of each other's presence and indeed need not be sup-posed to be near each other. The juxtaposition is symbolic, not illu-sionistic, making a point about two banished men who must disguise themselves and endure humiliation while villains prosper.

A large stage property can create the effect of simultaneous staging even when no character is visible there. A table set out with a light repast for Duke Senior at the end of Act 2 scene 5 of *As You Like It* must remain on stage during the following short scene, for it is there in scene 7 just where the Duke was told it would be.[45] In scene 6, then, Orlando and Adam look desperately for food while the table remains visible to the spectators. We do not need to suppose the two hungry men literally close to a table laden with food, for again the juxtaposition is symbolic: starvation and approaching savagery are mutely contrasted with an emblem of the hospitality that will introduce Orlando to the teachings of nurture. A curtained bed (or possibly a curtained recess)[46] provides a similar effect in *Romeo and Juliet*: Juliet drinks the potion given her by Friar Laurence and then lies asleep within the bed-curtains while Juliet's mother and father and the Nurse make preparations for the wedding that will never take place. The Nurse, bidden to awaken Juliet, does not make an exit to mark the next "scene" (conventionally called Act 4 scene 5); she need only proceed to the curtained bed, where she finds her young mistress apparently dead in her clothes. Juliet's unseen presence throughout scene 4 comments eloquently on the ironic gap of understanding between Juliet and her family. Visual juxtapositions in Shakespeare lend themselves to ironies of contrast between law and tyranny, banishment and insolent authority, savagery and humility, love's distress and parental misunderstanding.

Such juxtapositions through simultaneously visible scenes are rare, but they point to depictions of conflict that are much more common on Shakespeare's stage. The essential visual resource for many scenes in Shakespeare, with or without the assistance of the stage façade and the occasional large property, is the movement or grouping of characters. Shakespeare's nonillusionistic stage, as John Styan observes, encourages division of the acting space into "separately significant areas" more readily than on the naturalistic stage, and thereby lends meaning to spatial distinctions when an actor is left alone on the platform after a crowded scene or is taken aside from his group.[47] Symmetrical arrangements are essential to a concept of order, but they also serve in Shakespeare as a framework of disorder. Contending forces face one another in uncertain struggle, loyalties waver, shifts in staging configuration signal a fatal turning. Shakespeare's repertory players, evidently familiar with the sorts of groupings or "blockings" that Shakespeare frequently calls for, act out in the dual spatial language of their stage a series of visual contrasts between alliance and isolation, attraction and antagonism, harmony and misunderstanding.

A balanced tableau of opposing forces, so common in Shakespearean staging, invokes ideas of symmetry and structure even while its energies are consumed in conflict. Oppositions are often elaborately formal, with speech answering speech and character balanced against character. Considerable attention is paid to horizontal spatial distinctions of left and right, and to vertical distinctions of high and low. Bolingbroke and Mowbray confront each other "Face to face, / And frowning brow to brow," at the lists in Coventry, seconded by heralds and marshals whose ritual acts and speeches reinforce through visual and verbal elaboration the parallelism of the encounter (*Richard II*, 1.1.15–16, 1.3). The origin of the Yorkist-Lancastrian conflict is portrayed as an argument among various gentlemen in the Temple Gardens, London, who alternatively pick white roses and red roses as heraldic emblems of their allegiance to Richard Plantagenet or to the Duke of Somerset.[48] The followers of Duke Humphrey clash with those of Beaufort. The unceasing reciprocal violence of *3 Henry VI*, in which a Lancastrian must die for a Yorkist, eye for eye, is illustrated in the symbolic scene of a son who has killed his own father and a father who has killed his son.[49] An entire battle in *King John* and complex negotiations over Arthur Plantagenet's rights in France are rendered theatrically in terms of what Alan Dessen calls "the stage psychomachia," with the French king at the center of alternatives to left and right.[50]

Dessen's term reminds us that the device of military confrontation on stage as a metaphor for conflict enjoys a venerable tradition in plays like *The Castle of Perseverance* and *Wit and Science*. Yet we must also recognize that stage conflict in the morality tradition is morally absolute; it pits good against evil and is able to express allegory in dramatic terms because it shares a symbolic language of readily accepted signifiers. Shakespeare's use of this traditional language is iconoclastic in that it discovers ambiguity beneath the reassuring exterior of symbolic certitude. The elaborate chivalric symbolism and the providential assumptions of trial by combat in *Richard II* are at odds with the morally complex issues posed by the murder of Thomas of Woodstock. The extensive symmetries of the *Henry VI* plays cannot determine right or wrong; instead, they testify to an increasing savagery made all the more terrible by the ritual form in which the massacres are staged. Spectacular entrances of opposing forces from opposite doors on Shakespeare's stage are often vitiated by moral compromise and cynicism, as in Prince John of Lancaster's encounter with the rebels at Gaultree Forest in *2 Henry IV* (4.1), Antony's negotiations with Octavius about a disastrous arranged marriage in *Antony and Cleopatra* (2.2), the ill-considered choosing of an emperor in *Titus Andronicus* (1.1), the formal but unfriendly meeting in *Cymbeline* between the King with his courtiers "*at one door, and at another, Caius Lucius and Attendants*" (3.1), and the like. Even Henry V's treaty negotiations with the conquered French (*Henry V,* 5.2), or the confrontation between Oberon who enters "*at one door, with his train*" and Titania "*at another, with hers*" in *A Midsummer Night's Dream* (2.1.59), cannot conceal mistrust and inequality. The color symbolism of contrasting liveries or uniforms in these encounters labels the opposing sides only to accentuate their animosity.

Eavesdropping provides Shakespeare another staging configuration with which to juxtapose groups of characters and dramatize conflicting points of view. Eavesdropping is inherently iconoclastic on Shakespeare's stage; it examines status, protestations of sincerity, and self-importance from the outsiders' skeptical vantage and thereby enlists the spectators' sympathy for the irreverent perspective. Spatially, eavesdropping bestows centrality on the figure being observed, framing and structuring his or her function at the focus of attention while the eavesdropper shares with us as spectators a liminal borderland of onlooking and criticism.

The downfall of Cardinal Wolsey in *Henry VIII*, for example, is closely observed by Wolsey's political enemies as well as ourselves, and those onlookers sharpen our perception of the irony in Wolsey's self-undoing by their anticipation of his troubles and their evident satisfaction at his discomfiture (3.2.75–203). Our pleasure in Malvolio's infatuation with self in *Twelfth Night* is heightened by the satiric commentary of Sir Toby and his cohorts, who from their place of concealment continually inform us what he is doing: "He has been yonder i' the sun practicing behavior to his own shadow this half hour . . . How he jets under his advanc'd plumes! . . . Look how imagination blows him . . . Now is the woodcock near the gin" (2.5.16–82). The presumably invisible Puck and Oberon and Ariel overhear lovers' confessions or foil rebellious plots; Duke Vincentio, disguised as a friar, becomes a "looker on" in his city of Vienna.[51] The physical separation on stage of these persons from those they overhear gives visual definition to their role as interpreters.

More eavesdroppers than one in "observation" scenes[52] of this sort can intensify the iconoclastic function of eavesdropping by subjecting the central stage picture to varying interpretations that are incommensurate with one another. In the last act of *Troilus and Cressida*, Cressida's capitulation to Diomedes is observed from one vantage point by Troilus and Ulysses, and from another by Thersites. As Douglas Sprigg observes, the stage is almost schematically polarized into symbolic contrasts, with Troilus the naive romantic on one side and Thersites the "priapic gargoyle" on the other; lechery is opposed to love, decadence to innocence, venality to fidelity.[53] The conversations of those watching Cressida constitute in effect a series of stage directions. "Cressid comes forth to him," says Troilus. "You shake, my lord, at something," Ulysses says to him. "She strokes his cheek," observes Troilus (5.2.6–53). Cressida's position amid a multiplicity of views on the nature of physical love subjects her to a moral tug of war that is made pictorial through stage groupings. The stage picture also gives visual form to a difficulty of interpretation. How are we to judge Cressida's desertion? The judgers on stage not only fail to agree, but regard matters so much from their own bias that certainty remains elusive. The problematic character of this "problem play" takes form on stage as an abortive debate among speakers not in communication with one another. Reasoned discourse breaks down once more, as earlier in the council meetings of Trojans and Greeks.

This scene of overhearing takes place at night, as we learn from several verbal references to nighttime and from a torch burning on stage (l. 5). Nighttime on Shakespeare's stage is a notably liminal state of ambiguity, discrepant awareness, danger, and carnival inversion, paradoxically the more so because the stage is so totally visible in the Elizabethan theater. The absence of theatrical lighting means that darkness is conveyed to the spectators by movements and groupings of costumed actors as well as by their dialogue: by nightwear, by torches and torchbearers used not for illumination but as signals of darkness, by the stated inability of actors to see one another, by fearful or surprised encounters, by stealth, tiptoeing, and the like.[54] The spectators, accepting the convention of obscurity of vision, are in fact able to see everything and are thus omniscient. They are able to interpret the metaphoric significance of darkness in the visual context of the entire theater; human blindness is framed by the imposing theatrical façade with its connotations of order and hierarchy.

Human actions in the nighttime are perceived to be those of elopement and escape from authority, as in the masquerading atmosphere of Jessica's departure from her father's house in *The Merchant of Venice*, or the meeting of lovers as in *Romeo and Juliet*, or a lonely watch on the guard platform in the dead of night as in *Hamlet*. The extinguishing of a torch on stage accompanies the murder of Banquo in *Macbeth* (3.3).[55] The night before the assassination in *Julius Caesar* is marked by numerous prodigies, of which the chief participants in the drama offer interpretations as varying as their several philosophies. The dark encounters near Swinsted Abbey in *King John* (5.6) bespeak the confused and demoralized state into which England has fallen on the death of her dynastically flawed king. Stage conventions of darkness urge a sense of transition and mystery.

Above all, visible signs of darkness accentuate the ironic contrast between the all-knowing state of the spectators and the "benighted" condition of the characters on stage. The swift and violent action in *Othello*, occurring so often at night, makes use of visual signs to stress the blindness of human endeavor. Brabantio, searching for Othello with "some special officers of night" and "*with Servants and torches*," encounters him in a tense scene of arrest that bears a visible though fleeting resemblance to the nighttime arrest of Christ at Gethsemane, which in the medieval cycle plays was similarly staged with torchbearers in the full light of day.[56] The nighttime brawl of Cassio and Roderigo during the watch on Cyprus depends for its ominous atmosphere on the contrast between the feasting celebrations of the evening and the clash that suddenly erupts, amid the tolling of a "dreadful bell" and other evidences of encounter in the dark. Othello and Desdemona must be "wak'd with strife" from their "balmy slumbers" (2.3.169, 252). The second fight of Cassio and Roderigo produces a scene of threatening darkness (5.1) in which the wounded Cassio cries for help but for a time remains unassisted by Lodovico and Gratiano, who are fearful of some unseen villainy. As Alan Dessen observes, the scene acts out "various kinds of real and metaphoric darkness prevalent in this tragedy," since the situations of both Roderigo and Cassio bear a significant resemblance to that of Othello.[57] The actors, although in full view of the spectators, convey by their groping hesitancy and inability to distinguish one another a vivid sense of terror and isolation. Our ability as spectators to see more than the characters can see, combined with our inability to intervene, enhances a discrepant awareness that is essential to the scene's mood of anxiety and uncontrollable violence. We foresee tragic events, but cannot dispel the darkness of the soul that induces Othello to extinguish first the "flaming minister" he carries to Desdemona's bedside and then the "Promethean heat" of her innocent life. The visual signs of darkness on Shakespeare's stage are most distressing in their liminal suggestion when they invoke the passage to death itself.

Interior locations in Shakespeare use groupings of characters, the theatrical façade, and occasional movable properties to define visually a recurring set of interior spaces or enclosed areas through which a world of privacy, nighttime, inverted authority, and informal companionship is vividly contrasted with that of public function. Such recurring locales include the throne room, the feasting hall, the council chamber, the tavern room, the bedroom, and the garden. The Elizabethan stage façade, as we have seen, furnishes architectural detail, gallery, doors, and pillars that are visually applicable to a great hall or presence chamber, or even (George Kernodle would argue) to a garden, since exterior architecture is a familiar background motif in medieval painting and street pageantry for scenes located indoor or outdoors.[58] The tiring-house façade serves here not as an exterior wall for a siege or the like, but as an interior partition separating visible stage space from the unseen world lying beyond its doors. Movable properties like thrones, chairs, tables, and beds, though by no means in use for the majority of scenes in Shakespeare, are sometimes pressed into service for these recurring interior locations. When brought temporarily on stage they generate, in George Reynolds' phrase, "a symbolic rather than a picture stage, that is, a stage on which the properties are intended only to suggest the scene rather than to picture it completely, congruously, and realistically."[59] Movable properties are all the more distinctive because they are infrequently used. Our sense as spectators of where we are is strongly influenced by properties and their spatial relation to their surroundings, despite the general absence of verisimilar scenic devices like wall decorations and floor coverings.

Whenever the throne is thrust out on stage for a single scene or for a large sequence of action, for example, it at once establishes its own milieu, claiming its relationship to the world around it and becoming, as Kernodle says, "physically and expressively the center of the action." A throne scene, on the Elizabethan stage, as in the tableaux vivants of street pageants, is not constructed realistically to resemble a palace, but is "a set show built around a throne."[60] In the midst of architectural surroundings that suggest the ambiance of a royal court, the throne is augmented in its visual impressiveness by symbolic associations of a traditional character. Shakespeare certainly knows how to exploit the throne's power to invoke awesome majesty, as in *Henry V*, when the King speaks from "this imperial throne" as he defies the Dauphin of France (1.2.35).

Yet this theater of majesty, in which the very building seems to embody the idea of monarchical power, is most often in Shakespeare the symbolic reminder of greatness lost, of a once-noble authority now subverted by tyrants or factionalists. The throne, both symbolically and in a literal theatrical sense, is the center of dispute between Yorkists and Lancastrians in Shakespeare's first historical tetralogy, and between the two sides of the conflict in *Richard II*. Claudius, in *Hamlet*, knows how to bolster his claim to the kingdom with the potent symbolism of "the throne of Denmark," to which he repeatedly alludes (1.2.49, 109). Macbeth plunders for his use the same image of royal authority. No doubt the throne appears on stage more often than it is specifically mentioned,[61] a recurrent visual symbol of conflict as well as of structure. We shall see further violations of the throne as an object of ceremonial significance in the next chapter. Here our interest is in the function of the throne in establishing a sense of royal interior. Because the throne is present on stage and central to our view, the surrounding architecture of gallery, doors, pillars, and the like is subsumed into a picture of regal hierarchy whereby we can then measure the degree to which the symbol is vitiated by ignoble strife and ambition.

A bed thrust out or "discovered" on Shakespeare's stage becomes, like a throne, the physical center of the action, able to define the adjoining space and architectural detail as belonging to it for the duration of a bedchamber scene.[62] A bed is also expressive of its occupant. It is something private, like a ring, associated with personal qualities of the owner such as innocence and vulnerability. Its curtains close off a space that is intimate and mysterious, but which is also misunderstood and subject to duplicitous or violent attack.

Imogen's bed in *Cymbeline*, for instance, thrust on stage when, as the stage direction indicates, Imogen enters "*in her bed*" (2.2), suggests the purity and blamelessness of the woman whose chamber is violated by the presence of an evil intruder. Iachimo too is associated with a large stage property,[63] for he is to emerge "*from the trunk*" in her room while she sleeps in order to note intimate details about her person and belongings and to remove a bracelet from her arm. Desdemona's entrance in Act 5 scene 2 of *Othello* seems to be accomplished by a similar thrusting out, for she too enters "*in her bed*" and the mute presence of her bed with its curtains is an eloquent indictment of Othello's tragic error. The link between this bed and Othello's marriage is carefully developed throughout the play in preparation for the final scene and its dominating stage property. Juliet falls asleep from Friar Laurence's potion in her bed and is there discovered, a seeming corpse (*Romeo and Juliet*, 4.3–5).⁶⁴ Both the staging method and its symbolic import are found in Shakespeare's contemporaries as well, as in Thomas Heywood's *Silver Age* in which we find the stage direction "*Enter Semele drawne out in her bed*" or in Thomas Middleton's *Chaste Maid in Cheapside* with "*A Bed thrust out upon the Stage, Allwits Wife in it.*"⁶⁵

Because the bed is relatively uncommon and hence visually striking on Shakespeare's stage, it can be effective as a linking device to pair scenes or characters whenever it recurs. In *2 Henry VI*, for instance, a bed "*put forth*" on stage with the murdered Duke Humphrey in it (3.2.146) focuses attention on the extraordinary signs of his violent death, whereupon in the next scene Cardinal Beaufort is found also dying in bed—the very stage property he is credibly believed to have prepared for Humphrey. The visual continuity of bed-curtains links the two scenes and underscores the irony that the Cardinal dies in a bed so like that he had readied for his victim.⁶⁶ Beds in Shakespeare are thus apt to juxtapose innocence with intrusion and violation. The bed's traditional associations of peace and intimacy are invoked as a backdrop to violence and death, much as the throne serves to put spectators in mind of a majesty that is often desecrated.

Tables and chairs are not infrequently brought on stage to establish an interior scene, such as the council table "*with chairs and stools*" used in the interrogation of Cranmer in *Henry VIII* (5.3), or the council meeting in the Tower of London in *Richard III* "*at a table*" (3.4). When antagonists sit opposite one another to sort out their grievances or to negotiate terms, like Antony and Octavius or Hotspur and Glendower,⁶⁷ the stage furnishings assist materially in the spatial metaphor of symmetrical conflict through which Shakespeare often expresses a tension between order and disorder. The conflict is especially evident in feast scenes, as we shall see in the following chapter when we examine banqueting as a symbol of hospitality too often vitiated. Tables and chairs can also establish a sense of camaraderie, of intimacy among drinking companions in the Boar's Head tavern of *1* and *2 Henry IV* or (though furniture is not specifically mentioned) in a room of the Countess Olivia's house in *Twelfth Night* where Sir Toby carouses with Sir

Andrew and Feste (2.3). In scenes of this kind the movable furniture helps to establish an intimate sense of location in contrast to the world lying beyond the stage façade; the stage is a place of revelry, while the outer world belongs to Malvolio and his kind. The ambiance is created not by stage furniture alone but by the relation of the movable properties to the surrounding theater building. The properties suggest the purpose of the scene and group the actors at its focus, while the acting space defines for us an enclosed world set apart by partitions from what lies beyond our visible range.

Thus the role of the stage façade and its doors in creating scenes of interior location is no less visually essential than that of the movable furniture. The façade and its doors enclose the space and separate it from what lies beyond—usually an inner room, or the outer world, or both. The unseen space backstage establishes through contrast the understood location of the visible stage. As Michael Issacharoff argues, the theater exploits a useful tension between visible space that is represented on stage and invisible offstage space that must be evoked through language and stage movement into or out of its perimeter; the outside space can invade the inner or mimetic space and thereby define where and what it is.[68]

Shakespeare's way of contrasting stage space with what lies beyond the façade often involves two imagined offstage locations, one leading to an inner world and one to the outer world of public affairs. In the sequence of scenes leading up to and including the murder of Duncan in *Macbeth*, for example, backstage space must represent first the inner castle where Duncan dines and is murdered, and then the world exterior to the castle from which Macduff arrives to awaken Duncan. The inner castle is suggested first by the servants' entrances and exits ("*Enter a Sewer, and divers Servants with dishes and service, over the stage*") as though to the hall where Duncan is being royally feasted (1.7). When Macbeth enters on stage as though from that chamber, pondering in soliloquy the frightful act he is about to commit, we imagine him to be in some inner courtyard or antechamber of the castle adjacent to the great hall; the precise location is less important than the juxtaposition of Macbeth's isolation with the conviviality taking place in the adjoining room. The claustrophobic sense is intensified by the encounters of husband and wife in whispered conference, and by the nervous meeting of Macbeth and Banquo (2.1). The stage continues to represent the inner courtyard or some such space, vaguely defined in itself but precisely located in relation to Duncan's chambers lying backstage. "*A bell rings*"; Macbeth exits to the murder and in the scene immediately following reappears to his wife, who in turn exits to Duncan's chambers to plant the murder weapons on Duncan's grooms. The furtive scene of husband and wife is overwhelmed by the oppressive sense of the dead king lying within, beyond the stage façade.

An appalling knock at a stage door representing "the south entry" provides continuity in the theater between the retirement of Macbeth and his lady and what is conventionally (though misleadingly) marked as a new scene (2.3), the arrival of the Porter to admit Macduff and Lennox. The main stage still occupies flexible space within the castle, defined now in relation to the stage door where the knocking occurs—presumably not the door leading to Duncan's chambers. Macduff and Lennox come from the outside world. Theirs is a function of discovery and judgment, a calling to account derived from visual traditions of the visitation of Death,[69] and the imagined location from which they arrive is spatially contrasted both with the backstage location of the murdered Duncan and with the enclosed area on the main stage occupied by the murderer and his wife.

The visible contrast between two stage doors, one leading to an inner world and one to the outer world of public affairs, affords Shakespeare a spatial vocabulary for conflict that he uses elsewhere to powerful effect. In *Julius Caesar* he creates in succession a pair of interior locations made parallel to each other by their physical relation to inner and outer worlds backstage. Brutus and then Caesar, as they consciously or unconsciously approach the fateful moment of assassination, must choose between the counsel of their wives, who belong to a domestic inner world, and that of the conspirators, who arrive from without. First Brutus enters "*in his orchard*" (2.1) as though from his own sleeping chambers, and is joined by Lucius and later by Portia from the same presumed inner space; in the interim, the conspirators are "at the door" (l. 70) and are admitted as though from the outer world of Rome. The "orchard" or garden is defined by its proximity both to the interior of Brutus' house and to the street. Caesar's house in the following scene (2.2) is "placed" by just the same visual signals, by the entrance of Calpurnia and others from within the house and by the arrival of the conspirators from without. Conflict is defined in terms of the alternatives presenting themselves from backstage.

Although we cannot prove from stage directions that one stage door served for the inner domestic world in each of these scenes and another stage door for the outer world, this kind of dual imagined presence of inner and outer worlds lying beyond the stage façade is common enough in Shakespeare's establishment of interior scenes that it suggests a visual convention to which Shakespeare's spectators were attuned. The sense of locale for a tavern is created in the *Henry IV* plays not only by tables, stools, tapsters in their leather aprons, whores with their ruffs and jewels, "lack-linen" swaggerers with swords and "two points" on their shoulder, musicians, drinking companions with red countenances, talk of "moldy stew'd prunes and dried cakes," quantities of sack, and the like (*2 Henry IV*, 2.4.122–145), but by a sense of enclosed space defined by two unseen presences, one the interior rooms of the tavern and the other the outside world.[70] The saturnalian world of merriment located on stage lies figuratively between the two.

Within the tavern lie the "fat" room from which Ned Poins emerges, the "Pomgarnet" and other tavern rooms to which Francis the drawer scuttles back and forth, the offices of Vintner and Hostess, and the room where Falstaff has supped with Doll Tearsheet.[71] The world of sober accountability also lies beyond the tiring-house façade, however, pressing its demands on those who carouse no matter how long they try to stave off the moment of reckoning. A knock at the door is the audible manifestation of that other world. Falstaff bids the Hostess "clap to the doors" in the tavern scene of *1 Henry IV*, but the Hostess' news is that "there is a nobleman of the court at door" with a message for Hal from the King. The merriment turns to playacting on the subject of this summons. Another knocking is heard, announcing the Sheriff "with a most monstrous watch . . . at the door" (2.4.273–285, 477–478). In *2 Henry IV* as well, *"Peto knocks at door"* with news of a crisis in King Henry's civil wars, followed by "more knocking at the door" to signify that Sir John must, like Hal, "away to court, sir, presently. / A dozen captains stay at door for you" (2.4.350–371).

This visual convention of the main stage lying figuratively and theatrically between two offstage worlds, one inner and one outer, lends itself to a number of Shakespeare's recurring locales besides the tavern in which the values of self-expression and holiday are at odds with public accountability. The enclosed orchard or garden can depend upon this convention, such as Brutus' orchard in *Julius Caesar* or Justice Shallow's Gloucestershire orchard with its sense of the manor house at hand and also the outer world; *"One knocks at door"* to herald Pistol's arrival with news of the death of Henry IV (*2 Henry IV*, 5.3.70). The Capulets' walled orchard in *Romeo and Juliet* not only abuts the house itself in the tiring-house façade but is reached by Romeo from without; he "ran this way, and leapt the orchard wall," we are told, probably not surmounting an actual stage structure but entering on stage as though from outside the Capulets' property (2.1.6). Cressida and Troilus must part at her father's house when the arriving Aeneas knocks at the gate from within the tiring-house; the noise prompts Cressida to retire into her chambers, also within (*Troilus and Cressida*, 4.2.35–44). The two worlds backstage thus represent the terms of Cressida's dilemma, a private world of emotion and one of political negotiations requiring the exchanging of hostages.[72]

Two offstage locales help create a sense of the prison in *Measure for Measure* as between two similar worlds of inner secrecy and of public authority where truth is eventually revealed. The setting of the prison is evoked (as in other prison scenes in *King John*, *Cymbeline*, *Richard III*, and so on) by manacles, heating irons, instruments of torture, ropes, executioners in recognizable attire, keys, and visible symptoms of darkness,[73] and also by our awareness that the stage doors lead both to prison cells within and to the outer world from which a messenger arrives with renewed orders for Claudio's execution (3.1–2, 4.2–3). Shipboard in *Pericles* is suggested, as in *The Tempest*, by nautical uniforms and lingo, but in addition by a sense of offstage shipboard space "beneath the hatches" and by a barge of Mytilene that is understood to be alongside, enabling Lysimachus to "come aboard" (3.1.1–71, 5.1.5–66).[74] The stage door and the façade are thus essential in localizing for a time the protean image of the Elizabethan stage and what it signifies. In the theater, as in man's social life, to go through a door is to cross a boundary; it can be part of a ritual of separation, a moment of profound alteration in status.[75]

The "idea" of Shakespeare's theater that emerges from its spatial dimensions is one of majesty and grandeur subjected to conflict. The heavens above, the underworld below, the sweep of action on the intervening plane of human life, all excite our admiration for an ordered universe of physical beauty and meaningful subordination of lesser to greater. In this *theatrum mundi*, however, the rise and fall of princes and of more ordinary mortals take literal form in images of ascent and descent. Cities under siege are taken and retaken, royal persons negotiate their surrender by descending from their place of elevation, or leap to their death. Lovers elope or are separated by the distance between them, or are lifted up to reunion in death. Sudden discovery of persons thought lost or dead by means of a curtained recess can embody *peripeteia* in the very structure of the theater façade, and can hint at the mysteries of art lying behind what the spectators are able to see; but the same device is also a potent visual metaphor of concealment and misunderstanding. Scenic reversals from outside to inside eloquently convey the notion of reversal of fortune; simultaneous staging juxtaposes two scenes or characters with unstated ironic effect. Groups of characters confront one another in symmetrical conflict or offer detached perspective in "observation" scenes. The throne, potent symbol of majesty, is subverted by faction; the bed invokes an innocence that is attacked or destroyed; a claustrophobic atmosphere of conflict or conspiracy is intensified by the juxtaposed sense of an imagined offstage location; the tavern's intimacy is broken in upon by the importunate demands of duty. In such a dramatic world, as we shall see next, the ceremony and order upon which degree is based are themselves continually tested. Nevertheless, our sense of wonder at the resplendent edifice before us is not lessened by our perception of its capacity for expressing conflict and change.

❧ V

The Language of Ceremony

The breach of custom
Is breach of all.

—Cymbeline

CEREMONY was omnipresent in Elizabethan life because it gave overt form to the social roles through which members of that society found their place and identity. As Thomas Van Laan persuasively observes, role playing was by no means confined to the theater.[1] Queen Elizabeth and King James had dominant roles to play by virtue of their elevated position in the social structure; consequently their every action took on symbolic meaning as an expression of their public function. "We Princes," observed Elizabeth in 1586, "are set on stages, in the sight and view of all the world duly observed. The eyes of many behold our actions."[2] Courtiers too were instructed by Castiglione, Spenser, Norton and Sackville, Lyly, and many others in the proper role of statesman and adviser, though the advice was of course not always followed. In private life, a married woman found herself expected to act out the duties of a wife, a servant could justify his or her place by fulfilling the role of loyal and obedient follower, and the lover or the friend encountered elaborate rules governing the performance of his part in a ceremony of courtship or of sworn brotherhood.

This universal role playing in English society provided Elizabethan dramatists a significant model for their portrayal of characters and relationships. Persons in plays, as in the audience watching those plays, were expected to fulfill roles defined for them by the nature of the individual's position in a mimetic social structure.[3] The theatrical nature of English public life in fact served as a major source for pageantry on the Elizabethan stage; the royal entries and progresses of Elizabeth and

James, staged as elaborate entertainments, were emulated in the theater by Peele, Lyly, Marlowe, Shakespeare, and a host of other dramatists.[4] Shakespeare's familiarity with the language of ceremony owes much to the omnipresence of pageantry in his life, both on stage and in the world it mirrored. Street pageants, triumphs, tableaux vivants, mummings, dumb shows, masques, funeral processions, and the like were as integral to Shakespeare's theater as to the Tudor and Stuart dynasties for which they were so often devised.

A consequence in Shakespeare's theater is that characters are under constant pressure to fulfill a ceremonial role or roles assigned to them in the social structure. From society's point of view, identity is role. Adriana's identity in *The Comedy of Errors* is dependent on her being a wife, as Van Laan shows, and this identity can be taken away; her husband's philandering changes her character. At the play's end all the major characters are properly identified as fathers, sons, servants, brothers, and the like; the dispelling of the play's confusion of identities leads ultimately to a sense of being reborn. To be Antipholus of Ephesus is to be a husband, a brother-in-law, a master of servants, a friend, a business acquaintance, a pillar of the community, a son to old Egeon, a brother. Being a husband entails serious obligations. The very concept of character, argues Van Laan, is as a nexus of various social roles.[5] The "inner man" sought for in modern psychological terms may not always be determinable. Changes in character are often nothing more than a process of becoming fully what the character is destined to become. By the same token, a character can lose identity, especially in the tragedies, and thereby lose all reason for existence: "Othello's occupation's gone" (*Othello*, 3.3.362).[6]

The ceremonious gestures through which social roles are affirmed take on an extraordinary centrality in Shakespeare's presentational language of the theater. Kneeling, embracing, clasping of hands, bowing, removing the hat, assuming a proper place at table, deferring to others in going through a doorway—all are part of a rich vocabulary expressing contractual obligation, obedience, homage, submission, fealty, petition, hospitality, parental authority, royal prerogative. Ceremonious actions form the visible substance of what Belarius in *Cymbeline* calls "reverence, / That angel of the world," that "doth make distinction / Of place 'tween high and low" (4.2.248–250). As G. K. Hunter observes, the plays are "microcosms of life not only as lived but also as organized." Shakespeare's plays accordingly encompass a large repertory of gestures defining characters "by their social status rather than their individual existence." Such gestures include "the servant's cringe, the soldier's swagger, the grandee's frown, the fop's simper, and the whole vocabulary of social deference and authority."[7]

Shakespeare's presentation of ceremony is notable not merely for its ubiquitousness, however. To a remarkable extent, ceremony in his plays is the focus of dramatic conflict. We learn much about the visual nature of ceremony on Shakespeare's stage from the manner in which it is interrupted or violated. Moreover, his protagonists often awaken our deepest sympathy when they express impatience with the outward form of manners, as when Duke Senior finds among his "co-mates and brothers in exile" a life more sweet "Than that of painted pomp," or Henry V on the eve of Agincourt deplores the constraints and artificiality of "idol ceremony," or King Lear madly urges that pomp "Take physic" and expose itself to feel what wretches feel.[8] The failures of ceremony are no less far-reaching than its successes.

We must observe, nonetheless, that those who protest so cogently against ceremony are dissatisfied not with its proper form but with abuses of it. Sympathetic characters become rebels or outsiders only when ceremony is perverted to the use of tyrants and flatterers, like Duke Frederick in *As You Like It* or Cornwall, Regan, and their associates in *King Lear*. Hamlet is driven into antisocial behavior not by a dislike for ceremony but paradoxically by his being denied access to its proper observances; the funeral baked meats coldly furnishing forth the marriage tables for his uncle-father and aunt-mother render impossible the expression of a deeply felt grief and leave him no alternative but to devalue the "customary suits of solemn black" and other "forms, moods, shapes of grief" that cannot denote him truly.[9] Righting of wrong in Shakespeare's plays customarily takes the form not of escape from ceremonial observance but rather of a return to it, to a fulfillment of role that is also a fulfillment of self.

In Arnold van Gennep's terms, ceremony or ritual is essential to the threefold process by which the hazardous "rites of passage" are traversed: a separation from one's former status as child or unmarried person or aging parent, a transition that is threateningly unstable unless controlled or licensed by ritual performance, and a revitalization or reincorporation forming a new family unit or recognized place in this world or the next.[10] Victor Turner further explains the ritual function of transition or liminality, and its dramatic potential for the theater, by showing how the novices in "life-crisis" rites of passage such as the advancement from puberty to adulthood or from lower rank to chieftainship are subjected to humiliations that are meant to prepare the candidates for their new responsibilities. Conversely, those who are consigned to permanently inferior positions in the structure are raised up for a time in a symbolic make-believe designed to reconcile them to their ordinary lot. Those of high station are stripped of rank and humbled to remind them of the dangers of tyrannical authority, while those of low station are given the temporary role of mimicking their social betters and restraining their social pride. Communitas is thus a state of meaningful status reversal, one that expresses through inversion the reasonableness and necessity of hierarchical principle.[11]

The gestural language of inversion, of anticeremonial, offers Shakespeare a potent form of expression for what is unjust and hollow in the social order. It channels protest into playacting through which spectators in the theater can participate in drama as a rite of passage. At times, to be sure, the threat of disorder becomes distressingly real. Although King Lear's harrowing trials resemble those of the reviled chief-elect in a rite of passage, acting out inversion of status through which such a figure is made to confront (for the ultimate good of the community) the insolence of power and the dangers of confusing the office with its incumbent, Lear's tormentors are not in fact performing an instructive ritual licensed by social practice. Their deadly earnestness overwhelms the "game" of social ritual and denies at last to Lear, after an abortive restoration, the refound identity that social ritual has vainly promised. Still, this seeming exception proves by its very failure the powerful necessity of the rediscovered sense of structure to which Shakespearean drama, like other rites of passage, tends. Shakespeare's reincorporations often coincide with a reaffirmation of identity. Duke Senior identifies himself to Orlando as "the Duke / That lov'd your father"; Lear is restored to fresh kingly garments and to a daughter's love before his rediscovered identity as king and father is taken from him; Hamlet proclaims his return to England in his royal person as "I, Hamlet the Dane," and is borne in death with full dignity as one destined "To have prov'd most royal."[12] Violated ceremony craves to be answered in Shakespeare by a revitalized ceremony.

Shakespeare thereby tests and reaffirms not only the social values of ceremony but the stage language through which we perceive those social values. Ceremony is what presentational language in Shakespeare is frequently "about"; as Martha Fleischer argues, the basic visual sign in his plays is "order itself."[13] The struggle between order and disorder bespeaks the danger of failure, for the threat of hollowness and insincerity in the language of ceremony is an attack on what is central to meaning in drama as in all social intercourse. The battle between meaningful and corrupted ceremony takes place in all arenas of life: in family and personal relationships, as manifested in the ceremonious rites of passage such as christenings, betrothals, marriages, and funerals; in state occasions like coronations, triumphal entries, and the receiving of ambassadors; in judicial ceremonies like public penance, farewell speeches of condemned persons, and trials; and, most embracingly, in ceremonials of precedence and contract that are an integral part of daily ritual, such as greetings, farewells, taking of places at table, handclaspings, embracings, doffings of the hat, bowings, and kneelings. All of these common occasions, and others, take place before our eyes on Shakespeare's stage. They are occasions both of formal splendor and of divisive misunderstanding. Affirmation of meaning in ceremony is preciously won, for the threat of meaninglessness is never long absent.

Shakespeare seldom brings on stage the full-scale Elizabethan forms of ceremonial for rites of passage such as christenings, marriages, and funerals, but he is very much concerned with the impact of these important transitions on the lives of the chief participants. He also shows the response of the community in which these events take place, since rites of passage celebrate an ending and a beginning for society as well as for the initiates. The immense importance to England of the newborn Elizabeth in *Henry VIII*, for example, is shown not in the ceremonial of christening itself but in an elaborate procession with trumpeters, nobles, and burgesses in their regalia "*bearing great standing-bowls for the christening-gifts*," the Duchess of Norfolk under a canopy "*bearing the child richly habited in a mantle*," prayers for a long and prosperous life, flourishes, and Archbishop Cranmer on his knees to the King and Queen. The crescendo of splendor leads triumphantly to Cranmer's long and fervent speech of prophecy for Elizabeth's future reign (5.5.1–56).

These images of order derive their intensity of meaning from the conflict out of which they have grown, for the day of christening itself has begun in the tumult of a multitude whose heads must be cudgeled to maintain discipline (5.4.6–32). Even more, the christening procession is seen as the climax of a series of earlier ceremonials in which figures of high rank have been variously conducted to coronation or to trial or execution. The christening is both literally and figuratively a time of birth and renewal for a nation torn by conflict. The ceremonial betokens a better future and justifies the suffering of the past by interpreting it as a necessary prologue to England's greatness to come. Because ceremonial validates past tribulation and illuminates the meaning of an enigmatic and perilous transition, it serves a contractual function uniting past and future. The visual impressiveness on stage attests to the momentous responsibilities undertaken by the participants. Custom is fulfilled, but the fragile character of its achievement emphasizes the pervasive threat to tradition and hence the value of what is attained.

Marriage is a far more omnipresent ending and beginning in Shakespeare, especially in the comedies, yet once again we are shown not the ceremony itself so much as the attendant transition and conflict. Shakespeare is more apt to dramatize the betrothal which, although a formal ritual and solemn contractual obligation made by the couple in the presence of witnesses and signaled by their joining of hands, is a moment of choice. The young woman must redirect her commitment of love and enter irrevocably into a new family structure, the young man must accept responsibility for her welfare, and her father must renounce his primary claim of authority in favor of the younger man. Their doing so in a ceremony of "hand-fest," as it was commonly known in Shakespeare's day, anticipates the legal and financial process whereby the marriage ceremony completes a transfer of authority.[14] Marriage itself is usually dramatically uninteresting, however meaningful to the participants, but betrothal confronts the substance of transition. It is here that the father candidly reveals his reluctance to part with his daughter. The misunderstandings and deceptions that alienate one generation from another, the tensions and ambiguities that ritual is devised to conciliate and clarify, take the form on Shakespeare's stage of an interrupted or irregular ceremony.

In *The Winter's Tale*, for example, when Florizel takes Perdita by the hand at the sheepshearing festival, we are seemingly presented with all the elements ceremonially and legally necessary for a valid betrothal: witnesses, dowry settlement, the father's acknowledgment of transfer, and the symbolic gesture of the hands. "Take hands, a bargain!" says the Shepherd in his role as surrogate father. "And, friends unknown, you shall bear witness to 't. / I give my daughter to him, and will make

/ Her portion equal his" (4.4.383–386). In response to Florizel's importunate request that the Shepherd "Contract us 'fore these witnesses," the old man responds with alacrity, "Come, your hand; / And, daughter, yours" (ll. 390-391). Because Florizel's true father is present in disguise, however, the dramatic point of the ceremony is its abrupt termination. In response to Florizel's request to "Mark our contract," Polixenes replies, "Mark your divorce, young sir" (l. 417) and accompanies his words by the actions of revealing his identity and forcing the couple to separate their hands. Only in the play's final scene is the gesture of union restored, when Leontes is urged by Paulina to "present your hand" to the statue of Hermione, and Camillo too joins the throng of lovers by taking Paulina "by the hand" (5.3.107, 145). The ceremony of betrothal and its interruption lead us through the complication of this late romance to an eventual restoration of harmony.

The island of *The Tempest* provides Shakespeare an ideal valedictory location in which to discover what is truly essential about the reincorporating function of ritual. Isolation from all civilized institutions of law and church throws upon Prospero, as master of ceremonies in his world of contending art and nature, the role of devising the ceremonies to be performed by himself and the young people who fall in love. Instinct bids the lovers couple with no more ceremony than the courting rituals seen in a state of nature. A father's possessive love bids Prospero monopolize his daughter in their mutual banishment, like old King Lear going willingly to prison with Cordelia to "sing like birds i' th' cage" (*King Lear*, 5.3.9). Prospero knows that he and his children must channel the libidinous energies of transition into the form of ritual or lose themselves to savagery. He must reinvent the safeguards through which human community disarms the threat of separation from established family ties. Ferdinand and Miranda must become novices in a rite of passage, humbled and made anxious under Prospero's tutelage to prepare them for their new roles. Prospero himself must confront the ambivalent feelings about his daughter's marriage that produce in him such turbulent emotion despite his efforts to remain calm, for he is both priest and participant in the ritual over which he presides.

To answer all these needs, the stage gestures of betrothal in *The Tempest* stress contractual agreement, consent of the father, and control of erotic pleasure through ceremony. The lovers answer each other in contractual terms, as Ferdinand accepts from Miranda the title of "husband" with "a heart as willing / As bondage e'er of freedom" and, by

way of solemn pledge, offers the necessary gesture: "Here's my hand."
Her reply is to offer hers to him, "with my heart in 't" (3.1.88–90).
Their vows, using such phrases as "I am your wife" and "My husband,"
take the form of a contract *de praesenti* rather than *de futuro* and are thus
irrevocable according to English ecclesiastical law; prenuptial sex would
require penance as a sinful act, but would not invalidate the union.[15]
The father is present at the betrothal, albeit invisible to the lovers, and
after a testing of their constancy confirms the gift of Miranda by tend-
ering her to Ferdinand, "to thy hand" (4.1.3–5). The financial terms
in which Prospero speaks of transferring Miranda from his care to that
of Ferdinand are only partly metaphoric, for the ceremony does indeed
entail the transfer of one who is regarded as a property; Miranda is
"my gift and thine own acquisition / Worthily purchas'd" (ll. 13–14).[16]
The union is a "contract" (ll. 19, 84, 133) to which Alonso too gives
his eventual blessing by joining the hands of the young people (5.1.215).

   The wedding ceremony itself is never really performed in its entirety
on Shakespeare's stage. One reason may be, as suggested earlier, that
the occasion ordinarily lacks dramatic conflict. Another factor may have
been governmental strictures against derogation or abuse of the Book
of Common Prayer.[17] At any rate, we are more apt to be shown a
masquerade of marriage than the ritual itself, as in the pretended union
of Orlando and "Ganymede" in *As You Like It*, with Celia (disguised
as Aliena) officiating as priest. Here we witness the exchanging of vows
("Will you, Orlando, have to wife this Rosalind?") and the actions of
giving and taking; but the absence of a priest's "commission," and
especially the absence of a father, are pointed reminders that Rosalind
must still be reunited with her father before he can give her away
(4.1.120–139). The irregularities of forest life have already prompted
Touchstone to seek a union with Audrey before a hedge priest who is
not likely to marry them well, and with no man present to give the
bride away. "I will not take her on gift of any man," he jibes, though
even Sir Oliver Martext knows that "she must be given, or the marriage
is not lawful" (3.3.63–66).

   Both these imperfect ceremonies make dramatic capital out of what
is essential but lacking: the father's gesture of separation from the bride,
through which he renounces his claims to her first affection and guar-
antees that there are no impediments to her marriage. The fulfillment
of this lack can signal the happy ending of a comedy, as when Hymen
in *As You Like It* instructs Duke Senior to "join her hand with his /

Whose heart within his bosom is" (5.4.113–114). In a kind of theatrical synecdoche the gesture of the father's renunciation can stand for the remainder of the marriage ceremony, which need not then be performed as anticlimactic. As in betrothal, the conflict is resolved once the father has signified his determination to accept the loss of a daughter. The French King in *Henry V* similarly gives his daughter Katharine to Henry of England ("Take her, fair son") in full view of the French and English courts as a token not only of resigning a daughter but of acknowledging France's submission to her neighbor (5.2.346).[18]

The presence of witnesses to confirm a contractual obligation is as important as the father's renunciatory gesture in Shakespeare's ceremonious representation of marriage, for the interests of the community in the forming of a new family unit are paramount. This ceremonial function of marriage tends in several Shakespearean comedies to a theatrical emphasis on witnessing and on festive entertainment. We see not the weddings with which *A Midsummer Night's Dream* presumably ends, but an after-dinner play staged for the couples' recreation. The actual marriages are described as taking place offstage in *The Taming of the Shrew*, while the final wedding banquet affords an opportunity for everyone not only to celebrate but to consider what marital obligation entails. Those present have good reason to ponder the meaning of the event, for the actual marriage ceremony uniting Petruchio and Kate has been described to us as extraordinarily irregular.

Because the form of the marriage ceremony invokes such positive images of witnessing and of orderly transition, it functions eloquently in Shakespeare as a traditional or "received" language of gesture against which to measure the imperfections in human relationships that arise from misunderstanding and mistrust. The offstage wedding of Olivia and Sebastian in *Twelfth Night*, for example, is described in such a way as to stress the formal nature of the ritual. The priest insists that he has performed "A contract of eternal bond of love, / Confirm'd by mutual joinder of your hands, / Attested by the holy close of lips, / Strength'ned by interchangement of your rings." The "ceremony" of this "compact" has been "seal'd" or ratified by the priest's own sacred function and testimony (5.1.152–157). The priest thus emphasizes not only the ceremonial gestures performed, but their contractual and witnessing function: the gestures confirm, attest, strengthen, bear witness, ratify. Yet the event itself has been highly unusual, lacking witnesses or anyone to give away the bride. The very identity of one of the partners, it appears, is in serious doubt. The illusion of misplaced ceremony generates a breach between master and servant and between friend and friend, until a way is found at last for Viola to give her hand to Orsino in a restorative gesture of affiance. The language of ceremony directs our attention to what is lacking as much as to what is fully performed, and insists on the serious completion of forms before the transitional process can give way to reincorporation.

The interruption of Claudio's intended wedding to Hero in *Much Ado about Nothing* offers a still more vivid image of flawed ritual than the offstage ceremonies in *The Taming of the Shrew* or *Twelfth Night*, for this aborted wedding is actually staged to our view. It becomes a central visual picture of inverted order, one that juxtaposes the festive solemnity of the ceremony itself with Claudio's mistaken perception that the ceremonial signs are all hollow. The couple are evidently sumptuously dressed for the occasion, for Hero has spent the previous evening in girlishly animated conversation about her elegant new gown and headdress. The priest is at hand, as are the bride's family and witnesses. Yet the contractual terms of the ceremony, lightly assumed by Hero's father to be pro forma and hence requiring no more than a brief "plain form of marriage," unexpectedly become an issue of substance. The priest's routine inquiry about any "inward impediment" why the couple should not be conjoined elicits a charge of promiscuity, which if true would indeed invalidate the contractual premises of transfer of property upon which the service is based; the father's delivering of his daughter to the altar is a mute testimonial of guarantee that she is without legal encumbrance (4.1.2–11). Leonato's surmise that he has been tricked into vouching for tarnished goods, with all the loss of honor that such an act would entail for him, may explain his rage at Hero for the supposed discovery.[19]

Accordingly, a new and inappropriate gesture must replace the one provided by the service in the Book of Common Prayer: instead of taking the seeming maid given him by the father, "as God did give her me," Claudio undertakes to "render her again" and so hands her back (ll. 25–28). His motive in this public gesture of denial, however misinformed, is to proclaim Hero as a menace to the contractual sacredness upon which the marriage ceremony depends for its efficacy. Claudio answers ceremony with inverted ceremony. Later, as a penance, he must reenact the ceremony he has aborted, taking another lady, as he thinks, by the hand from her father: "Which is the lady I must seize upon?" (5.4.52). He is not to see the face behind her veil until he agrees to "take her hand / Before this friar and swear to marry her" (ll. 55–56). Once he has actually done so, Hero unveils to reveal the woman he has traduced and now accepted, a woman reborn of the slander from which she died in reputation. Only by a renewed ceremony, then, can the impediments of a desecrated ceremony be removed. Stage picture answers stage picture in a theatrical motif of rebirth.

The wedding ritual is an important model for dramatic action in Shakespeare not only in interrupted wedding ceremonies, but more broadly in depictions of the father as he struggles to relinquish his daughter to a younger man. As Lynda Boose argues, van Gennep's ritual pattern of separation, transition, and reincorporation describes an ideal completion of the ritual process that is achieved only seldom in Shakespeare and at great personal cost.[20] Comedy, to be sure, can end "with the scattered elements of ritual regrouped and correctly enacted," as when Portia in *The Merchant of Venice* finds a way to fulfill her dead father's will, but even in this play Jessica serves as a dramatic foil to Portia by enacting an escape and theft from her father's house that leaves the willing bestowal by the father unperformed.

Shakespeare's tragedies view the reluctance of the bride's father as an increasingly essential factor in the protagonists' downfalls, one that takes the form on Shakespeare's stage of an empty or inverted ritual. Old Capulet in *Romeo and Juliet* quarrels with his daughter over her marriage, and is left at last with the futile role of bargaining with Montague over a bridal portion for the young woman who is now married to her deathbed. The "nunnery scene" in *Hamlet* is a savage parody of a wedding ritual: the bride's father is present only as a spy, Ophelia gives back Hamlet's gifts to her rather than receiving a ring, and Hamlet's dowry to her is a curse of sterility. Brabantio, frustrated in his attempt to block the "unnatural" marriage of Desdemona to Othello and confronted with her open challenge of the obedience he has demanded from her, mocks the ceremony of joining their hands even as he unwillingly performs it: "I here do give thee that with all my heart / Which, but thou hast already, with all my heart / I would keep from thee" (*Othello*, 1.3.196–198).

An intended ritual of engagement for Cordelia in the opening scene of *King Lear* becomes instead a counterritual of banishment and curse ("Will you, with those infirmities she owes . . . Dow'r'd with our curse, and stranger'd with our oath, / Take her, or leave her?" 1.1.203–206), as a consequence of which the King and his daughter are condemned throughout the play to a tragic circularity of uncompleted ceremonial forms. Unable to free himself of the wish to be rejoined with Cordelia to the exclusion of all others, Lear must see his wish fulfilled at last in terrible fashion: Cordelia recalled by dire event from her marital responsibilities in France, father and daughter together in prison, father and daughter united in death. Lear repossesses Cordelia for all time, but at an intolerable cost. Even in Shakespeare's late romances, the specter of imperfect separation pursues Pericles and Leontes, for they are unable to go forward with their own lives until they resolve the riddle of possessive attachment to a daughter. Prospero's success, in *The Tempest*, in giving away his daughter and thereby enacting his proper role of renunciation, is all the more wondrous because so many fathers have failed before him and because his own temptation to remain forever on the island with Miranda is so great. Thus the shattered human world of the late romances, "through obsessive reenactments of broken rituals, strives to recapture what has been lost and thus to reconnect itself with the sacred world of its origins."[21]

A sense of the incomplete weighs heavily upon public ceremonials of mourning in Shakespeare, as though some essential lack once again will not allow ritual to ease a difficult transition from a secure state to one that is uncertain and perilous. As with the marriage ceremony, the formal service of burial and its comforting words of rest eternal are not depicted on stage. Instead, elaborate funeral processions juxtapose public solemnity and magnificence with a mood of desecration and failure. The show of splendor befits an age in which death was the most common occasion for display and edification,[22] but the occasion itself is almost always interrupted or otherwise maimed. The incorporating function of funereal ritual, intended to reassure the bereaved that the dead person is joining a new spiritual world, seems lost in doubt about the survivors' own troubled futures. The formal stage language of ceremony frames a liminal world of conflict and disillusionment.

A common theme, especially in the history plays, is that of ancient honor new besmirched and national greatness despoiled. Shakespeare begins his dramatization of England's civil wars, in fact, with the interrupted funeral procession of Henry V (*1 Henry VI*, 1.1).[23] The "*Dead March*" and procession are elaborate, for it befits the corpse of the renowned Henry V to be "*attended on*" by his royal family and the aristocracy of England, but the enmity of those he has left behind soon expresses itself in the sudden appearance of messengers with grave news from the battlefields of France. These sad eruptions strike the mourners as a desecration of the ceremony for which they are gathered. "What say'st thou, man, before dead Henry's corse?" asks the Duke of Bedford, of the first messenger, who speaks of the loss of Orleans, Paris, and other territories. "Speak softly, or the loss of those great towns / Will make him burst his lead and rise from death" (ll. 62–64). The funeral of Henry V becomes a symbol of the demise of England's primacy. Its somber warnings are borne out in the funeral of Henry VI in *Richard III*, in which, as the Lady Anne protests, a "black magician" brazenly undertakes to "stop devoted charitable deeds" (1.2.34–35). The image of the murderer at the funeral of his victim implicates King Henry IV in *Richard II* as well, for his own actions have led to his following after the "untimely bier" of Richard (5.6.52).

Those who are dead are seldom laid to quiet rest; the mourners speak of them as bleeding afresh, of returning to reproach those left behind, of longing for vengeance. The unceasing struggle in *Titus Andronicus* between sacred ritual and savage vengeance is rendered in a series of contrasting tableaux; the opening funeral procession in honor of Titus' sons is incongruously mingled with the ceremonies of imperial election, triumphal entry, and the ritual slaughter of Alarbus,[24] whereas the concluding obsequies for Titus and Lavinia, "closed in our household's monument," are vividly opposed to Tamora's unsung departure. "No funeral rite, nor man in mourning weed, / No mournful bell shall ring her burial," declares the new emperor (5.3.194–197). The final exeunt in formal procession accompanying the dead bodies is therefore undercut by a reaffirmation of the violence to ceremony that first gave rise to the play's tragic excitement. Portentous irregularities similarly mar the obsequies in *Hamlet, Julius Caesar, King Lear,* and *Cymbeline.*[25]

Ceremonies of state in Shakespeare, including coronations, triumphal entries, and the receiving of ambassadors, are perhaps to be viewed as the rites of passage of the body politic, for they celebrate moments of transition in the social order. As such they must celebrate a separation and a reincorporation as well, for the life of the nation is no less dependent than is the individual on ceremonious completion in which all the participants fulfill their proper roles. Coronations especially are often synchronous with the death of a monarch and the accession of his heir. The individual is subsumed in the sacred office; the symbolic death and rebirth of the state are enacted in the drama of the king's two bodies. Role playing thereby enhances the significance of the occasion and the symbolic character of the ritual devised for it. Coronation is an awesome ceremony on Shakespeare's stage, one that embodies all the hierarchical values that are visually implicit in the theater building as *theatrum mundi*. Yet the event itself, more often than not, is deeply marred by anxiety and disillusionment.

Consider, at the very start of Shakespeare's career, the doleful litany of interrupted rituals, disputed claims, and ironic undercuttings that mar the ceremony of coronation in the first historical tetralogy. The coronation and procession for the inept young Henry VI in Paris are solemn affairs in which the chief persons of the realm cry "God save King Henry" as the Lord Bishop sets "the crown upon his head" and the Governor of Paris kneels to take his oath of allegiance, but these events are repeatedly interrupted by the quarrels of Vernon and Basset and by the plucking off the Garter from the leg of the craven Falstaff (*1 Henry VI*, 3.4–4.1).[26] *2 Henry VI* commences in political difficulties because the lovesick young King insists that the coronation be performed with all speed for his new Queen, whom Suffolk has brought back from France (1.1.72). Edward of York's ascending the throne in *3 Henry VI* is a symbolic coronation which quickly degenerates into a raw struggle for the "chair of state" on which he has dared to sit (1.1.51). In due course Warwick is able to see the coronation of Edward, whom he has made king, but almost immediately the Yorkist alliance falls apart over a marriage treaty with France (2.6.96). Edward's final victorious scene in this play allows him once more to occupy the royal throne (5.7.1), but only as an ailing monarch whose younger brother is already plotting the downfall of his house. The "stately triumphs," "mirthful comic shows," "drums and trumpets," and flourishes of this ceremonial (ll. 43–45) can only mock the impressive occasion for which they were devised.

When Richard III enters "*in pomp*" to assume England's throne, accordingly, we see the hollowness of his pretense to such splendor as the culmination of a dismaying series of imperfect coronations. Richard is seated "Thus high" by the advice of Buckingham and others, and hopes to wear "these glories" for many a day (*Richard III*, 4.2.1–5). The music for the event—a "*sennet*" for his royal entrance and another "*Sound*" when he mounts the throne—calls attention to the ceremonial weight of the entire action. Yet Richard's order of business on this momentous occasion is to suborn the murder of his nephews and to break with Buckingham. As Bridget Gellert Lyons points out, Richard is never able to "project a real connection between himself and the signs of his office"; because he usurps those signs, the effect is inevitably one of dissonance and incongruity. His coronation displaces that of his young nephew, Edward, an event that never takes place but is anticipated often in the play.[27]

To this distressing panorama of profaned coronations we might add the extraordinary irregularity of King John's "double coronation," in which he is once again crowned by the Pope in a "superfluous" ceremony of "double pomp" that disfigures "the antique and well noted face / Of plain old form" (*King John*, 4.2.4–40),[28] and the inverted ritual of deposition through which Richard II undertakes to give "this heavy weight from off my head / And this unwieldy scepter from my hand" (*Richard II*, 4.1.205–206).[29] In such a context we are perhaps able to understand why the deposition of Richard had to be censored from early texts—and why, conversely, the coronation of Henry V assumes such symbolic importance as the culmination of a long sequence of ceremonials in Shakespeare's history plays. Hal's coronation procession at the end of *2 Henry IV* must answer the fears of those who, like the dying King Henry IV, anticipate that now "a time is come to mock at form" (4.5.118). Hal's removing of the crown from his father's pillow and trying it on is hardly the reassuring ceremony that the occasion demands; as a coronation of sorts, yet wholly irregular, it recalls all too vividly the rebellion of his youthful years. In its place must come a public new beginning, as Hal promises to the Lord Chief Justice and other advisers: "Our coronation done, we will accite, / As I before rememb'red, all our state" (5.2.141–142). Not coincidentally, Hal chooses his coronation procession as the occasion on which to reject Falstaff publicly, for the symbolism of the ceremony demands an acceptance of order and responsibility. The diminution of personal warmth in Hal that must accompany such a rejection of an old companion is intensified by the visual contrast in this ceremony that is at once so wrenching and so politically auspicious.[30]

A similar contrast informs the coronation procession of Queen Anne in *Henry VIII*. Its glittering parade of trumpeters, officers of state in full array, and countesses in coronets of gold, coming after a ceremony in which Anne has had "all the royal makings of a queen, / As holy oil, Edward Confessor's crown, / The rod, and bird of peace, and all such emblems / Laid nobly on her," puts observers in mind of all the

personal misfortunes and political uncertainties that have paradoxically
led to this moment of "general joy" (4.1.6–90).[31] Even at its best in
Shakespeare, the ceremony of coronation is symbolic of an order achieved
only through trial and dissension.

Triumphal entries of generals returning from successful battle or
rulers receiving homage from their citizens are virtually never, on
Shakespeare's stage, visual celebrations of princely magnificence such
as we see in contemporary illustrations of the Roman triumph.[32] The
Roman plays especially stage triumphal entries or allude to them as
warnings against vainglorious pride and the mutability of power. In
Julius Caesar, for example, while the commons of Rome "make holiday
to see Caesar and to rejoice in his triumph," draping his statues with
"ceremonies" or trappings of state (1.1.30–65), conspiracy against him
feeds on these visible signs of his fatal inclination toward one-man rule.
His first appearance in a public procession, surrounded by his entourage
and insisting that his followers are to "Set on, and leave no ceremony
out" (1.2.11), is hardly reassuring to those who suspect him of coveting
the crown. These images of self-blinded greatness intensify through
ironic anticipation the necessary end of such ceremonial dignity. "O
mighty Caesar! Dost thou lie so low? / Are all thy conquests, glories,
triumphs, spoils, / Shrunk to this little measure?" (3.1.149–151).

Antony and Cleopatra offers edifyingly opposed images of triumphal
entry, performed by those who understand the limits of victorious
gesture and those who do not. Ventidius, entering *"as it were in triumph"*
from his conquest of Parthia, has to consider carefully how too successful an accomplishment and too glorious a celebration may danger-
ously outshine those of his master Antony; too many "triumphant
chariots" and "garlands" on his head will earn for him the ironic fate
of Sossius, undone by too quick an accumulation of renown (3.1.1–
19). Antony, in vivid contrast, is not hesitant to indulge in the elaborate
ceremonial acclaim that Ventidius wisely disclaims for himself. The
celebration in honor of Antony's temporary victory at Alexandria is to
be monumental. "Trumpeters," Antony cries, "With brazen din blast
you the city's ear, / Make mingle with our rattling taborines, / That
heaven and earth may strike their sounds together, / Applauding our
approach" (4.8.35–39). This ranting display of triumphal ritual signals
the loss of control for which Antony must pay the price of defeat and
humiliation. Octavius is mocked in turn for his cynical plan to lead
Cleopatra "in triumph" and to expose her to "the shouting varletry /

Of censuring Rome" (5.2.55–108). Cleopatra will, by her regal suicide, upstage Octavius in his politically self-serving manipulation of ritual; she will "call great Caesar ass / Unpolicied" (ll. 307–308). Neither Antony's nor Octavius' triumphal entry is shown on stage, but the way in which these rituals are invoked suggests the taste for pageantry to which both men are inclined. The protagonist of *Coriolanus* too is known for his triumphal entries, into Rome and into Corioles, and we are invited to make ironic contrast between the adulation showered upon Coriolanus and his subsequent fate as public enemy of both cities.[33]

The triumphal entry has its use as political ceremonial, to be sure, but it succeeds only when employed by rulers who understand that the language of such visual discourse must be directed to a ritual of passage for the state rather than for the person at its head. For the soldiers' procession into the village of Agincourt after their victorious battle, Henry V allows no boast to take from God that which "is his only," and he similarly denies his followers' request that "His bruised helmet and his bended sword" be borne "Before him through the city" upon his return to London. The full triumphal entry would be too redolent of "vainness and self-glorious pride"; Henry's wish is to give "full trophy, signal, and ostent / Quite from himself to God" (*Henry V*, 5 Prol. 18–22). The Duke in *Measure for Measure* knows too how to use a proper circumspection in his ceremonial return to the city of Vienna. "Give me your hand," he instructs Angelo and Escalus, "And let the subject see, to make them know / That outward courtesies would fain proclaim / Favors that keep within" (5.1.14–17). Roman triumphs and royal entries are familiar images in Shakespeare's theater, but their symbolic language is too often abused by those who confound enlightened image making with idolatry of the self. Ceremonious receivings of ambassadors display a similar tendency toward polar contrasts on Shakespeare's stage; their stately protocol and display can be used as instruments of wise public policy by Henry V in his confrontation with the Dauphin's representatives, but tend more often to hollow visual splendor in the hands of Cymbeline or Claudius of Denmark.[34]

Shakespeare's representations on stage of the judicial ceremonies of his era—public penance, return of the prisoner from sentencing, trials—seem extraordinarily public and instructional from a modern point of view. As Shakespeare presents them, they appear directed less at determining guilt or innocence, or at assuring just result, than at making an example of those who have presumably offended. Justice serves the interests of the body politic by offering warnings and drawing moral conclusions. Hence the visual impact is by design public and didactic. Shakespeare conveys to us the weight and impressiveness of such a symbolic language of justice, while suggesting at the same time that its traditional formulas do not always tell the whole truth. The splendid visual tableau of justice is qualified by ambiguities about the guilt of the central figure, or at least the ironic possibility that worse offenders may have escaped censure.

The Duchess of Gloucester's public penance in *2 Henry VI*, for example, subjects her to the degrading symbols of shame normally reserved for fornicators and adulterers like Jane Shore who, in Thomas Heywood's *2 Edward IV*, must enter on stage with two "Parators" or officers of an ecclesiastical court *"in a white sheet barefooted with her hair about her eares, and in her hand a waxe taper."*[35] The Duchess' offense of witchcraft requires her public appearance barefoot and *"in a white sheet"* with verses pinned upon her back *"and a taper burning in her hand."* She is accompanied by officers and a crowd who "point / And nod their heads and throw their eyes" upon her. Shakespeare thus provides striking visual details in his staging of a scene for which the chronicles report merely that the Duchess was sentenced "to do open penaunce, in iii open places, within the citie of London."[36] That a once-powerful and haughty duchess, envied at court for her rich finery, should experience the cut of the "ruthless flint" on her "tender-feeling feet" is an instructive fall from pride to humbleness, but it is also a wry comment on those allies of the Queen who have their own motives for bringing Eleanor down (2.4.9–34).

"The ceremony / Of bringing back the prisoner" in *Henry VIII* juxtaposes awesome public instruction with a sense of the vanity of all pomp and circumstance. No requirement of etiquette is omitted for the Duke of Buckingham as he is brought from his arraignment with *"tipstaves before him; the axe with the edge towards him; halberds on each side; accompanied with Sir Thomas Lovell, Sir Nicholas Vaux, Sir Walter Sands, and common people, etc."* (2.1.4–53). He is afforded opportunity for a last address, modeled on death speeches for such an occasion. His barge is ready and fitted out with "such furniture as suits / The greatness of his person." The Duke cannot overlook the irony, however, of being provided such courtesy by those who have brought about his downfall. "Let it alone," he says of the ritual devised for his last hours, "my state now will but mock me. / When I came hither, I was Lord High Constable / And Duke of Buckingham; now, poor Edward Bohun" (ll. 99–103). Whether he is guilty of the offense for which he must die is, moreover, an issue on which the play is studiously noncommittal. The political reasons for his demise are much more apparent than the purportedly criminal ones.

Trials in Shakespeare can present us with an even more dismaying sense of the hollowness of ceremonial proceedings, as when Queen Katharine in *Henry VIII* is summoned into consistory court to face an impressive assembly of vergers, scribes, clergymen, ministers, and the King "*under the cloth of state*" (2.4.1), all bent on finding public justification for her divorce, or when Queen Hermione in *The Winter's Tale* enters "*as to her trial*" to confront an official proceeding the result of which has been predetermined by the King (3.2.10). Justice presents a ceremonial visage in Shakespeare, but the very dignity and formalism of the undertaking sometimes do as much to question the results as to affirm the high principles of order visually embodied in the stage picture of the courtroom.

Ceremonious rites of passage and rituals of state, with their visual splendor and momentousness of occasion, are exceptional events on Shakespeare's stage; though we see many such events, each is a special occurrence. Daily ritual, on the other hand, provides a ubiquitous ceremonial language of greeting, parting, and deferring to authority that we must add to our vocabulary of signals if we are to appreciate the full range of Shakespeare's expressions of relationship and obligation.[37] Many of his ceremonial gestures, such as offcapping, handclasping, bowing, and kneeling, are acknowledgments of familial authority, contractual obligation, or hierarchical dependency. As such, they appear to reflect Elizabethan social custom and to reinforce traditional values of bond and subordination. Yet the very familiarity of such gesture generates also a language of nuance by means of which Elizabethan spectators might recognize, through subtle variations from the norm, signals of estrangement, defiance of authority, and other kinds of social inversion. Hierarchical formalism in the language of gesture necessitates its own opposite, a visual language of social anomaly.

Children in well-bred Elizabethan households, for example, were expected to make a daily obeisance to their parents as a sign of submission to parental authority.[38] This customary visual language is useful to Shakespeare not simply as a mirroring of Elizabethan life, or as a way of demarcating rank and status within the family, but as a subtle instrument of communication in which the least departure from normality demands interpretation. In *Cymbeline* Imogen's unexpected absence from the court is first detected by her failure to perform the ceremonial daily routine expected of her; she has not yet tendered to her father "The duty of the day" (3.5.32). The King makes no point of the ceremony itself, which is entirely traditional, but of its sudden omission. Clearly the custom is observed at other times in Shakespeare without comment, for as a matter of expected form it need draw no attention.[39] Juliet's resolution in *Romeo and Juliet* to "fall prostrate here" before her father, and to seek pardon for having ventured to oppose his will regarding her marriage to Count Paris, is thus no extraordinary stage business as measured by Elizabethan social custom; it is merely the seeming return of Juliet to the pattern of daily obeisance that Capulet believes he has every right to expect. The meaning she intends her gesture to convey is one of accustomed obedience: "Henceforward I am ever rul'd by you" (4.2.20–22). In dramatic context, however, the gesture is also eloquent because of what it implies for the omniscient spectator: Juliet has resolved on the desperate course of drinking Friar Laurence's sleep-inducing liquor, and uses her customary gesture of submission as a means of misleading and even defying parental authority.

Daily greetings among persons of rank demand precise and meaningful gestures of acknowledgment, so much so that omission or negligent performance is an unmistakable sign of disruption. The "customary compliment" with which Polixenes greets Leontes in *The Winter's Tale* is met with "Wafting his eyes to th' contrary and falling / A lip of much contempt," leaving the royal visitor at the Sicilian court to wonder at such an alteration in his entertainment (1.2.370–372). The Grecian generals in *Troilus and Cressida* convey their displeasure toward Achilles by putting on the "form of strangeness" as they pass by his tent and "either greet him not, / Or else disdainfully" (3.3.51–53). A decay of manners, then, is a manifest sign of the discord that must follow, according to Ulysses' famous speech, when "proportion, season, form, / Office, and custom" are no longer observed in the proper "line of order" (1.3.87–88).

Often the disruption in the form of greeting is caused by some crisis and consequent need for haste that abort accustomed ceremony. "My lord, I scarce have leisure to salute you, / My matter is so rash," says

Aeneas to his brother Troilus as he arrives with the unwelcome news that Cressida is to be returned to the Greeks (*Troilus and Cressida*, 4.2.61–62). "Now, good Camillo, / I am so fraught with curious business that / I leave out ceremony," apologizes Florizel to Camillo in *The Winter's Tale* at a particularly critical juncture in Florizel's defiance of his father's injunction against his marrying Perdita (4.4.514–516). "Come, come; sans compliment, what news abroad?" inquires the Bastard of Hubert in *King John* as Hubert brings comfortless news of the poisoning of the King (5.6.16). "The time will not allow the compliment / Which very manners urges," says Albany of Kent in *King Lear*; the otherwise notable event of an earl's return from exile must be temporarily overlooked in the extremity of so many deaths and reversals of fortune (5.3.237–238). Lord Stanley in *Richard III* cannot bestow on his son-in-law, the Earl of Richmond, the observances appropriate to their reunion on the eve of battle: "The leisure and the fearful time," he explains, "Cuts off the ceremonious vows of love / And ample interchange of sweet discourse, / Which so long sund'red friends should dwell upon." These expressions attest to the customary nature of such greetings and to the ceremonious nature of their form, and evince the symbolic function of such observances in proclaiming a return to ordered happiness: "God give us leisure for these rites of love!" (5.3.97–101). Seemingly small matters are portents because they announce departures from what is expected.

Ceremonial partings in Shakespeare are barometers of unrest in another way.[40] The etiquette of departure is a matter of precedence; persons of rank are afforded the courtesy of leaving first, and normally the characters on Shakespeare's stage observe this formality as a matter of course. In *Coriolanus*, for example, as Caius Marcius prepares to depart for the war against the Volscians, the officers who will accompany him under the generalship of Cominius insist that Caius Marcius be the first to leave after the general himself. To Cominius, Lartius says, "Lead you on," and then to Caius Marcius, "Follow Cominius. We must follow you; / Right worthy you priority." The citizens are to follow after (1.1.245–248). When Don John, the villain of *Much Ado about Nothing*, has finished conferring with his cohorts about a mischievous plan to embarrass Claudio and Don Pedro, Borachio and Conrade step aside to allow their master to leave first: "We'll wait upon your lordship" (1.3.70). They also mean by this that they will be attentive to his every command, but the stage action used to signify their alacrity centers on their deference at the doorway. Macbeth, rapt in contemplation of the witches' prophecies, emerges from his reverie to discover that Banquo, Angus, and Ross are politely waiting for him to leave first. "Worthy Macbeth, we stay upon your leisure," says Banquo, and Macbeth graciously replies to them, as he goes ahead, "Come, friends" (*Macbeth*, 1.3.148–156). No doubt these instances speak for many other occasions in which precedence is routinely observed on the Shakespearean stage.

Yet deferential ceremony of this sort can be idiotic or unsettling when carried to extremes, and the custom sometimes invites satiric criticism in Shakespeare. Slender's refusal to go before Anne Page to dinner in *The Merry Wives of Windsor*, even when he has been told that the meal waits for him, is a sure sign of his ludicrous bumptuousness. "I'll rather be unmannerly than troublesome," says he, as he manages to be both (1.1.292). When Queen Elinor in *King John* tries to send her new follower, the Bastard, ahead to the wars in France, the Bastard makes a jest out of the prospect of his preceding her through a door: "Our country manners give our betters way" (1.1.156). When the ceremony of precedence is abandoned, at any rate, the omission signals not a social disruption so much as a liberating spontaneity and avowal of comradeship like that shared by novices in a rite of passage. The ending of *The Comedy of Errors* resolves the insignificant question of which Dromio is elder by acknowledging that their reunion and mutual happiness are far more important. "Nay, then, thus," says one of them, as they propose to exit together, "We came into the world like brother and brother, / And now let's go hand in hand, not one before another" (5.1.424–426). In *Much Ado about Nothing*, Don Pedro ends a contest of politeness between himself and his host, Leonato, by placing them on a basis of equality. To the request of Leonato, "Please it your Grace lead on?" Don Pedro replies, "Your hand, Leonato. We will go together" (1.1.153–154). In *Hamlet*, the protagonist can find no more expressive way to indicate his closeness to Horatio and Marcellus, in the face of so much hostility and misunderstanding elsewhere in the Danish court, than to refuse their customary deferring to him in departure: "Nay, come, let's go together" (1.5.191).[41]

Stage music, as an essential part of the ceremonial in entrances and departures, can define both the impressiveness of an occasion and the irregularity that so often disfigures the outward appearance of pomp. Sennets, flourishes, tuckets, and other aural signs accompany and interpret the pageantry adorning the Shakespearean stage. These signals are sufficiently precise in the information they convey about rank that an Elizabethan audience often can know the title of an entering dignitary before he is visible. The symbolic associations of music with hierarchical degree, the body politic, and every kind of order known to the Renaissance enhance the dignity of a royal appearance.[42] Yet the effect is not infrequently ironic, as when a sennet greets the entry of King Richard III "*in pomp*," or employs the musical language of royal arrival and departure for Julius Caesar shortly after he has refused the crown of Rome.[43] In *Macbeth*, the trumpet flourishes for the arrival and exit of Duncan and his eldest son Malcolm are juxtaposed with the soliloquizing of Macbeth as he contemplates the step on which he must fall down or else o'erleap (1.4.1–58). Other sound effects, like ringing bells and the knocking at the door, are contrasted in *Macbeth* with the oboes that officially welcome the King into Macbeth's castle.[44] Music suggests an ordered world that is too often under attack or undermined by its own failures. In war, to a degree unfamiliar to us today, drum, trumpet, and fife present in the theater "A fearful battle rend'red you in music,"[45] through which alarms and retreats signal the course of events to an audience attuned to the military significance of each sound.[46] The familiar opening stage direction of "*Alarums, excursions, retreat*" (as for example in *King John*, Act 3 scene 3) is to be expressed not only in the token movement of soldiers across the stage but in meaningfully distinct sounds that indicate at every turn which way the battle is going. Symbolic use of music in this way reinforces, not without irony, Renaissance concepts of war as musical harmony and classical conventions translating war into elevated, sonorous discourse.

Arrivals and departures from the banqueting table, matters of ceremonial precedence in Shakespeare, establish a sense of order that often contrasts with the violations of hospitality to which the custom is all too prone. Two feasts in *Macbeth* are connected visually by signs of disrupted order. The first, for Duncan on the night of his murder, takes place backstage with servants in attendance while Macbeth, on the main stage, plays the irregular part of a host who has deserted his function. His wife joins him from the banqueting hall to ask, distraught, "Why have you left the chamber?" She is at pains to insist that the King has noticed Macbeth's extraordinary absence and has asked for him. "Know you not he has?" Macbeth has already contemplated in soliloquy the horrifying significance of his contradictory dual role as host and killer of the king; he should, as host, "against his murderer shut the door, / Not bear the knife myself" (1.7.15–31).

In the second banquet, honoring among others the supposedly absent Banquo on the night that he has been murdered, close attention to etiquette and arrangement of seating by rank once again prepares the way for disruption. The stage is sumptuously fitted out, with a "*Banquet prepared*" and the court of Scotland in attendance. "You know your own degrees; sit down," Macbeth greets his guests. He himself graciously condescends to "mingle with society, / And play the humble host," while "Our hostess keeps her state," but is soon called to the door to converse apart with the man he has suborned to murder Banquo and Fleance. Lady Macbeth notes the symbolic irregularity of his absence from table. By not giving the cheer properly, she says, he seems only a grudging host. "The sauce to meat is ceremony. / Meeting were bare without it" (3.4.1–37). Yet Macbeth cannot adequately play the host, just as he could not with Duncan, since the man he pretends to honor as his guest lies secretly murdered.

The ceremony of hospitality, thus violated, turns to mock its master of ceremonies. Macbeth apostrophizes Banquo and wishes him present, whereupon "The table's full." Disruption paradoxically takes the form of the belated arrival of one who, though invited, is unexpected. In the disorder of the table that quickly follows, the guests rise at Macbeth's distress, are bidden to sit, and finally must retreat in visible disarray. "At once, good night," Lady Macbeth instructs them, "Stand not upon the order of your going, / But go at once." To her husband, she protests that he has "displac'd the mirth, broke the good meeting, / With most admir'd [that is, wondered at] disorder." But what is one to do, Macbeth ponders, when ghosts rise from the grave to which they were committed "And push us from our stools?" (ll. 46–121). Throughout this scene the emptiness of Macbeth's new regal authority is conveyed through stage images of ceremonial feasting that repeatedly dissolve into confusion and aborted hospitality.

Visual juxtaposition of true and false hospitality is a part of Shakespeare's dramatic heritage. In the Saint Nicholas play of Adeodatus the Son of Getron (late twelfth century), for instance, a heathen king enjoys an opulent repast that is pointedly contrasted with charitable bread and wine set out for the clerics and the indigent. King Herod, in the N Town Corpus Christi cycle, feasts in insolent pride as he is about to be struck down by Death. Christ's Last Supper, featured in all the Corpus Christi cycles, contrasts the great feast of charity with the sharp bargaining of the chief priests.[47] Often these juxtaposed symbols of charitable hospitality and of worldly vainglory are simultaneously visible.

Shakespeare's use of two contrasting languages of the stage banquet, while indebted to the medieval tradition, shifts away from the morally absolute antitheses of religious drama to a stance of ironic complexity. The ceremony of feasting represents not so much God's gift of charity as a civilizing ritual of reincorporation too often inverted into its very opposite. The banqueting table is at its best not on rigidly formal occasions but as in King Simonides' idiosyncratic entertaining of a stranger knight in *Pericles*, or in the informal egalitarianism of the Forest of Arden in *As You Like It*—though even in this latter instance the communal banquet where Orlando finds sustenance is set in debate against Jaques' melancholy view of the Seven Ages of Man. The banquet that ends *The Taming of the Shrew* (5.2) resolves the "jarring notes" of Kate and Petruchio into a tableau of peace and quiet life, but not before we are made comically aware of the shrewishness that Lucentio and Hortensio will discover in their new wives.

Elsewhere in Shakespeare the banquet is subject to a still more disillusioned view of lifeless artificiality. The flattering guests who disport themselves at Timon's ornate "sweep of vanity" and who "*rise from table, with much adoring of Timon*" in order to "*show their loves*," richly deserve to be invited to a second feast in mocking celebration of Timon's financial ruin that his friends have done nothing to prevent. Here they find "*Tables and seats set out*" and "*Servants attending*" as before, yet their elaborately "cover'd dishes" contain nothing but warm water. This second banquet confirms what Timon suspected even in his prosperity, that "ceremony was but devis'd at first / To set a gloss on faint deeds, hollow welcomes" (*Timon of Athens*, 1.2.16–144, 3.6.1–48). The final ceremonial table in *Hamlet* from which Gertrude takes the stoup of poisoned wine and carouses to her son's fortune, the grisly banquet in *Titus Andronicus* at which the guests are elaborately bidden to "take your places" at table for a cannibalistic repast, the elaborate feasting in *Troilus and Cressida* and *Antony and Cleopatra* among enemies who will be at one anothers' throats next day, all suggest how frequently in Shakespeare the ceremony of the table is glaringly juxtaposed with violence and hypocrisy. The ceremony itself is not at fault. Instead, its regular form and sense of hospitable order impress upon us visibly the contrast between a civilized institution and the shortcomings of those who too frequently debase it.

Gestures of handclasping and embracing in Shakespeare go well beyond their commonplace function in greeting and parting to express in ceremonial form the confirmation of a pledge or contract, and thus to underscore the seriousness of an agreement that is too often violated.[48] As symbolic stage actions, they enable us to follow visibly the formation of an alliance or conversely the abrogation of it, the shifting of sides in a conflict, the estrangement of friends or kinsmen, the desecration of a promise. The ceremonial act takes on a special dramatic significance when it is inverted, for then the sense of order implicit in the gesture mocks those who abuse its true form.

The stage imagery of hands in *Julius Caesar*, for example, allows us to follow from its fervent beginnings to its disillusioning collapse a conspiracy that depends above all on mutual pledges of agreement among gentlemen.[49] Casca and Cassius shake hands to confirm Casca's joining the conspiracy against Caesar: "Hold, my hand . . . There's a bargain made" (1.3.117–120). Brutus similarly asks that each conspirator "Give me your hands all over, one by one" (2.1.112) when he joins their cause. This series of handshakes signifies not only a solemn promise but the gentlemanly commitment that Brutus prefers to an oath, and it anticipates the visually similar scene in which Antony also takes the hands of each conspirator—although without meaning to abide by what he seems to promise.

Hands are prominent in the assassination itself. "Casca, you are the first that rears your hand," instructs Cinna, and Casca's gesture is accordingly eloquent: "Speak, hands, for me!" (3.1.30, 76). The conspirators bathe their hands in Caesar's blood "Up to the elbows," but realize that this gesture might be misinterpreted by the bereaved Antony. "Yet see you but our hands / And this the bleeding business they have done," says Brutus, "Our hearts you see not." Antony has offered to die by their "purpled hands" that "do reek and smoke," but instead invites each man to "render me his bloody hand" in seeming token of reconciliation, however much it may offend Caesar's ghost "To see thy Antony making his peace, / Shaking the bloody fingers of thy foes" (ll. 107–199).

Later, when Brutus and Cassius have had a falling out, Cassius asks his fellow general to "Give me your hand" and embrace in token of mutual forgiveness, but their magnanimity cannot forestall the final scene of separation in which the opponents of Caesar embrace and take one another's hands for an "everlasting farewell" (4.3.117, 5.1.115). Strato asks Brutus to "Give me your hand first" before Brutus runs on Strato's sword (5.5.49). On stage the recurrent device of hands gives visual force to an ironic metaphor that is all-pervasive: however much the conspirators may believe that "every bondman in his own hand bears / The power to cancel his captivity" (1.3.100–101), experience shows that whoever had a "hand in his [Caesar's] death" shall perish by his own hands, "by traitors' hands" (5.1.56).

The ceremonial nature of handclasps and embraces in Shakespeare is evident in the remarkably public occasions on which they are employed. Leaders seek formal pledges of loyalty from their followers or attempt to reconcile factions; those who change sides proclaim their new affiliation through public gesture. As a result, the crucial turnings in a political conflict are apt to be signaled on Shakespeare's stage by symbolic action. The defection of the kingmaker Warwick from the Yorkist to the Lancastrian side of the civil wars in *3 Henry VI* takes the visible form of a hand extended by the Lancastrian Prince Edward to his welcome new ally: "And here, to pledge my vow, I give my hand." The stage direction is explicit: "*He gives his hand to Warwick*" (3.3.250). When the Duke of Clarence joins Warwick in defection, the event is ceremonially confirmed by King Henry himself: "Warwick and Clarence, give me both your hands. / Now join your hands, and with your hands your hearts" (4.6.38–39). The dying King Edward IV, in *Richard III*, makes a futile attempt to reconcile the factional lords to Queen Elizabeth and her ambitious kindred by urging them to "take each other's hand; / Dissemble not your hatred, swear your love" (2.1.7–8). The many "embracements" (l. 30) of this scene cannot conceal the enmity that will soon break out anew. Bolingbroke, in *Richard II*, commits himself to sacred obligation in his alliance with the Percies: "My heart this covenant makes, my hand thus seals it" (2.3.50). Elizabethan spectators would know that this public assurance of covenant is no more destined to survive than Richard's public embracing of Bolingbroke in the lists at Coventry (1.3.54).

The handclasp and the embrace thus establish themselves as recurrent gestures in the history plays, gestures that generally offer a grave indictment of political hypocrisy and opportunism. They are, as in *Julius Caesar*, testimonials against the swearers to which the audience is witness; their truth cannot be denied. Monarchs who forswear themselves may hope also to equivocate themselves out of their promises, but the gestures will not let them get away with this. "I may disjoin my hand, but not my faith," argues King Philip of France, whom Cardinal Pandulph has at length persuaded to "Let go the hand of that arch-heretic," King John of England, and thereby cancel the pact of peace over which the two kings have just embraced. The visible fact nevertheless remains: "This royal hand and mine," that were so "newly knit . . . Married in league, coupl'd, and link'd together / With all religious strength of sacred vows," are now parted and prepared for war (*King John*, 3.1.192–262). The gesture of handclasping is redeemed, in the history plays, only by the accession of Henry V. Just as Henry's coronation procession restores the dignity of a ceremony profaned in one interrupted coronation after another in earlier plays, his clasping the hand of the Lord Chief Justice in *2 Henry IV* signals his commitment to a rule of law that England has long awaited: "There is my hand" (5.2.117).

In personal and family conflicts no less than in political struggle, the joining of hands and embracings connote a harmony and reconciliation that can be cruelly violated. These gestures provide, as we have seen, the central stage action both for betrothals and marriages and for profanations of those ceremonial forms. As tokens of alliance among friends or family, too, these gestures speak of hope and of terrible disappointment. The final tableau in *Romeo and Juliet*, of two grieving fathers joining hands in sorrow, gains its visual strength from its ironic recapitulation of the lovers' brief touching and embracing. "O brother Montague," says Capulet, "give me thy hand" (5.3.296). The gesture does much to express the regret they both feel at having unknowingly contributed to the tragic ending, and the hope they now feel that the feud will be ended. As the play's prologue assured, their childrens' death has been a means to end the continuance of the parents' rage.

In *King Lear*, on the other hand, the gesture is inverted into its devastating opposite, as are so many images of order and harmony in this play. King Lear's confrontation with his two ungrateful daughters reaches the point of impasse when Goneril, arriving from Scotland at the Duke of Gloucester's house, is joined in a clasping of hands by her sister. "O Regan, will you take her by the hand?" cries Lear. "Why not by th' hand, sir?" is Goneril's reply. "How have I offended?" (2.4.193–194). Regan's gesture is an open signal of her siding with Goneril and seeing no wrong in her conduct toward her father. As in the history plays, this gesture gains resonance if we are able to measure the extent of its inversion from the orderly norm.

Gestures of obedience such as offcapping, kissing hands, bowing, and kneeling express not a contractual relationship of vow as in hand-clasping and embracing, but a relationship of dependency and subordination. These gestures are an acknowledgment of inferiority to one whose aid is sought. As such they are the omnipresent outward form on Shakespeare's stage of hierarchy and degree, enjoining our respect for ordered social and political institutions. They are also the language of flattery and obsequiousness. No visual language in Shakespeare is more capable of signaling the sharp contrast between order and its opposite, for ceremonies of obedience are as necessary as they are fatally subject to abuse.

The gesture of "cap and knee," with cap in hand and on bended knee, is a conventional token of submission to authority, as when the commoners are reported to have greeted Bolingbroke upon his return to England "with cap and knee" (*1 Henry IV*, 4.3.68). Flinging up the cap can also be a token of submission. Lord Clifford in *2 Henry VI* asks that each of Cade's followers embrace the King's pardon, "Fling up his cap, and say 'God save his Majesty!' " (4.8.14), and in *3 Henry VI* Warwick promises that "he that throws not up his cap for joy" in honor of great Edward of York will forfeit his head (2.1.196). Iago reports, in *Othello*, how three influential men of Venice "Off-capp'd" to the general on behalf of Iago's candidacy for lieutenant, though without success (1.1.11). Othello, for his part, says proudly that his deserts "May speak unbonneted to as proud a fortune / As this that I have reach'd" (1.2.23–24), and from the context it is evident that "unbonneted" means without removing the hat, standing on equal terms. Acknowledgment of differences in social rank and submission to authority must have been signaled by gestural use of the hat far more frequently on the Elizabethan stage than Shakespeare's dialogue directly indicates.

When offcapping is overtly mentioned, on the other hand, its connotations are apt to be pejorative. Bolingbroke is accused by Richard II of pandering to the commoners for their political favor: "Off goes his bonnet to an oyster-wench" (*Richard II*, 1.4.31). The Clown in *All's Well That Ends Well* makes fun of manners at court: "He that cannot make a leg, put off 's cap, kiss his hand, and say nothing, has neither leg, hands, lip, nor cap" (2.2.9–11). Osric, in *Hamlet*, cannot leave off saluting his interlocutors with an exaggerated gesture of deference. "Put your bonnet to his right use," Hamlet instructs him, " 'tis for the head" (5.2.93). The gesture in *Timon of Athens* is at first fawning—"the cap / Plays in the right hand, thus"—but soon converts to "certain half-caps and cold-moving nods" as Timon's fortune deserts him (2.1.18–19, 2.2.218). Apemantus' sardonic advice to Timon is to play the game of courtly flattery for personal advantage: "Hinge thy knee, / And let his very breath whom thou'lt observe / Blow off thy cap" (4.3.213–215).

Coriolanus refuses to "practice the insinuating nod" and be "off" to the commoners "most counterfeitly," like some politicians who are "supple and courteous to the people"; he will not show his "unbarb'd sconce" to those who in his estimation desire his "hat" rather than his heart (*Coriolanus*, 2.2.26, 2.3.99–100, 3.2.101). Coriolanus' distaste for such compliance with flattering forms is excessive, to be sure, but his fellow patrician Menenius is no less offended by the tribunes for being "ambitious for poor knaves' caps and legs," or the wavering commons who cast their "stinking greasy caps in hooting at / Coriolanus' exile" (2.1.68–69, 4.6.133–134). The gesture of offcapping is apt to seem particularly hypocritical when it is practiced by a politician seeking favor from those who are ordinarily obliged to offcap to him.

Kneeling is more likely to be taken seriously. Whereas offcapping and curtseying or "making a leg" may connote craven surrender, cringing, or toadying, kneeling is a profound gesture of acknowledgment of the claims of hierarchy. It occurs often on Shakespeare's stage, more often than indicated in stage directions or dialogue, and is thus a conventional action, yet its visual significance gives it a crucial impact at moments of conflicting loyalty. It can serve as the dominant expressive gesture at the point of dramatic reversal. Its range of expression is large: it can depict a critical shift of power in a political struggle, or the choice between mercy and justice in the presence of a judging figure, or the ironic reversal of the deference due a parent by a child, or the erosion of fealty owed an aging king. The seriousness of the gesture does not mean, however, that it is used as a straightforward sign of obedience; on the contrary, its most telling function is to delineate an idea of obedience that is harshly tested by political or moral ambiguity and by the misappropriation of its ceremonial forms to unjust ends.

The stage image of kneeling in *Richard II* functions somewhat like the oft-noted verbal image of the sun rising and setting; both continually inform us as spectators how the balance of power shifts delicately but decisively from Richard to Bolingbroke.[50] Whereas the verbal image of the sun (or buckets in a well, or still other verbal images) is evoked through speech, the image of kneeling is incorporated in the actors' gestures. It is not always commented upon; the image pattern must be perceived by the eye, whether literally so in the theater or by the eye of the imagination.

The image commences in the first scene, as Mowbray throws himself at the feet of Richard to beg for the privilege of combat against Bolingbroke (1.1.165); the King is very much the monarch still, but must nonetheless grant this request and that of Bolingbroke. At the tournament itself, Bolingbroke craves permission to "bow my knee before his Majesty" and "take a ceremonious leave" by kissing the King's hand; Richard responds by descending and folding his cousin in his arms (1.3.47–54). The nuances of feudal obligation and of kinship are nicely balanced in this exchange, intended to give public disclaimer to the animosity that both men feel. These political gestures can scarcely have been part of the prescribed trial ritual.[51] Richard fears, no doubt correctly, that Bolingbroke is all too ready to give "the tribute of his supple knee" to the commoners of England in a bid for their support, "As were our England in reversion his" (1.4.33–35). The seeming inversion of authority in which a ruler kneels to his countrymen does much to characterize the "vile politician" that Hotspur and the Percies soon learn to mistrust. Hotspur kneels to Bolingbroke in order to "tender you my service" (2.3.41), though he will look back in *1 Henry IV* with resentment upon this occasion when "I first bow'd my knee / Unto this king of smiles" (1.3.241, 245–246).

The political ambiguity of Bolingbroke's return to England from exile takes visible form in the contrast between Bolingbroke's gestures and his seeming intentions. "Show me thy humble heart, and not thy knee," York protests to his nephew, by way of attempting to arrest the movement of one "Whose duty is deceivable and false" (*Richard II*, 2.3.83–84). The confrontation between Bolingbroke and Richard at Flint Castle, examined in Chapter IV in terms of vertical motion from gallery to main stage, is no less rich in visual metaphors of kneeling and other obeisance. Bolingbroke commences the negotiation by offering "On both his knees" to "kiss King Richard's hand" and "Even at his feet to lay my arms and power," yet the audience knows that Bolingbroke is really in command; he will kneel only when Richard's capitulation to his demand for enfranchisement is firmly understood. Richard insists on the gestures of obedience that would signify his retention of authority, but in vain. "We are amaz'd," he says to Bolingbroke's envoy, Northumberland, "and thus long have we stood / To watch the fearful bending of thy knee." If Richard is indeed king, "how dare thy joints forget / To pay their aweful duty to our presence?" (3.3.36–76).

Only when Richard descends into the base court in a gesture of surrender does Richard receive the tokens of obeisance that are now transparently hollow. "You make a leg, and Bolingbroke says ay," Richard cuttingly observes of Northumberland's belated politeness to the King. "Stand all apart, / And show fair duty to his Majesty," Bolingbroke orders. The Quarto stage direction is explicit—"*He kneels down*"—but the delayed timing of this gesture is so apparent that Richard can do no more than point out its inappropriateness: "Fair cousin, you debase your princely knee / To make the base earth proud with kissing it" (ll. 175–191). During the scene of abdication as well, Richard calls attention to the strangeness of his new role as subject by lamenting that he has hardly yet learned "To insinuate, flatter, bow, and bend my knee" (4.1.166). Shakespeare thus invests with symbolic meaning a ceremonial event that in Holinshed is reported more matter-of-factly; Holinshed merely relates how Bolingbroke, as he first got sight of the King, "shewed a reuerend dutie as became him, in bowing his knee, and comming forward, did so likewise the second and third time, till the king tooke him by the hand, and lift him vp, saieng; Deere cousine, ye are welcome."[52]

Bolingbroke's new role as king places him in the nearly comic position of being petitioned through a veritable contest of kneelings,[53] when Aumerle and his two parents all beg King Henry to forgive or denounce the son for his treasonous plotting. "Rise up, good Aunt," urges the King, but the Duchess protests that "For ever will I walk upon my knees" until Aumerle is pardoned. "Unto my mother's prayers I bend my knee," Aumerle joins in, prompting York to bend his "true joints" against them both (5.3.92–98). The incongruity of conflict within the family shows itself on stage in the strange inversions that prompt a father to kneel against his son. As Ernest Gilman observes, the incongruity is further intensified when we perceive a visual similarity between these kneelings to a monarch and those of Act 1, scenes 1 and 3, in which Mowbray and Bolingbroke humbled themselves before Richard. The repetition of these stage images, like the repeated banishings of Mowbray, Bolingbroke, and then Exton, conveys the impression of a tragic cycle; history repeats itself only to discover in Bolingbroke's role in the murder of his cousin a recapitulation of the sin of Cain. The "cycle of homicide" links the new King Henry IV to his predecessor, for Richard too stained his hands with Abel's blood when he consented to the execution of Thomas of Woodstock. The recapitulated image of kneeling marks Henry as the new king, one whose act of pardon is symbolic of renewal for a warworn kingdom, but the image also mocks and distorts that ideal by impressing upon our vision the dark parallelism of events from which Henry has not escaped.[54]

The structural function of kneeling in *Measure for Measure* is notably different. Rather than serving, as in *Richard II*, as an image pattern shifting progressively from one protagonist to his nemesis in the course of the play, kneeling in *Measure for Measure* is concentrated in the final scene of reversal where it becomes the expressive gesture of the reversal itself. The gesture is, to be sure, anticipated when Isabella is urged by Lucio, in her first conference with Lord Angelo, to "Kneel down before him, hang upon his gown," and again when she bitterly retorts to her condemned brother Claudio, "Might but my bending down / Reprieve thee from thy fate, it should proceed" (2.2.48, 3.1.143–144).[55] Both of these anticipations, however, are directed forward to the final climactic scene and derive their symbolic meaning from it; Isabella's refusal to kneel for Claudio, in her anger and disappointment at his begging her to save his life by submitting to Angelo's will, prepares for the scene in which she will kneel for her wronger and forgive the offense she before found unforgivable.

In the final scene itself, the insistent kneelings pace the struggle between justice and mercy as Isabella's moment of decision approaches. Isabella is once again urged to "kneel before" an authority figure, this time the returned Duke, and to beg again for "justice, justice, justice, justice" (5.1.20–26). The repetition of her earlier gesture seems to mock her, for it appears that her efforts are once more in vain. Mariana too has her petition, and insists that she will rise from her knees only when her claim to Angelo is recognized; "Or else for ever be confixed here, / A marble monument!" (ll. 237–238). As a result of the Duke's surprising revelations, however, Isabella's kneeling is enlarged from a gesture of supplication to one of choosing; paradoxically, she who has sought justice must now judge Angelo through her kneeling or refusing to do so. She must also thereby preserve Mariana's happiness or else destroy it. "Sweet Isabel, take my part! / Lend me your knees," urges Mariana, who is already down before the Duke. Vincentio makes plain what Isabella's gesture of kneeling would mean: "Should she kneel down in mercy of this fact [the seeming execution by Angelo of Isabella's brother Claudio], / Her brother's ghost his paved bed would break, / And take her hence in horror." Yet Mariana persists: "Sweet Isabel, do yet but kneel by me! . . . O Isabel, will you not lend a knee?" (ll. 435–447). The repetition suggests the hesitation on Isabella's part that is dramatically necessary for such a moment of choice.

When Isabella does at last kneel, it is to beg mercy for her enemy and also to beg a husband for Mariana; it betokens her acknowledgment of both sinful nature in humanity and legitimate sexual desire, and indicates that she is ready to accept in herself what it is to be a woman.[56] No gesture could more eloquently encompass the changes that she has undergone. Angelo of course has knelt too, to acknowledge that the Duke "like pow'r divine" (l. 374) has seen the truth about him and rightfully possesses the power to sentence or to forgive. The Duke's alteration is no less apparent in the language of stage gesture: from one who shunned ceremony, loving his people but being unwilling to "stage me to their eyes" (1.1.69), he has become a ruler who understands the importance of public symbolism as a means of instructing his subjects in the necessity of order and rule. The kneelings of Act 5 are a measure of the potency of both his justice and his mercy.

The kneeling in the last act of *Coriolanus* shows still another use to which this climactic gesture can be put, for, although the gesture serves as in *Measure for Measure* to mark the protagonist's crucial choice, its visual statement mocks and inverts the military might to which Coriolanus has aspired. Coriolanus' mother must kneel to him, but in doing so brings about his capitulation to her. In preparation for this ironic reversal, the image of kneeling throughout the play traces Coriolanus' relation both to his mother and to the commoners of Rome whom he so despises. He kneels to his mother when he returns from his first great victory at Corioles (2.1.170), giving visible demonstration to the widely held view that he has performed brave acts in the wars chiefly "to please his mother" (1.1.37). He finds it impossible, on the other hand, to bend his knee to the people (2.2.26). Like the gown of humility and the deferential removing of the hat, kneeling represents for him the submission to popular opinion that he will not tolerate. When his mother urges him to go with bonnet in hand and with "Thy knee bussing the stones," because "in such business / Action is eloquence," he is outraged at the suggestion that his "arm'd knees, / Who bow'd but in my stirrup," should "bend like his / That hath receiv'd an alms" (3.2.77–122). The image of kneeling sharply differentiates the submission he acknowledges to his mother and that he denies to the popular will of Rome.

It is ironically appropriate, therefore, that Coriolanus' forcing the issue of submission upon Rome should lead to his own obeisance and surrender. Clearly his return from exile has as one of its goals the humiliation of Rome's citizens by forcing them to bow down before him; he turns the tables on those who before insisted on receiving the tribute of his cap and knee. "Go you that banish'd him," Menenius sardonically suggests when Coriolanus' threat to the city has become known, "A mile before his tent fall down, and knee / The way into his mercy" (5.1.4–6). Yet those who must now kneel to Coriolanus are friends as well as enemies, and not all of them owe professions of obedience to him. Cominius' tale of his reception at the camp of Coriolanus suggests how much the ceremony of obedience is amiss. "I kneel'd before him; / 'Twas very faintly he said 'Rise'; dismiss'd me / Thus, with his speechless hand" (ll. 68–70).

Coriolanus has in this way withstood the painful prospect of being knelt to by his own former general, to whom he deferred so readily in Act 1 (1.1.246). Coriolanus buckles, however, when he must confront an even more overwhelming gesture of obedience on the part of one to whom he acknowledges deference. "My mother bows," he says, "As if Olympus to a molehill should / In supplication nod" (5.3.29–31). She too is struck by this inversion of authority and love; although he of course attempts to kneel to her, she insists that he stand while "I kneel before thee, and unproperly / Show duty" (ll. 54–55). Although Coriolanus rises from his seat and attempts to cut short this painful interview, his mother and the other women resort once more to the most potent weapon they have at their disposal: "Down, ladies! Let us shame him with our knees" (l. 169). The cause of his capitulation is summed up in the paradoxical stage image of a mother kneeling to her son.[57]

King Lear too kneels to his child, and this stage image of inverted authority acts visibly as in *Coriolanus* to remind us of the kneelings we have seen throughout the play. The stage picture gains poignancy from an awareness of how the motif has been used previously, and indeed how the language of ceremonial gesture resonates in all Shakespearean drama. The visual reminiscences in *King Lear* are quite unlike those of *Coriolanus*, however, for Lear's kneeling to Cordelia is no capitulation or ironic defeat; it is instead an atonement for the terrible inversions of authority that have preceded it.

To look at *King Lear* in terms of kneeling and other signs of ceremony is to see a steady erosion of proper custom, and a transfer of deferential tokens from Lear to those who take away his authority. The play commences with what the King has intended to be a ceremony of obeisance.[58] In his eyes those whom he has loved most choose to defy him: Kent resolves to be "unmannerly," and Cordelia has "obedience scanted" (1.1.145, 280). At the Duke of Albany's palace, however, Lear begins to discover what disobedience can truly mean. Goneril instructs Oswald to "Put on what weary negligence you please" (1.3.13), and the upshot is a brawl that gives specious confirmation to Goneril's charge that Lear's knights undermine her authority in her own home. As a consequence, those who serve Lear and kneel to him are taken away from him or humiliated. Kent, disguised as Caius and acting as messenger for the King, shows his "duty kneeling" as a matter of course to the Duke of Cornwall; but this routine gesture cannot conceal Kent's disrespect for the "smiling rogues" who "bite the holy cords a-twain / Which are too intrinse t' unloose." Kent is thrown in the stocks for insolence, while Oswald and his fellow "silly ducking observants" are free to practice their craven flattery (2.2.74–104, 2.4.29).

Cornwall and others who enjoy power may now command the knee more effectively than Lear, who has given away his perquisites of ceremony along with his title. The dawning realization of this change appalls him. "Do you but mark how this becomes the house," he observes with biting irony to Regan as he kneels to the absent Goneril and apostrophizes her as his superior: " 'Dear daughter, I confess that I am old; / Age is unnecessary. On my knees I beg / That you'll vouchsafe me raiment, bed, and food' " (2.4.151–154). When Goneril arrives at Gloucester's house and joins hands with Regan, thus confirming their intention that their father bow to the necessity of his diminished stature, Lear's mind turns to another daughter to whom he might kneel instead. Rather than return with Goneril, he protests, he would humble himself before Cordelia and her husband: "I could as well be brought / To knee his throne, and, squire-like, pension beg / To keep base life afoot" (ll. 212–214). He is not consciously ready to do so, and indeed his lips cannot yet name Cordelia as the object of this imagined kneeling, but his longing for a symbolic act of contrition toward her is evident in the image itself.

The image anticipates the event; once he has suffered the harrowing experience of the storm and of losing his sanity, Lear will find some measure of comfort in kneeling to Cordelia. She for her part longs to kneel to him, and asks that her father hold his hand in benediction over her. "You must not kneel," she urges (4.7.60). A father and king should not kneel to a daughter. From his experience of madness, however, Lear has begun to discover how cruelly the forms of obedience had blinded him when he relied overly on their sustenance. Restored to Cordelia, offering to her the homage he no longer craves for himself, Lear shares with her a mutuality of kneeling and an equality of love that will sustain them until they are joined in death. Indeed, even as they are taken off to prison together, Lear avers to Cordelia that "When thou dost ask me blessing, I'll kneel down, / And ask of thee forgiveness" (5.3.10–11), and his last act is to kneel over her dead body in a futile attempt to determine if she still lives.[59]

No play offers a more jolting challenge than *King Lear* to the conventions of ceremonial language, for every ceremonial action (kneeling, embracing, clasping of hands) is pressed into the corrupted service of those who gain cruel ascendancy over their victims. Even at the last, when the villains have paid a reckoning for their crimes, ceremonial attentiveness to the return of the Earl of Kent from exile or to proper mourning rites for Goneril and Regan must be set aside in the terrible expediency of death. The memorable stage images of the last two acts are those in which all order and authority appear to have been overwhelmed: Lear madly arraigning a footstool in lieu of his daughter Goneril, Gloucester being blinded and attempting suicide, Lear bedecked with weeds and Gloucester blind in a sorrowful encounter of two broken old men, Lear kneeling to Cordelia, and finally "*Lear, with Cordelia in his arms*" in a "side-piercing sight" that reminds its viewers both of the *pietà* and of the "promis'd end," the Last Judgment.[60] Even Lear's regaining some of his regal authority mocks him. The blind Gloucester kneels in order that he may "kiss that hand" (4.6.132), and the returning Kent greets Lear as "my good master!" (5.3.271), but Lear is finally denied the roles upon which his identity and his very existence depend.[61] He is restored to his "fresh garments" and to his daughter, and thus to his roles as king and father, only to have these identities snatched from him by the death of Cordelia. His final howl of grief, as Van Laan suggests, lacks all coherence; Lear is not mad, but in a far worse state, having lost all identity and reason to exist.[62]

The stage images of the play's last scenes are almost unutterably painful in their effect, since they portray a reality so overpowering that language seems defeated. The inability of words to describe adequately what his eyes have beheld calls forth from Edgar, as he witnesses the encounter of mad Lear and blind Gloucester, an acknowledgment that the event must be left to interpret itself:

> I would not take this from report; it is,
> And my heart breaks at it.   (4.6.141–142)

"It is" may be, in Inga-Stina Ewbank's fine phrase of tribute, "the greatest line of Shakespeare, the theatre poet." As evidence of Shakespeare's abiding interest in the power of the stage image, it is also the "ultimate stage direction."[63] Words alone cannot convey the awful truth of Lear's ruin. The incomparable language is there too, of course; the apparent defeat of language is in part a theatrical illusion calling forth Shakespeare's greatest verbal as well as visual eloquence. Word and image are unforgettably paired; to the pregnancy of words, Shakespeare supplies a stage picture that can speak "More pregnantly than words" (*Timon of Athens*, 1.1.97).[64]

Through such stage pictures we see that ceremony in Shakespeare—whether of betrothal, marriage, burial, coronation, trial, banquet, greeting, farewell, or tending of obeisance—is a thing of fragile beauty, sumptuously theatrical but too frequently hollow in performance, more often desecrated than properly fulfilled. The many disruptions of ceremony call into question the very language of visual signs, for, despite their critical importance at moments of dramatic reversal, their encompassment of failure in a play like *King Lear* suggests a terrible meaninglessness to what we see, a failure of language and of human action. Yet our final response to *King Lear* as high tragedy rather than as existential nightmare not only affirms a value in what is brutally attacked, but argues that the value is enhanced by the nature of the attack. Ceremony is all the more precious because it is so terribly perverted to unjust ends, and conversely the picture in Shakespeare of disrupted ceremony gains significance because of the ideal of ordered behavior that it implies. The true meaning of ceremony in Shakespeare is to be found only through testing and conflict.

❧ VI

"Maimed Rites":
Violated Ceremony in *Hamlet*

And so, without more circumstance at all,
I hold it fit that we shake hands and part.

(1.5.128–129)

"T H' APPURTENANCE of welcome is fashion and ceremony,"
says Hamlet to Rosencrantz and Guildenstern in a rare
moment of seeming relaxation when he is looking forward to the arrival
of the players at Elsinore. "Let me comply with you in this garb, lest
my extent to the players, which, I tell you, must show fairly outwards,
should more appear like entertainment than yours. You are welcome"
(2.2.371–375). As he offers the two young men his hand, he bids them
accept this gesture as his well-meant observation of the proper civilities
of the court. He appears to acknowledge the validity of such ceremony,
yet he characteristically refers to it as "complying," a word he later
uses pejoratively of Osric,[1] and as "garb," that is, fashion or outward
appearance. His apparent concern is that his old acquaintances—he
calls them "excellent good friends" at first, but quickly finds reason to
qualify that epithet—should not feel snubbed by the outward show of
a greeting to their social inferiors, the players. He has received the two
young men, as they later report to Claudius, "Most like a gentlemen,"
but with "much forcing of his disposition" (3.1.11–12). Even in this
moment of playful acceptance of social convention, Hamlet's way of
describing it is wry, quizzical, bordering on the satiric. He goes on
in the very next part of this scene to answer the entering Polonius
and his prolix ceremoniousness with studied though artful rudeness,
and then to aggravate this insult by a genuinely warm greeting to the
players.

Hamlet's antipathy to ceremony is more striking elsewhere in the play. It helps focus our attention on a pattern of "maimed rites" that extends from the very first scene, with its inversions of precedence on the guard platform, to the final scene, in which a banqueting table becomes a feast of death and a gentlemanly duel becomes a scuffle over a poisoned sword. The "o'erhasty marriage" of Gertrude and Claudius before the play begins is a maimed rite; so is the awkward public scene at court in which the marriage is announced in the presence of Gertrude's inconsolable son, the dramatic entertainment presented by the players to Claudius but broken off by his sudden rising, Claudius' abortive attempt at prayer, the "obscure funeral" of old Polonius, the substituting of a forged death warrant sent by Claudius to the King of England, and the burial of Ophelia without the singing of "the service of the dead." As Francis Fergusson puts it, the maimed rites of Ophelia are full of cross-references: to Polonius' funeral, to Gertrude's corrupt marriage, to the marriage of Ophelia and Hamlet that never takes place, and to Ophelia's mad mixture of funeral and marriage.[2] Even the last ceremonial entrance of Fortinbras with his army, and the military funeral in which four captains "Bear Hamlet, like a soldier, to the stage," represent a disruption of the nominal ceremony of reconciliation with which the play's climactic scene begins. These and other inversions of ceremony, some of them visible on stage and some of them presented only to our imagination, function as signs of disorder in the play. Stage images of public ceremony alternate with those of isolation, darkness, and terror, allowing the more private glimpses of intense emotion to comment unfavorably on the hollow reassurances of public life in Denmark. Image patterns of clothes, of poison, and of the theater, both verbal and actualized on stage, contribute to the graphic picture of dislocation and misplacing of ceremonial observance.

The Elizabethan public theater itself, as Fergusson points out, fulfills a similar purpose.[3] Its potent symbolism of the cosmos provides an admirable backdrop for Hamlet's speech on the nature of man; its inclusive depiction of the heavens above and hell beneath gives a spatial immediacy to Hamlet's notion that "this goodly frame, the earth" is also "a foul and pestilent congregation of vapors." In the Elizabethan theater the spectators see a painted heavens corresponding to Hamlet's stirring invocation of "this most excellent canopy, the air . . . this brave o'erhanging firmament, this majestical roof fretted with golden fire" (2.2.299–304), but the spectators have also witnessed the "wondrous strange" workings of the Ghost in the "cellerage" beneath the stage (1.5.152–165). The "idea of the theater" embodied in this play begins with a majestic conception of order and "the celebration of the mystery of human life"; the spectators can see, in the very architecture of the Elizabethan stage as interpreted by George Kernodle, an image of monarchical authority and the dependency upon the throne of all social well-being.[4] Yet the central theatrical icon of this play is based on a premise that is shattered from the start by Claudius' secret crime. The terrible failure of the throne in *Hamlet* to meet the all-encompassing demands placed upon it is one source of the philosophical and moral conflict in which Hamlet, and we, are so absorbed.

In the play's opening scene, two sentinels, meeting on the guard platform in the dead of night, at the changing of the watch, betray their nervousness by reversing the customary roles of challenger and challenged. "Who's there?" asks the soldier who is coming on watch, usurping the challenge to be spoken by the man already on duty, and is properly corrected: "Nay, answer *me*. Stand and unfold yourself" (emphasis added). As Lawrence Danson suggests, their exchange is "an inversion of ceremonial order," the first of many in the play.[5] The intense darkness is conveyed not through the theatrical convention of burning torches, as later in the full court scene when King Claudius sees "The Murder of Gonzago"; in this scene the darkness is conveyed by guards who cannot recognize one another or who must rely on their sense of hearing. "I think I hear them," says Francisco of the approaching Horatio and Marcellus. "Stand, ho! Who is there?" (1.1.1–14). Disembodied sound is important to this and the later scenes played on the battlements, in the crowing of the cock causing the Ghost to start "like a guilty thing / Upon a fearful summons," in the offstage braying of Claudius' kettledrum and trumpet that is so at variance with the eerie stillness of the castle battlements, in the cry of the Ghost "*under the stage*," "Swear by his sword."[6]

The silent language of gesture assumes a significant role in these scenes of darkness, of whispered conferences, of terrifying otherworldly appearances. "See, it stalks away . . . 'Tis gone, and will not answer." "*It spreads his arms.*" "*Beckons.*" "It beckons you to go away with it . . . Look with what courteous action / It waves you to a more removed ground."[7] We learn in fact a good deal about the appearance of the Ghost. It comes "In the same figure, like the King that's dead," as like the King "As thou art to thyself. / Such was the very armor he had on / When he the ambitious Norway combated. / So frown'd he once when, in an angry parle, / He smote the sledded Polacks on the ice" (1.1.41– 63). It evades the attempts of Marcellus and the rest to strike at it with their partisans, and "starts" guiltily at the crowing of the cock.

Horatio's report to Hamlet in scene 2 of what the soldiers have seen in the night is as fully descriptive as any theatrical producer could wish; it reads almost like a promptbook:

> A figure like your father,
> Armed at point exactly, cap-a-pe,
> Appears before them, and with solemn march
> Goes slow and stately by them. Thrice he walk'd
> By their oppress'd and fear-surprised eyes
> Within his truncheon's length, whilst they, distill'd
> Almost to jelly with the act of fear,
> Stand dumb and speak not to him.   (1.2.199–206)

Not only are the accoutrements exactly described, but also the pace, the gesture, the relative positioning of the figures on stage, the distance between them. The report would make no theatrical sense if it did not correspond fairly closely with what we as spectators have seen. Horatio adds more details from his own observation on the third night of watch: the Ghost "wore his beaver up," revealing "A countenance more / In sorrow than in anger," "very pale," with his eyes fixed upon Horatio "Most constantly." His beard was "as I have seen it in his life, / A sable silver'd." On one occasion the Ghost "lifted up it head and did address / Itself to motion, like as it would speak," but instead shrank away "in haste" at the crowing of the cock and "vanish'd from our sight" (ll. 216–241).

We learn a good deal about the physical appearance and gesture of the men on the battlements as well. Bernardo says to Horatio, "You tremble and look pale." They strike at the Ghost with their partisans, attempt to restrain Hamlet from following it, and reluctantly move from place to place at the Ghost's behest to swear secrecy on Hamlet's sword. One or two of these details, like the pallor, depend more on Elizabethan commonplace symptoms of sorrow and fear than on what spectators would actually be able to see, but the rest of the description points to the actors' performance on stage.

The emphasis on visual means of communication in these early scenes is appropriate to a play that poses so many enigmatic questions.[8] How are we, and Hamlet, to interpret these signs? What do they bode? As soon as Hamlet is informed of what Horatio and his companions have seen, he perceives at once the problem of interpretation. "My father's spirit in arms! All is not well. / I doubt some foul play . . . Foul deeds will rise, / Though all the earth o'erwhelm them, to men's eyes" (ll. 254–257). It is through his cross-examining that we learn so much about the Ghost's appearance. To the Ghost, when it reappears, his first questions are those of interpretation. "What may this mean, / That thou, dead corse, again in complete steel / Revisits thus the glimpses of the moon, / Making night hideous? . . . Say, why is this? Wherefore? What should we do?" (1.4.51–57). Hamlet later mistrusts his ability to interpret this apparition accurately because of his melancholy and because "the devil hath power / T' assume a pleasing shape" (2.2.600–601), and he is in fact misled by the seeming earnestness of Claudius at prayer (3.3). Hamlet's iconoclasm grows out of his perception of the complexity of signs.

As Hamlet nonetheless intuits and as the Ghost soon confirms, the terrible secret justifying so much alarm and puzzlement is one that attacks all basis of human order and civilization. The act of which the Ghost must speak represents at least three appalling disruptions: the killing of a king, the murder of a brother, and the desertion of a husband by his wife.[9] The act is thus an assault on monarchy, on blood relationship, and on marriage. The early part of *Hamlet* is filled with graphic visual images of this threefold horror. When the Ghost has led Hamlet to the crucial point of revealing how and by whom the Ghost was slain, he states the essential fact in an image of perverted monarchy:

> know, thou noble youth,
> The serpent that did sting thy father's life
> Now wears his crown.   (1.5.39–41)

The ensuing account repeatedly uses a tripartite rhetorical pattern to emphasize the crime of one who is a regicide-usurper, *bruder-morder*, and incestuous adulterer: "Thus was I, sleeping, by a brother's hand / Of life, of crown, of queen, at once dispatch'd, / Cut off even in the blossoms of my sin, / Unhous'led, disappointed, unanel'd" (ll. 75–78). The assault on the rite of marriage and on its sacred vows galls the Ghost, especially the "falling-off" of his queen, "From me, whose love was of that dignity / That it went hand in hand even with the vow / I made to her in marriage" (ll. 49–51). Later, in the play within the play, the player King similarly recalls his marriage in sacramental terms: thirty years have passed, he notes, "Since love our hearts, and Hymen did our hands / Unite commutual in most sacred bands" (3.2.157–158).

Hamlet too, even before the revelation of the murder to him, has been preoccupied with images of violated ceremony. His imagination dwells on the sad conflation of funeral and marriage, whereby the ceremonial objects properly devoted to the expression of grief have been perverted to the expression of joy. Gertrude has shown her frailty and change of appetite within "A little month, or ere those shoes were old / With which she followed my poor father's body, / Like Niobe, all tears." In a similar gesture of "thrift," as Hamlet wryly calls it, "The funeral bak'd meats / Did coldly furnish forth the marriage tables" (1.2.147–181). The violation of rites sacred to funeral or marriage, and the violation of the bonds of brotherhood, are seen as integral to the violation of a duty a subject owes his monarch.

Some of these pictures of disrupted custom in Denmark are reported to us as historical and social background rather than through direct visual signs in the theater; but even such verbal images of disorder are relevant to a presentational analysis of *Hamlet* because they anticipate the many ceremonial actions through which the play is rendered. The murder of Hamlet's father and his funeral (also, later, the funeral of Polonius) are not shown directly on stage, but they live in Hamlet's memory as in ours to be theatrically reincarnated in "The Murder of Gonzago," the abortive funeral of Ophelia, and Hamlet's killing of Claudius. Similarly, we do not literally see shipwrights and other workers exert themselves out of season, preparing for military action against Norway with a "sweaty haste" that "Does not divide the Sunday from the week" and makes "the night joint-laborer with the day" (1.1.76–78). Nor can we behold what makes this preparation necessary, the attempt by young Fortinbras to recover "by strong hand / And terms compulsatory" (ll. 102–103) the land won by old Hamlet from old Fortinbras of Norway in fair and chivalrous fight. We do, however, behold the consequence of these inversions of order in the figure of a King who must now walk nightly among men as a ghost, subjecting himself to further affronts undeserved by such a regal figure. "It is offended," says Marcellus, as the Ghost "stalks away" and refuses to answer Horatio's challenges (l. 50). When the soldiers strike at the Ghost with their partisans, the fruitlessness of their endeavor brings home to them that they are offending a figure of unparalleled dignity.

"We do it wrong, being so majestical, / To offer it the show of violence," Marcellus concludes (ll. 143–144).

This image of a kingly figure struck at by his own former soldiers accentuates the gravity of his recent fall from monarch to corpse and sufferer of the unspeakable torments of Purgatory. The image of this fall will recur visually in "The Murder of Gonzago," when we behold in dumb show and then in full performance the killing of a king, witnessed on stage by the usurping king who will also, in the fullness of time, be slain in public view. Several Shakespearean tragedies— *Richard II, Richard III, Henry VI, Macbeth*—make use of the devastating symbol of a killed king, but nowhere other than in *Hamlet* is the symbol used with such visible and murderous violence, practiced (in the case of the old King Hamlet) upon a reigning legitimate monarch. Richard II and Henry VI are deposed before they are slain, and have not reigned well; Richard III and Macbeth are usurpers killed in battle; Duncan is murdered offstage. King John, if in fact he is poisoned by a monk, is another weak ruler with a defective claim, like Henry VI. Even *Hamlet* depicts the murder of the old King Hamlet indirectly, through report and through the play within the play. Truly, as Rosencrantz observes (though he applies it with unconscious irony to the usurper, not the true king), "The cess of majesty / Dies not alone, but like a gulf doth draw / What's near it with it . . . Never alone / Did the King sigh, but with a general groan" (3.3.15–23).

This central image of disruption, the killing of a king, is reinforced throughout the play of *Hamlet* by a repeated juxtaposition of King Claudius' fulsomely ceremonial royal presence and Prince Hamlet's lonely rejection of such hollow ritual. In scenes that roughly alternate with one another, we see on the one hand Claudius in full regalia, surrounded by his court, and on the other hand Hamlet, standing by himself in strikingly different costume from all the rest, or on the battlements in the cold night with a few trusted associates, or in soliloquy. The ritual scenes at court, as Fergusson points out, focus on the Danish body politic and its hidden malady; they are "ceremonious invocations of the well-being of society, and secular or religious devices for securing it."[10] Claudius' first entrance is to an official court function. The stage direction in the second Quarto measures the formality and extent of the processional appearance: "*Flourish. Enter Claudius, King of Denmark, Gertrude the Queen, Councilors, Polonius and his son Laertes, Hamlet, cum aliis*" (1.2).[11] "*Cum aliis*" includes the ambassadors Voltimand

and Cornelius, whose dispatch to Norway is a first order of business. The stage is filled with richly costumed persons, and (although the stage directions do not so specify) the occasion would seem to demand a throne on stage, centrally located.[12] Certainly when they later watch "The Murder of Gonzago" on a state occasion, the King and Queen are seated. Gertrude is at Claudius' side throughout the play, enabling them to confer confidentially. Those advisers on whom the new king will rely most, such as Polonius, are evidently closest at hand. Stage business requires repeated signs of obeisance to the King: Cornelius and Voltimand undertake to "show our duty" to Claudius before they depart, and Laertes, similarly on hand to "show my duty in your coronation," now "bows" his thoughts and wishes of departure for France "to your gracious leave and pardon" (ll. 40–56). The flourish of trumpets announces the King's departure in procession as it has announced his arrival.

The positioning of Hamlet's name last in the opening stage direction of the second Quarto text suggests that he does not occupy a place in the procession appropriate to one who is proclaimed in this scene "the most immediate to our throne" (l. 109). The order of court business, proceeding from an official explanation of the King's marriage to the negotiations with Norway to the request for Laertes' departure and at last to Hamlet's situation, underscores once again his physical and psychic distance from the throne. Although he protests that his "inky cloak" and "customary suits of solemn black" cannot truly denote his inner grief, there can be no doubt that he is dressed in mourning black, while the rest of the court tries politicly to keep pace with Claudius' "auspicious and a dropping eye, / With mirth in funeral and with dirge in marriage, / In equal scale weighing delight and dole."[13] Nor can his mordant view of "windy suspiration of forc'd breath," of "the fruitful river in the eye," and of "the dejected havior of the visage" as woefully inadequate "forms, moods, shapes of grief" deny the fact that Hamlet's gestures are those of grief. His mother tells us that with "vailed lids" he continually seeks for his father "in the dust." The point of contention between Claudius and Hamlet logically becomes one of determining the proper extent of "mourning duties" for a dead father, of "filial obligation for some term" in what Claudius calls "obsequious sorrow"— that is, sorrow suited to obsequies or funerals, though the choice of term may also betray Claudius' complacency (ll. 11–92). How should sorrow manifest itself? And what are the signs of true monarchy? In the contest between these outward showings, presented to us as stage images, lies much of the dramatic conflict of the early scenes.

These same images, when Hamlet appears on the battlements, call upon our perception of what we see and what is to be imagined offstage. The juxtaposition of court and lonely battlements creates what Fergusson calls a "rhythm of performance" as we shift from scenes of hollow ceremony to "improvisational" scenes that "throw doubt upon the efficacy of the official magic."[14] Hamlet is with a few trusted followers, in the cold night air, awaiting the Ghost, but for the moment (scene 4) listening to Claudius' noisy revelry inside the castle. "*A flourish of trumpets, and two pieces go off,*" specifies the stage direction, indicating that Claudius is now fulfilling his earlier command that trumpet and cannon are to greet each occasion of the King's drinking: "No jocund health that Denmark drinks today / But the great cannon to the clouds shall tell, / And the King's rouse the heaven shall bruit again, / Respeaking earthly thunder" (1.2.125–128). The blasphemy of this inversion, whereby the heavens are to ape their human counterpart and master, is made still more offensive by its being a custom—"a custom," as Hamlet wryly qualifies it, "More honor'd in the breach than the observance" (1.4.15–16). Claudius' vast gift for evil can be seen in his ability to usurp custom, to make ceremony and observance serve his debased interests. He is the true corrupter of ceremony, by perverting its forms to his own use.[15] As a result, Hamlet, despite the reverence for proper ceremony that is suggested in his sorrow over the debasements of his father's funeral, is driven into the posture of a rebel.

Hamlet's "antic disposition" is more than a test of Claudius' guilt; it is also a protest aimed at the conventionality he sees perverted to the use of one who is a "cutpurse of the empire and the rule" (3.4.102).[16] The "wild and whirling words" with which Hamlet perplexes Horatio and the rest after the Ghost's departure are only one mark of his erratic behavior; he also makes an emphatic point of dispensing with ceremony. "And so, without more circumstance at all, / I hold it fit that we shake hands and part," he enjoins his comrades (1.5.128–129). After bidding them swear an oath of secrecy upon his sword, in a ceremony that is almost a comic travesty because of the Ghost's bizarre movements under the stage, after bidding them to hold "your fingers on your lips, I pray," and not to indulge in courtly games of leaking secret information through insinuating nods and folded arms, Hamlet insists on an exit that is fraternal rather than hierarchical. "Nay, come, let's go together," he insists, objecting to their habitual deference to him (ll. 188–191). Horatio has become indeed Hamlet's "good friend," one with whom he can honestly exchange that precious name of "friend" (1.2.163), one whom he can trust never to "flatter" or "crook the pregnant hinges of the knee / Where thrift may follow fawning," letting "the candied tongue lick absurd pomp" (3.2.59–61). Horatio's most precious gift for Hamlet is his ability to sort out what is real from what is specious in the elaborate ritual of courtly ceremony.

Most members of Claudius' court fail by this exacting standard, and their failure provokes in Hamlet further unconventional behavior as a protest against their conformity to a corrupted ethic. Stage image accentuates the contrast between a hollow ceremonial order and Hamlet's piercing through that apparent hierarchical structure; the metaphor of clothes, of inky cloaks and solemn suits of black, becomes literalized in Hamlet's aberrant dress. A notable instance of this, though described as happening offstage rather than before our eyes, is Hamlet's appearance to Ophelia in her closet in his "doublet all unbrac'd, / No hat upon his head, his stockings fouled, / Ungart'red, and down-gyved to his ankle, / Pale as his shirt, his knees knocking each other, / And with a look so piteous in purport / As if he had been loosed out of hell / To speak of horrors" (2.1.75–81). These costume effects and gestures, so minutely particularized, are in part a trap for Polonius, into which he obligingly falls: "Come, go with me, I will go seek the King. / This is the very ecstasy of love" (ll. 98–99). As such, these visual effects serve a major purpose of stage picture in the play, which is to test the nature of interpretation.[17] Polonius reads too simplistically, as Hamlet intends him to do, in the complex book of outward signs and their inner signification. Hamlet evokes in exaggerated fashion the "signs" of love melancholy, and Polonius is taken in.

The gestures and costume are more than love signs, however, for they reveal something to us of Hamlet's bitter disappointment at Ophelia's willingness to let her father interpret for her. It is surely no coincidence that Hamlet's "To be or not to be" soliloquy, with its profound questioning of "the law's delay," "The insolence of office," and other indicators of a corrupted ceremonial order, should be spoken while Ophelia is nearby, reading (or pretending to read) in a book of devotion, no doubt on her knees, and watched secretly by the King and Polonius. Her assumed piety is a stage literalization of what Polonius has just conceded, "that with devotion's visage / And pious action we do sugar o'er / The devil himself" (3.1.47–49). The stage business of kneeling at empty prayer is all the more arresting in the theater because it anticipates the scene, again witnessed by Hamlet, of Claudius' bowing his "stubborn knees" (3.3.70) to no effect. No matter how much we may pity Ophelia, and recognize the genuineness of her lament for the overthrow in Hamlet of "The courtier's, soldier's, scholar's, eye, tongue, sword," we find ourselves confronted with stage images in which her failure is, in Hamlet's eyes, all too apparent. Her suffering, appropriately, is to lose her sanity and to lament a father who, as Laertes protests, is interred with "No trophy, sword, nor hatchment o'er his bones, / No noble rite nor formal ostentation." Polonius' defective funeral anticipates Ophelia's own (4.5.214–216).[18] The elaborate procession of "*King, Queen, Laertes, and the Corse*," attended by priests, a lord, and others, conducting a young woman "of some estate" to an interment bereft of the sung requiem (5.1.217–221), is an overpowering token in this play of the end to which ceremonial observance has come.

Polonius and his son Laertes are no less foils for Hamlet's mordant observations on ceremonial forms.[19] Polonius is, after all, the author of that infamous advice to his son, "Costly thy habit as thy purse can buy, / But not express'd in fancy; rich, not gaudy, / For the apparel oft proclaims the man" (1.3.70–72). This conventional approach to signs, usefully employed in Shakespeare's earlier plays, is inadequate to measure Hamlet's tragedy, and it leads to a contest between empty formality and inner truth in which Hamlet's sentiments often border on the satiric. Polonius' windy expostulation on "What majesty should be, what duty is" (2.2.87) characterizes the tediousness of his bowings and observances; the scenes in which he appears as chief adviser to the King are, with fitting contrast, either scenes of court ritual with flourishes, obeisances, and escorting of noble visitors, or scenes of concealment behind arrases where, in Hamlet's phrase, he may "play the fool . . . in 's own house" (3.1.134). Hamlet's unfeeling response to Polonius' death is no doubt deplorable, but we cannot forget the very different roles that these two men play, at court or in amateur drama; Polonius' prophetic role while at the university was that of Julius Caesar, being "so capital a calf" that he was killed in the Capitol.

Laertes is more admired by Hamlet and indeed becomes outwardly like him in his fury of protest at a father slain. Laertes is prepared "To cut his throat i' th' church" if he can encounter his father's slayer (4.7.126). No image could better convey the assault on rite and observance to which the tragic events of the play have led Laertes. He is similarly ready to mount a palace revolution in command of a "riotous head" or "rabble" who shout, "Choose we! Laertes shall be king!" and his bursting in upon Claudius is accompanied by that most telling stage sign of violent disorder: "The doors are broke" (4.5.104–114). It seems for the moment that Laertes is Claudius' nemesis, the revolutionary who will throw out the regicide and thereby demonstrate how murderous usurpation teaches others in turn to rebel. The irony, however, is that Laertes is still his father's son, unable to read beneath the plausible outward signs of Claudius' monarchical façade, and so condemned at last to serve the interests of this "king of shreds and patches." His first appearance in the play, as Lynda Boose observes, explicitly pairs and contrasts him with Hamlet, for he is dressed in ceremonial garb and presents a petition in the most courtly terms to be allowed to return to Paris, the city of fashion and gaming, whereas Hamlet clings stubbornly to unfashionable mourning clothes and is denied his petition to return to Wittenberg, a city of reform and intellectual ferment. Laertes is, like his father, concerned "with the exterior surfaces of objects, emotions, thoughts, and actions," and for that reason is obsessed with the lack of public ceremony at his father's funeral.[20] The assaults on correct courtly behavior to which he is goaded by his father's death— the poisoned sword, the unbated point, the poisoned cup as a last resort—are all directed ultimately not at achieving a true unconventionality but at a defense of the false monarchy Claudius has devised.

Hamlet's growing contempt for the obedient forms practiced by Rosencrantz and Guildenstern is fitly expressed in the mocking show of ceremony with which he greets their summons of him to the Queen's chambers, following the performance of "The Murder of Gonzago." "You are welcome," he jokes at their announcement that the Queen has sent for him "in most great affliction of spirit." Guildenstern's annoyed response to Hamlet's rudeness sums up the apparent case against irreverent treatment of social forms: "Nay, good my lord, this courtesy is not of the right breed" (3.2.310–314). Hamlet's mockery continues, directed always against their subservience to the outward forms of ceremony: "We shall obey, were she ten times our mother" (l. 331). Appropriately, Rosencrantz and Guildenstern are the persons appointed to wait upon Hamlet, to serve as his entourage, and, after his killing of Polonius, to guard him at the King's "pleasure" or convey him to England. Hamlet's impertinent response to this function is to play hide-and-seek: "Hide, fox, and all after" (4.2.31–32). Rosencrantz and Guildenstern are not practiced villains—"there is a kind of confession in your looks which your modesties have not craft enough to color," Hamlet tells them (2.2.280–282)—but they can never rise above the kind of superficial obedience to forms that Claudius knows how to exploit.

Hamlet's finest impatience with ceremonious behavior manifests itself in Act 5, after his return from England, in his encounter with the gravedigger and with Osric.[21] The gravedigger throws out various skulls, one of which might be that of a courtier, "which could say 'Good morrow, sweet lord! How dost thou, sweet lord?'," though now, in a "fine revolution" of the ironies of history, he is being knocked about the mazard with a sexton's spade; or of a lawyer, with his "quillities, his cases, his tenures, and his tricks"; or of an important buyer of land, with his "recognizances, his fines, his double vouchers, his recoveries" (5.1.82–105). The almost good-natured satire of such behavior, the distance from it, the perception of its universality in human history embracing even Alexander the Great and Julius Caesar, all prepare us for Hamlet's conversation with Osric, who, like the anonymous landowner, "hath much land, and fertile," but who cannot put his bonnet "to his right use" or refrain from posturing in his description of "six French rapiers and poniards, with their assigns, as girdle, hangers, and so on," including their "carriages" (5.2.86–151). Osric is the ultimate creature of Claudius' court, one who in Hamlet's phrase "did comply, sir, with his dug, before 'a suck'd it" (ll. 186–187), and his comic discomfiture is essential to establishing the mood of resignation and ironic detachment, side by side with the deeply passionate caring about his father's death and his mother's remarriage, that Hamlet brings to his final rendezvous with Claudius and Laertes.

Claudius is of course Hamlet's principal antagonist, the man against whom Hamlet's protesting of corrupted ceremony is ultimately directed. Thus it is appropriate that this mockery king, most of whose entrances and exits have been marked by flourishes and processions, who dispatches ambassadors and receives petitioners, who sits in regal splendor in the midst of courtiers and torchbearers to behold a play on the subject of his own crime, but who also hides behind arrases and appoints men to spy and poison, should preside over a final scene in which the hollow splendor of his court appears in all its fatal glory. This final scene is, as Fergusson observes, "the last time we see all the dramatis personae gathered to celebrate the social order upon which they all depend."²² "*A table*" is "*prepar'd*" for the duel of Laertes and Hamlet. "*Trumpets, drums, and Officers with cushions*" arrive, followed in regal procession by the "*King, Queen, and all the State*," including Osric. Foils, daggers, and wine are borne in with a flourish. Once more, as he has done throughout the play, Claudius orders that "all the battlements" are to fire their ordnance when "The King shall drink to Hamlet's better breath." "Give me the cups," he proclaims, "And let the kettle to the trumpet speak, / The trumpet to the cannoneer without, / The cannons to the heavens, the heaven to earth, / 'Now the King drinks to Hamlet.' Come, begin." And the stage direction in Q2 specifies "*Trumpets the while*" (ll. 222–276).

This is Claudius' finest moment, the most impressive ceremony of his life as king, and the climactic moment of his secret plot on Hamlet's life. It is also the moment before he falls. The ritual act of throwing a pearl in Hamlet's cup, and the ceremonial drinking, conceal an attempt at poisoning Hamlet that instead becomes the means of Gertrude's death. The swordplay, ostensibly one more chivalrous manifestation of Claudius' royal magnificence, is instead the mechanism of his treachery. It fittingly precipitates the killing of a king, one who deserves to die, one whose violent death answers in visual terms the murder of old Hamlet and "The Murder of Gonzago" that have provided so dominant an image—to our imaginations and to our eyes—of inverted order. Through the killing of Claudius the stage action of regicide is at last legitimized; it enacts the vengeance demanded of Hamlet by his father, yet its unpremeditated suddenness on Hamlet's part makes it, in his eyes at least, the work of providential "rashness."

Hamlet's status as one likely "To have prov'd most royal" is confirmed by the play's final ceremonial in which he is borne to his grave accompanied by "The soldiers' music and the rite of war" (ll. 400–401). It is explicitly a rite of "passage," as Fortinbras insists (l. 400), a ceremony of death intended to offer some measure of comfort to those who must "draw [their] breath in pain" in this world and seek to understand the meaning of tragic events. For all the terrible sense of loss, the final ceremony does at least hint at a kind of reincorporation, one that we share in the liminal experience of theatergoing. The military orderliness of Hamlet's funeral procession may seem incongruous for one who was not a soldier, but it also completes something left unfinished in the abortive rites of passage for old Hamlet, Polonius, Ophelia, and others who have died—including Claudius, for whom no obsequies at all are proposed. Ceremony is at last not simply masquerade, as it was for Claudius, but a thing of substance that restores some hope of perceivable meaning in the ceremonial signs that hold together the social and moral order.[23] Hamlet's iconoclasm toward those signs, and his lament for a lost world in which those signs once had meaning, are answered to some degree (though not without irony as well) in the ritual solemnity of Hamlet's passage toward death.

ᥰ VII

Epilogue

To th' dumbness of the gesture
One might interpret.

—*Timon of Athens*

"THE *STAGE* feeds both the *eare* and the *eye*," wrote Owen Feltham in 1628, "and through this *latter sence*, the *Soule* drinkes deeper draughts. Things *acted*, possesse vs more, and are too more retaineable, then the *passable tones* of the *tongue*."[1] Feltham deftly summarizes an assumption central to this present study—that drama, more effectively than any other art form, encourages interplay between the spoken word and the visual image, thereby bestowing upon the physical image in the theater a remarkable power too often overlooked by readers of dramatic texts. At the same time, Feltham's neoplatonic preference for vision over discourse produces its own distortions if applied too rigorously to Shakespeare's plays. Shakespeare is at once profoundly sensitive to the theatrical image and mistrustful of icon worship.

The point that drama joins speech and picture in mutually profitable collaboration needs to be remembered as a corrective to Mario Praz, Wylie Sypher, and like-minded critics who pursue suggestive but imprecise analogies among the sister arts, invoking the concept of *zeitgeist* or an *air de famille* that can link a baroque building to a poem by Crashaw or a painting by Rubens.[2] Such critics transfer terms from one art form to another in a kind of critical synesthesia, enabling them to talk of a "vocabulary" of colors or "composition" and "line" in a poem. Simonides of Ceos' famous prescription that "painting is mute poetry and poetry a speaking picture," and Horace's no less famous dictum of "*Ut pictura poesis*," encourage the discovery of parallelisms based on "unity of taste," as for instance the purported similarities between Renaissance lyrical refrains and the repetitions of a Renaissance façade.[3] Too often, as G. Giovannini warns, the correspondence is inherently unstable because one side of it is based on something physically real and objective to our senses, whereas the other involves a metaphoric leap through which we attempt to describe our affective response to the comparison.[4]

The manifest dangers of *zeitgeist* criticism can nonetheless be avoided in the study of drama by attention to practical and historical (rather than affective and synesthetic) connections between speech and picture. Even outside the theater, as John Steadman points out, poetry and painting were regarded in Shakespeare's day as especially close because they held in common so many ethical and mythological traditions; "though working in different media, they often selected the same subjects and endeavored to communicate the same 'meanings.' "[5] Iconographic and mythological treatises were consulted by poets and painters alike; the mutual borrowings had gone on for so long that distinctions were no longer recognized as precise or valid. Poetry and painting shared ethical convictions that all art should teach, delight, and perhaps also persuade or move. Writers on painting talked in Horatian or Aristotelian fashion about imitation of actions, verisimilitude, decorum, the unities, distinctions in genre, and other literary terms, while writers on poetry or rhetoric urged pictorial vividness. The parallel between the poetic and visual arts, says Steadman, "was still critical orthodoxy." However imprecise, such cross-disciplinary analysis by its very existence brought poetry and painting closer together. These two sister arts were further united by the use of similar technical devices, such as exemplum, personification, allegory, enigma, metaphor, and appeals to forensic, deliberative, or epideictic commonplaces. Art forms in which poetry and painting actually converged, such as emblem books, hieroglyphs, drama, pageantry, masques, and processions, were popular and omnipresent.

Nowhere was this convergence more evident than in drama. The special place of drama in a study of verbal and visual signals is that its two worlds of word and picture are simultaneously perceptible to a theatergoing audience. The relationship between the two is complicated by the differences of media through which they communicate, but both have an objective theatrical existence. The spoken language is audible, as it is not in an emblem, and the balance between sound and spectacle is more mutual and rich than in pageants, processions, masques, or other chiefly visual entertainments. Unlike the hypothetical world of art conjured up by *zeitgeist* criticism, in which word and picture are too often connected by unequalizing analogies between something physically perceived and something metaphorically invoked, drama has the immense advantage of addressing itself directly to both ear and eye. For this reason alone we are obliged to account for their interaction in the theater.

We cannot afford to overlook Lessing's often-noted objection to the blurring of the distinctions between poetry and painting. The signs through which they operate, he insists, are incommensurate. Poetry employs "articulate sounds in time" that follow one another sequentially and therefore best express actions whose parts are consecutive, whereas visual art uses "figures and colours in space" that coexist simultaneously in our vision and are therefore best applied to "bodies with their visible properties."[6] This distinction, important as it is for the criticism of both poetry and art, must nevertheless be viewed in perspective as the product of late eighteenth-century sensibility. As Mark Rose observes, Renaissance writers "tended to think of poetry spatially, in terms of painting," whereas romantic writers "tended to think of poetry more in terms of music, in terms of time."[7] When we examine the Renaissance, with its dominant conception of poetic form in spatial terms, and especially when we examine the drama of that age, we need to account for a theatrical experience in which our ears and eyes are constantly engaged.

Instead of dismissing comparison between language and picture as impossible because the modes of expression seem so unlike, we must, as Ernest Gilman successfully argues, welcome the clash and interplay of these different modes. We must recognize that their juxtaposition in the theater obliges us to find means of transplanting one art form into the other's terms. However incompatible the media in which they operate, both are at work expressing the idea of the play; if they use dissimilar signs, those signs aim alike at communicating what the dramatist wishes to "say." Both art forms arise, that is, from the dramatic situation, and both take part in the process by which the play is perceived and understood. As Gilman suggests, the relationship between word and picture can vary from reinforcement and intensification to divergence and ironic undercutting, with a wide and subtle range of possibilities between these extremes.[8] Our task, if we want to appreciate the whole of drama, must be to study the reinforcing or contrasting ways in which, as Feltham says, "The *Stage* feeds both the *eare* and the *eye*."

To make such a study of Shakespeare, on the other hand, is to become aware of the dangers of iconographic overinterpretation. The aesthetic of correspondences found in medieval iconography, in emblem books, in street pageantry, and the like, offers to Shakespeare an appealing set of visual correlations through which to convey social class, sex, profession, wealth, age, nationality, political affiliation, emotional state—or to signal alterations in those traits. Yet Shakespeare does not use these signals merely to affirm hierarchical principle. He contrasts the symbolic and ordered world of his *theatrum mundi*, drawn largely from the traditions of the Tudor morality play and public pageantry, with the more illusory world of neoclassic theater, a world that accentuates disguise and holiday. In this intimate world of lovers' escapes, nighttime, and protests against conformity, Shakespeare explores liminal values of social egalitarianism and divestiture of rank like those in the transitional process of a rite of passage. He in fact portrays marriage, coronation, death, and other turning points in human life in terms both of necessary ritual forms and of iconoclastic inversions through which the limits of custom are perceived.

The unceasing dialectic in Shakespeare between a visually structured world of seemingly fixed meaning and one of ambiguous transformation vastly extends the complexity of the observable "image" (*imago*, likeness, statue, picture, representation of the external form of an object) in Shakespeare's plays and poems. It provides him contrasting ways of interpreting the theater façade, behind the actors, as housing a royal citadel under siege or as a private dwelling in an illusory spectacle of misunderstanding. Costumes and costume changes attest to the dominance of role in the social structure, or conversely betoken a theatrical metamorphosis in which identity is misapprehended and then reaffirmed. Devices of scenic reversal and discovery, reliant not on scenery but on spatial relations of one acting space to another, hint at *peripeteia* and *anagnorisis* in the constantly changing spectacle and offer a glimpse through the theatrical façade into the essence of theatrical illusion. Vertical descents of characters repeatedly challenge the hierarchical assumptions of the architectural frame in which such action takes place. In their gestures of emotion the actors test and transcend the commonplaces of visual language upon which Elizabethans base their understanding of meaning in gesture.

Ceremonial forms are put to the severest test of all by human violations of custom that seem to render meaningless the conventional language in which ceremony is dressed. Yet by questioning the complacent certitudes of visual language in his theater, Shakespeare achieves the only kind of affirmation capable of lasting credibility. Just as, in Turner's words, no society can long flourish without the dialectical process through which its members periodically move from "the mediacy of structure" into "the immediacy of communitas" and thence to a return,[9] Shakespeare's venture into a similar world of visual inversion and complexity is prized most of all for the iconoclastic perspective it gives on the limits and the potentialities of gestural language in the theater.

ও Notes

I. Visual Interpretation: Text and Context

1. Citations to the text throughout this study are to David Bevington, ed., *The Complete Works of Shakespeare*, 3rd ed. (Glenview, Ill.: Scott, Foresman, 1980).

2. James Edward Siemon, *Shakespearean Iconoclasm* (Berkeley: University of California Press, 1984), chap. 1; and Jonas Barish, *The Antitheatrical Prejudice* (Berkeley: University of California Press, 1981), pp. 66–79.

3. T. W. Craik, *The Tudor Interlude: Stage, Costume, and Acting* (Leicester: Leicester University Press, 1958), chaps. 3 and 4.

4. Maurice Charney, " 'We Put Fresh Garments on Him': Nakedness and Clothes in *King Lear*," in *Some Facets of "King Lear": Essays in Prismatic Criticism*, ed. Rosalie L. Colie and F. T. Flahiff (Toronto: University of Toronto Press, 1974), pp. 77–88.

5. Siemon, *Shakespearean Iconoclasm*, intro.; and René Girard, "Lévi-Strauss, Frye, Derrida and Shakespearean Criticism," *Diacritics* 3.3(1973):34–38.

6. I am indebted to Wilbur Sanders, *The Dramatist and the Received Idea* (Cambridge: Cambridge University Press, 1968), for the useful concept of received idea or tradition.

7. Northrop Frye, "The Argument of Comedy," in *English Institute Essays, 1948*, ed. D. A. Robertson, Jr. (New York: Columbia University Press, 1949), pp. 58–73: C. L. Barber, *Shakespeare's Festive Comedy* (Princeton: Princeton University Press, 1959); and Alvin Kernan, "Place and Plot in Shakespeare," *Yale Review* 67.1(1977):48–56. Cited by Marjorie Garber, *Coming of Age in Shakespeare* (London: Methuen, 1981), p. 7.

8. Arnold van Gennep, *The Rites of Passage*, trans. Monika B. Vizedom and Gabrielle L. Caffee (London: Routledge & Kegan Paul, 1960); and Victor W. Turner, *The Ritual Process: Structure and Anti-Structure* (Chicago: Aldine, 1969). Discussed by Garber, *Coming of Age in Shakespeare*, pp. 6–13.

9. Turner, *The Ritual Process*, p. 95. See also Mircea Eliade, *Rites and Symbols of Initiation: The Mysteries of Birth and Rebirth* (New York: Harper & Row, 1958), esp. pp. 21–40.

10. Turner, *The Ritual Process*, esp. pp. 106–107, and "Variations on a Theme of Liminality," in *Secular Ritual*, ed. Sally F. Moore and Barbara G.

Myerhoff (Assen: Van Gorcum, 1977), pp. 36–52. The liminal character of slavery, as manifested by the losing of name and identity, tattooing, branding, shaving of the head, change of clothing, and the like, is discussed by Orlando Patterson, *Slavery and Social Death: A Comparative Study* (Cambridge, Mass.: Harvard University Press, 1982), pp. 35–76. Richard F. Hardin, " 'Ritual' in Recent Criticism: The Elusive Sense of Community," *PMLA* 98(1983):846–862, though objecting to the slowness of literary critics to come to terms with the meaning of "ritual" because of outdated notions about the origins of myth in ritual, proposes Victor Turner as the anthropologist whose work is "the most adequate for criticism today" (p. 847).

11. R. A. Foakes, "Suggestions for a New Approach to Shakespeare's Imagery," *Shakespeare Survey* 5(1952):81–92, reviews the New Criticism in these terms, citing Cleanth Brooks, *Modern Poetry and the Tradition* (Chapel Hill: University of North Carolina Press, 1939), p. 15; Robert Heilman, *This Great Stage: Image and Structure in "King Lear"* (Baton Rouge: Louisiana State University Press, 1948), p. 12; S. L. Bethell, *Shakespeare and the Popular Dramatic Tradition* (Durham, N.C.: Duke University Press, 1944), p. 80; G. Wilson Knight, *The Wheel of Fire*, 4th ed. (London: Methuen, 1949), p. 15; and others. See also Mark Rose, *Shakespearean Design* (Cambridge, Mass.: Harvard University Press, 1972), p. 2; and Oscar J. Campbell, "Shakespeare and the 'New' Critics," in *Joseph Quincy Adams Memorial Studies*, ed. James G. McManaway et al. (Washington, D.C.: Folger, 1948), pp. 81–96. Edward Partridge, "Re-Presenting Shakespeare," *Shakespeare Quarterly* 25(1974):201–208, makes a similar point, citing L. C. Knights, *Explorations: Essays in Criticism* (London: Chatto & Windus, 1946), pp. 18–20; and John Holloway, *The Charted Mirror: Literary and Critical Essays* (London: Routledge & Kegan Paul, 1960), pp. 220–221.

12. Caroline F. E. Spurgeon, *Shakespeare's Imagery and What It Tells Us* (Cambridge: Cambridge University Press, 1935), esp. pp. 125 and 344–345.

13. Barish, *The Antitheatrical Prejudice*, passim.

14. Maurice Charney, *Shakespeare's Roman Plays: The Function of Imagery in the Drama* (Cambridge, Mass.: Harvard University Press, 1961), p. 8.

15. Foakes, "Suggestions for a New Approach," pp. 81–92; Alan S. Downer, "The Life of Our Design: The Function of Imagery in the Poetic Drama," *Hudson Review* 2(1949):242–263; Paul A. Jorgensen, "Vertical Patterns in *Richard II*," *Shakespeare Association Bulletin* 23(1948):119–134, and *Shakespeare's Military World* (Berkeley: University of California Press, 1956). See also Una Ellis-Fermor, *The Frontiers of Drama*, 2nd ed. (London: Methuen, 1946); and Alfred Harbage, *Theatre for Shakespeare* (Toronto: University of Toronto Press, 1955).

16. Foakes, "Suggestions for a New Approach," pp. 81–92.

17. Charney, *Shakespeare's Roman Plays*, pp. 41–78. On stage blood in *Julius Caesar* see also Leo Kirschbaum, "Shakespeare's Stage Blood and Its Critical Significance," *PMLA* 64(1949):517–529; and P. Jeffrey Ford, "Bloody Spectacle in Shakespeare's Roman Plays: The Politics and Aesthetics of Violence," *Iowa State Journal of Research* 54.4(1980):481–489.

18. Philip C. McGuire and David A. Samuelson, eds., *Shakespeare: The Theatrical Dimension* (New York: AMS Press, 1979); Sidney Homan, ed., *Shake-

speare's "More Than Words Can Witness" (Lewisburg, Pa.: Bucknell University Press, 1980); and Ann Pasternak Slater, *Shakespeare the Director* (Totowa, N.J.: Barnes & Noble, 1982). See also Alan C. Dessen, *Elizabethan Drama and the Viewer's Eye* (Chapel Hill: University of North Carolina Press, 1977); and Maynard Mack, "The Jacobean Shakespeare: Some Observations on the Construction of the Tragedies," in *Jacobean Theatre*, ed. John Russell Brown and Bernard Harris (London: Arnold, 1960), pp. 11–41.

19. G. K. Hunter, "Flatcaps and Bluecoats: Visual Signals on the Elizabethan Stage," *Essays and Studies*, n.s. 33(1980):16–47.

20. Slater, *Shakespeare the Director*, p. 6.

21. Those who speak of stage symbolism include Kenneth Burke, *The Philosophy of Literary Form: Studies in Symbolic Action*, 2nd ed. (Baton Rouge: Louisiana State University Press, 1967), esp. pp. 8–18, and *Language as Symbolic Action: Essays on Life, Literature, and Method* (Berkeley: University of California Press, 1966); Walter J. Ong, "Space and Intellect in Renaissance Symbolism," *Explorations* 4(1955):95–100; and Don Cameron Allen, "Symbolic Color in the Literature of the English Renaissance," *Philological Quarterly* 15(1936):81–92. "Emblem" is a useful term to John Shaw, "The Staging of Parody and Parallels in *1 Henry IV*," *Shakespeare Survey* 20(1967):61–73; Dieter Mehl, "Emblems in English Renaissance Drama," *Renaissance Drama*, n.s. 2(1969):39–57; John Reibetanz, "Theatrical Emblems in *King Lear*," in *Some Facets of "King Lear*," ed. Colie and Flahiff, pp. 39–57; Glynne Wickham, *Early English Stages, 1300 to 1660* (London: Routledge & Kegan Paul, 1966–), vol. 2, pt. 1, pp. 206–244, and vol. 3, p. 79; and others. The concept of iconography is central to the critical method of Martha Hester Fleischer, *The Iconography of the English History Play* (Salzburg: Institut für englische Sprache und Literatur, 1974); Bridget Gellert, "The Iconography of Melancholy in the Graveyard Scene of *Hamlet*," *Studies in Philology* 67(1970):57–66; Huston Diehl, "Iconography and Characterization in English Tragedy, 1585–1642," *Comparative Drama* 12(1978–79):113–122; and others.

Perhaps the most frequently used terminology is that of stage imagery, as in Clifford Lyons, "Stage Imagery in Shakespeare's Plays," in *Essays on Shakespeare and Elizabethan Drama in Honor of Hardin Craig*, ed. Richard Hosley (Columbia: University of Missouri Press, 1962), pp. 261–274; Martha Hester Golden, "Stage Imagery in Shakespearean Studies," *Shakespearean Research Opportunities* 1(1965):10–20, and "Stage Imagery," in *The Reader's Encyclopedia of Shakespeare*, ed. O. J. Campbell and Edward G. Quinn (New York: Crowell, 1966), pp. 819–820; Alan C. Dessen, "Hamlet's Poisoned Sword: A Study in Dramatic Imagery," *Shakespeare Studies* 5(1969):53–69, and other articles; Michael Goldman, "Acting Values and Shakespearean Meaning: Some Suggestions," in *Shakespeare: Pattern of Excelling Nature*, ed. David Bevington and Jay L. Halio (Newark: University of Delaware Press, 1978), pp. 190–197; David Daiches, "Imagery and Meaning in *Antony and Cleopatra*," *English Studies* 43(1962):343–358; Wolfgang Clemen, *The Development of Shakespeare's Imagery* (Cambridge, Mass.: Harvard University Press, 1951); Jacqueline E. M. Latham, "The Imagery of *Hamlet*: Acting," *Educational Theatre Journal* 14(1962):197–

202; and Dieter Mehl, "Visual and Rhetorical Imagery in Shakespeare's Plays," *Essays and Studies*, n.s. 25(1972):83–100. Some German criticism speaks of "Schaubild," as in Dieter Mehl, "Schaubild und Sprachfigure in Shakespeares Dramen," *Shakespeare Jahrbuch* (West) 1970, pp. 7–29; see also Robert Fricker, "Das szenische Bild bei Shakespeare," *Annales Universitatis Saraviensis*, Philosophie, 5(1956):227–240.

22. See, for example, Alan C. Dessen, "Shakespeare's Patterns for the Viewer's Eye: Dramaturgy for the Open Stage," in *Shakespeare's "More Than Words Can Witness*," ed. Homan, pp. 92–107; and Slater, *Shakespeare the Director*, pp. 6–7.

23. Raymond B. Waddington, "Moralizing the Spectacle: Dramatic Emblems in *As You Like It*," *Shakespeare Quarterly* 33(1982):155–163; and John M. Steadman, "Falstaff as Actaeon: A Dramatic Emblem," *Shakespeare Quarterly* 14(1963):231–244. See also Douglas L. Peterson, *Time, Tide, and Tempest: A Study of Shakespeare's Romances* (San Marino, Calif.: Huntington, 1973).

24. Siemon, *Shakespearean Iconoclasm*, intro., in discussing excesses of emblematic interpretation, cites Mehl, "Emblems in English Renaissance Drama," pp. 39–57, and John Doebler, *Shakespeare's Speaking Pictures: Studies in Iconic Imagery* (Albuquerque: University of New Mexico Press, 1974). See also Fleischer, *Iconography of the English History Play*, and Henry Green, *Shakespeare and the Emblem Writers* (London: Trübner, 1870).

25. For a useful summary and bibliography see Fleischer, *Iconography of the English History Play*, pp. 3–9; and John Doebler, "Bibliography for the Study of Iconography in Renaissance English Literature," *Research Opportunities in Renaissance Drama* 22(1979):45–55.

26. Ernst Gombrich, "Icones Symbolicae," *Journal of the Warburg and Courtauld Institutes* 11(1948):163–192, also in *Symbolic Images* (New York: Phaidon, 1972); and Huston Diehl, "Iconography and Characterization," pp. 113–122.

27. See for example the analysis of Bach's choral prelude "Durch Adams Fall" in Manfred F. Bukofzer, *Music in the Baroque Era: From Monteverdi to Bach* (New York: Norton, 1947), p. 283, cited by W. Moelwyn Merchant, *Shakespeare and the Artist* (London: Oxford University Press, 1959), pp. 8–9. See also Bukofzer, "Allegory in Baroque Music," *Journal of the Warburg and Courtauld Institutes* 3(1939–40):1–21.

28. Joseph Anthony Mazzeo, "A Critique of Some Modern Theories of Metaphysical Poetry," *Modern Philology* 50(1952–53):88–96, esp. p. 88.

29. Quoted in Jean H. Hagstrum, *The Sister Arts* (Chicago: University of Chicago Press, 1958), p. 10. See Rosemary Freeman, *English Emblem Books* (London: Chatto & Windus, 1948), intro. and chap. 1; Mario Praz, *Studies in Seventeenth-Century Imagery* (Rome: Edizioni di storia e letteratura, 1964); Peter M. Daly, *Literature in the Light of the Emblem* (Toronto: University of Toronto Press, 1979); and Don Cameron Allen, "Ben Jonson and the Hieroglyphics," *Philological Quarterly* 18(1939):290–300. On emblems in pageantry see David M. Bergeron, "The Emblematic Nature of English Civic Pageantry," *Renaissance Drama*, n.s. 1(1968):167–198; and Wickham, *Early English Stages*, vol. 2, pt. 1,

pp. 209 ff.

30. Stephen Orgel, "The Poetics of Spectacle," *New Literary History* 2(1971):367–389, quotes *Timber, or Discoveries*, in C. H. Herford, Percy and Evelyn Simpson, eds., *Ben Jonson* (Oxford: Clarendon Press, 1947), 8:610, ll. 1514–24. See also Samuel C. Chew, *The Virtues Reconciled: An Iconographic Study* (Toronto: University of Toronto Press, 1947), pp. 3–8. Horace offers classical authority for the idea of the eye's primacy over the ear: "the mind is less actively stimulated by what it takes in through the ear than by what is presented to it through the medium of the eye—permitting the spectator to see for himself." *Ars Poetica*, in T. S. Dorsch, trans., *Classical Literary Criticism* (Baltimore: Penguin, 1965), p. 85.

31. *The Complete Works of John Webster*, ed. F. L. Lucas (London: Chatto & Windus, 1927), 4:42–43. Cited by Diehl, "Iconography and Characterization," p. 115.

32. Thomas Heywood, *"Londini Speculum*, The Third Show," in *Dramatic Works* (Pearson reprint ed.), 4(1874):312; cited by Hunter, "Flatcaps and Bluecoats," pp. 16–17.

33. John Calvin, *Two Epistles . . . whether it be lawfull for a chrysten man to communicate or be partaker of the masse of the papysts, without offending God and hys neyghbour* (London: R. Stoughton, 1548).

34. On Shakespeare's reflection of a Protestant bias in favor of the ear rather than the eye, especially in his comedies, see William G. Madsen, *From Shadowy Types to Truth: Studies in Milton's Symbolism* (New Haven: Yale University Press, 1968), p. 161; and Siemon, *Shakespearean Iconoclasm*, chap. 1.

35. Judith Dundas, "Shakespeare's Imagery: Emblem and the Imitation of Nature," *Shakespeare Studies* 16(1983):45–56.

36. Ibid.

37. George F. Reynolds, *On Shakespeare's Stage* (Boulder: University of Colorado Press, 1967), and *The Staging of Elizabethan Plays at the Red Bull Theater, 1605–1625* (New York: Modern Language Association, 1940); W. J. Lawrence, *The Elizabethan Playhouse and Other Studies*, 1st and 2nd ser. (Stratford-upon-Avon: Shakespeare Head, 1912, 1913).

38. Wickham, *Early English Stages*, vol. 2, pt. 1, pp. 206–244.

39. George R. Kernodle, *From Art to Theatre: Form and Convention in the Renaissance* (Chicago: University of Chicago Press, 1944); and Bernard Beckerman, *Shakespeare at the Globe, 1599–1609* (New York: Macmillan, 1962), pp. 102–106.

40. Kernodle, *From Art to Theatre*, p. 2.

41. See Richard Southern and C. Walter Hodges, "Colour in the Elizabethan Theatre," *Theatre Notebook* 6(1952):57–60; and Hodges, *The Globe Restored* (London: Benn, 1953), esp. pp. 68–69.

42. Kernodle, *From Art to Theatre*, p. 15; and Wickham, *Early English Stages*, vol. 1, chaps. 2–7.

43. Andrew Gurr, *The Shakespearean Stage, 1574–1642*, 2nd ed. (Cambridge: Cambridge University Press, 1980), p. 1. See also the illustrations on pp. 34–84 in Kernodle, *From Art to Theatre*.

44. Beckerman, *Shakespeare at the Globe*, p. 164.

45. Hunter, "Flatcaps and Bluecoats," pp. 21, 22. See also Maurice Charney, *How to Read Shakespeare* (New York: McGraw-Hill, 1971), pp. 95–97.

46. Hunter, "Flatcaps and Bluecoats," p. 18.

47. Beckerman, *Shakespeare at the Globe*, p. 67.

48. Ibid., qualifying earlier analysis by Victor E. Albright, *The Shaksperian Stage* (New York: Columbia University Press, 1909), pp. 1–9 and passim.

49. Lawrence J. Ross, "The Use of a 'Fit-up' Booth in *Othello*," *Shakespeare Quarterly* 12(1961):359–370, esp. p. 363, cited by Alan C. Dessen, "Two Falls and a Trap: Shakespeare and the Spectacles of Realism," *English Literary Renaissance* 5(1975):291–307.

50. Hunter, "Flatcaps and Bluecoats," p. 21; and Werner Habicht, "Tree Properties and Tree Scenes in Elizabethan Theater," *Renaissance Drama*, n.s. 4(1971):69–92.

51. Beckerman, *Shakespeare at the Globe*, pp. 72–73, discussing George F. Reynolds, "*Troilus and Cressida* on the Elizabethan Stage," in *Joseph Quincy Adams Memorial Studies*, ed. McManaway et al., pp. 229–238.

52. Beckerman, *Shakespeare at the Globe*, p. 168, citing *Twelfth Night*, 1.5.295–302 and 2.2.1.

53. Richard Hosley, "The Origins of the So-Called Elizabethan Multiple Stage," *Tulane Drama Review* 12.2(1968):28–50; and "The Gallery over the Stage in the Public Playhouse of Shakespeare's Time," *Shakespeare Quarterly* 8(1957):15–31.

54. Beckerman, *Shakespeare at the Globe*, p. 106; and John Styan, *Shakespeare's Stagecraft* (Cambridge: Cambridge University Press, 1967), p. 24.

55. On the question of the trapdoor for the Ghost in *Hamlet*, see Beckerman, *Shakespeare at the Globe*, p. 203; cf. Maurice Charney, *Style in "Hamlet"* (Princeton: Princeton University Press, 1969), pp. 170–172: and George F. Reynolds, "*Hamlet* at the Globe," *Shakespeare Survey* 9(1956):49–53.

56. George Kernodle, "The Open Stage: Elizabethan or Existentialist?" *Shakespeare Survey* 12(1959):1–7, esp. p. 7.

57. Bertram Joseph, *Elizabethan Acting* (London: Oxford University Press, 1951), and "The Elizabethan Stage and the Art of Elizabethan Drama," *Shakespeare Jahrbuch* 91(1955):145–160. See also Arthur Gerstner-Hirzel, *The Economy of Action and Word in Shakespeare's Plays* (Bern: Francke, 1957).

58. Tadeusz Kowzan, "The Sign in the Theater: An Introduction to the Semiology of the Art of the Spectacle," *Diogenes* 61(1968):52–80, esp. p. 57; and Jiří Veltruský, "Man and Object in the Theater," in *A Prague School Reader on Esthetics, Literary Structure, and Style*, trans. Paul L. Garvin (Washington, D.C.: Washington Linguistics Club, 1955), pp. 97–107, esp. p. 99. See also Charles Morris, *Signs, Language, and Behavior* (New York: Prentice-Hall, 1946), chap. 1.

59. Patrice Pavis, "Problems of a Semiology of Theatrical Gesture," *Poetics Today* 2.3(1981):65–93, esp. p. 83.

60. Keir Elam, *The Semiotics of Theatre and Drama* (London: Methuen, 1980), p. 9.

61. Ibid., pp. 56–69; Edward T. Hall, *The Silent Language* (Greenwich, Conn.: Fawcett, 1959).

62. Elam, *The Semiotics of Theatre and Drama*, pp. 69–78; Ray L. Birdwhistell, *Kinesics and Context: Essays on Body-Motion Communication* (Philadelphia: University of Pennsylvania Press, 1970).

63. Grotowski and Artaud are quoted by Pavis, "Problems of a Semiology," pp. 84–87, and Michael Issacharoff, "Space and Reference in Drama," *Poetics Today* 2.3(1981):211–224. See "Interview with J. Grotowski," *Drama Review* 58(1973):113–135; and Antonin Artaud, *Le Théâtre et son double* (Paris: Gallimard, 1944).

64. In addition to the works cited above see Patrice Pavis, *Languages of the Stage: Essays in the Semiotics of Theatre* (New York: Performing Arts Journal Publ., 1981); Jean Alter, "From Text to Performance: Semiotics of Theatricality," *Poetics Today* 2.3(1981):113–139; and Ruth Amossy, "Toward a Rhetoric of the Stage," *Poetics Today* 2.3(1981):49–63.

65. Pavis, "Problems of a Semiology," pp. 81, 82.

66. Ernest B. Gilman, "Shakespeare's Visual Language," *Gazette des Beaux-Arts* 96(1980):45–48.

67. Dessen, *Elizabethan Drama and the Viewer's Eye*, pp. 50 ff.

68. Brownell Salomon, "Visual and Aural Signs in the Performed English Renaissance Play," *Renaissance Drama*, n.s. 5(1972):143–169. For an example in which stage picture devastatingly undercuts what is said by the characters, see David J. Houser, "Armor and Motive in *Troilus and Cressida*," *Renaissance Drama*, n.s. 4(1971):121–134.

69. See Tommy Ruth Waldo, "Beyond Words: Shakespeare's Tongue-Tied Muse," in *Shakespeare's "More Than Words Can Witness*," ed. Homan, pp. 160–176; and William H. Matchett, "Some Dramatic Techniques in *The Winter's Tale*," *Shakespeare Survey* 22(1969):93–107.

70. See Joyce Van Dyke, "Making a Scene: Language and Gesture in *Coriolanus*," *Shakespeare Survey* 30(1977):135–146; John Russell Brown, *Shakespeare's Plays in Performance* (London: E. Arnold, 1966), p. 42; Styan, *Shakespeare's Stagecraft*, pp. 62, 107–108; and Michael Goldman, *Shakespeare and the Energies of Drama* (Princeton: Princeton University Press, 1972), pp. 119–121.

71. See Inga-Stina Ewbank, " 'More Pregnantly Than Words': Some Uses and Limitations of Visual Symbolism," *Shakespeare Survey* 24(1971):13–18.

72. Discussed in Donald A. Stauffer, *Shakespeare's World of Images* (Bloomington: Indiana University Press, 1946), p. 22; Mehl, "Visual and Rhetorical Imagery," pp. 83–100; Habicht, "Tree Properties and Tree Scenes," pp. 69–92; and Daly, *Literature in the Light of the Emblem*, p. 158.

73. Clark Hulse, *Metamorphic Verse: The Elizabethan Minor Epic* (Princeton: Princeton University Press, 1981), pp. 180–181. William S. Heckscher, "Shakespeare in His Relationship to the Visual Arts: A Study in Paradox," *Research Opportunities in Renaissance Drama* 13–14(1970–71):5–71, argues that Shakespeare's interest in actual art works is ancillary, though he goes to great lengths in describing imaginary works like this one for their iconographic value.

74. David Rosand, " 'Troyes Painted Woes': Shakespeare and the Picto-

rial Imagination," *Hebrew University Studies in Literature* 8(1980):77–97. For possible sources of inspiration for Achilles' "imaginary puissance" in one of the *Imagines* of Philostratus the Elder or in Timanthes' representation of the sacrifice of Iphigenia, see also E. H. Gombrich, *Art and Illusion: A Study in the Psychology of Pictorial Representation* (Princeton: Princeton University Press, 1960), p. 211. The approving remarks of Pliny the Elder on this kind of artistic strategy are to be found in *Naturalia Historiae*, bk. xxxv, 61–96, in *The Elder Pliny's Chapters on the History of Art*, trans. Katherine Jex-Blake (London: Macmillan, 1896), pp. 106–133; see also S. Clark Hulse, " 'A Piece of Skilful Painting' in Shakespeare's *Lucrece*," *Shakespeare Survey* 31(1978):13–22.

75. See Henry Peacham, *The Compleat Gentleman*, 2nd impression (London: Francis Constable, 1634), p. 103: "Yea, in my opinion, no Rhetoricke more perswadeth, or hath greater power over the mind: nay, hath not Musicke her figures, the same which Rhetorique? What is a *Revert* but her *Antistrophe*? her reports, but sweet *Anaphora's*? her counterchange of points, *Antimetabole's*? her passionate Aires but *Prosopopea's*? with infinite other of the same nature." Cited by Linda Austern, "Music in English Choirboy Drama, 1597–1613," Ph.D. diss., University of Chicago, chap. 4. See also Joseph, "The Elizabethan Stage," pp. 145–160.

76. Siemon, *Shakespearean Iconoclasm*, chap. 2, points out a further hazard in Lucrece's mistaking the icon for the thing represented; she tears at the picture of Sinon as though it were the cause of her sorrow, thereby committing an error of literalism that to Protestant sensibilities smacks of belief in a Real Presence.

77. Merchant, *Shakespeare and the Artist*, pp. 170–173; Hagstrum, *The Sister Arts*, pp. 66–70; Hulse, *Metamorphic Verse*, pp. 141–194; Rosand, " 'Troyes Painted Woes,' " pp. 81–83; and Anthony Blunt, "An Echo of the 'Paragone' in Shakespeare," *Journal of the Warburg and Courtauld Institutes* 2 (1938–39):260–262.

78. Merchant, *Shakespeare and the Artist*, pp. 172–173.

79. Gotthold Ephraim Lessing, *Laocoön, Or The Limits of Painting and Poetry*, trans. and ed. William A. Steel (London: Dent, Everyman's Library, 1930), p. 55 and chap. 16.

80. See Hagstrum, *The Sister Arts*, intro. and chap. 1; and John M. Steadman, "Iconography and Renaissance Drama: Ethical and Mythological Themes," *Research Opportunities in Renaissance Drama* 13–14(1970–71):73–122.

81. On Shakespeare's concern more with metaphoric comparisons between art and poetry than with technical aspects of the painter's craft, see Margaret Farrand Thorp, "Shakespeare and the Fine Arts," *PMLA* 46(1931):672–693; Hulse, *Metamorphic Verse*, pp. 141–143; Ernest B. Gilman, *The Curious Perspective: Literary and Pictorial Wit in the Seventeenth Century* (New Haven: Yale University Press, 1978), pp. 88–90; and Claudio Guillén, "On the Concept and Metaphor of Perspective," in *Comparatists at Work: Studies in Comparative Literature*, ed. Stephen G. Nichols, Jr., and Richard B. Vowles (Waltham, Mass.: Blaisdell, 1968), pp. 28–90.

82. On the dual character of iconographic images in this play see Robert C. Fulton III, "Timon, Cupid, and the Amazons," *Shakespeare Studies* 9(1976):283–299.

83. Sir Laurence Olivier scored a notable success with *Titus* at Stratford-upon-Avon in 1957.

84. Lawrence Danson, *Tragic Alphabet: Shakespeare's Drama of Language* (New Haven: Yale University Press, 1974), pp. 1–21; and S. Clark Hulse, "Wresting the Alphabet: Oratory and Action in *Titus Andronicus*," *Criticism* 21(1979):106–118.

85. D. J. Palmer, "The Unspeakable in Pursuit of the Uneatable: Language and Action in *Titus Andronicus*," *Critical Quarterly* 14(1972):320–339, esp. p. 320.

86. Ibid. See also Albert H. Tricomi, "The Aesthetics of Mutilation in *Titus Andronicus*," *Shakespeare Survey* 27(1974):11–19; Mehl, "Visual and Rhetorical Imagery," pp. 83–100; and Eugene M. Waith, "The Metamorphosis of Violence in *Titus Andronicus*," *Shakespeare Survey* 10(1957):39–49.

II. The Language of Costume and Hand Properties

1. Hal H. Smith, "Some Principles of Elizabethan Stage Costume," *Journal of the Warburg and Courtauld Institutes* 25(1962):240–257, esp. p. 242. For a similar remark that costume is "scenery worn by actors" see Brownell Salomon, "Visual and Aural Signs in the Performed English Renaissance Play," *Renaissance Drama*, n.s. 5(1972):143–169, esp. p. 159.

2. Fitz Roy R. S. Raglan, *The Hero* (New York: Vintage, 1956), p. 251. Quoted in James Laver, *Drama: Its Costume and Décor* (London: Studio Publ., 1951), p. 16.

3. Wilfred D. Hambly, *Tribal Dancing and Social Development* (London: Witherby, 1926); and W. O. E. Oesterley, *The Sacred Dance: A Study in Comparative Folklore* (New York: Macmillan, 1923). See Laver, *Drama*, p. 14.

4. Van Gennep, *The Rites of Passage*, chap. 1.

5. Laver, *Drama*, p. 18.

6. Sir Henry Wotton to Sir Edmund Bacon, July 2, 1613. Printed in E. K. Chambers, *William Shakespeare: A Study of Facts and Problems*, 2 vols. (Oxford: Clarendon, 1930), 2:344.

7. *Diary* of Philip Henslowe, ed. R. A. Foakes and R. T. Rickert (Cambridge: Cambridge University Press, 1961), pp. 291–293.

8. *Thomas Platter's Travels in England, 1599*, trans. Clare Williams (London: Jonathan Cape, 1937), p. 167. Cited by Gurr, *Shakespearean Stage*, p. 178, and J. R. Brown, *Shakespeare's Plays in Performance*, p. 35. On conspicuous clothing consumption at the Elizabethan and Jacobean courts see Lawrence Stone, *The Crisis of the Aristocracy, 1558–1641* (Oxford: Clarendon Press, 1965), chap. 10, esp. pp. 562–566.

9. G. K. Hunter, "Flatcaps and Bluecoats: Visual Signals on the Elizabethan Stage," *Essays and Studies*, n.s. 33(1980):16–47, esp. pp. 25, 29. On

sumptuary laws see Frances Elizabeth Baldwin, *Sumptuary Legislation and Personal Regulation in England* (Baltimore: Johns Hopkins University Press, 1926); and Wilfrid Hooper, "The Tudor Sumptuary Laws," *English Historical Review* 30(1915):433–449.

10. Hunter, "Flatcaps and Bluecoats," p. 28.

11. Henslowe's *Diary*, March 1598 inventories, pp. 317–323.

12. Hunter, "Flatcaps and Bluecoats," pp. 42–43. Louis Adrian Montrose, "The Purpose of Playing: Reflections on a Shakespearean Anthropology," *Helios*, n.s. 7(1980):51–74, astutely argues that the public theater and the professional player were viewed as abominations by some Londoners because of the players' escape from vocation and vestiary restraints; as "men who made their living by pretending to be what they were not," they were "a stunning anomaly" (p. 56).

13. Bernard Beckerman, "Shakespearean Playgoing Then and Now," in *Shakespeare's "More Than Words Can Witness,"* ed. Homan, p. 150. Oscar Wilde is perceptive about Shakespeare's use of costuming for illusionistic and holiday effects; see "The Truth of Masks," in *Intentions* (London: James R. Osgood McIlvaine, 1891), pp. 217–258.

14. Turner, *The Ritual Process*, pp. 94–112.

15. Barbara Mowat, " 'The Getting Up of the Spectacle': The Role of the Visual on the Elizabethan Stage, 1576–1600," forthcoming in *Elizabethan Theatre*, ed. George Hibbard.

16. Ibid. For a similar polarity of traditions in Shakespeare's theatrical gestures, one derived from exemplary moral drama of the public actors and the other from the technical virtuosity of the private companies, see John Reibetanz, "Theatrical Emblems in *King Lear*," in *Some Facets of "King Lear,"* ed. Colie and Flahiff, pp. 39–57.

17. Mowat, " 'The Getting Up of the Spectacle.' "

18. Craik, *The Tudor Interlude*, p. 56, illustrates the use of royal dress to identify the king figure in *Wisdom Who Is Christ* (ca. 1460–74).

19. *Richard II*, 2.2.59, 2.3.27; *1 Henry IV*, 5.1.34–35.

20. *Richard II*, 2.1.21; *Romeo and Juliet*, 2.4.33–35; *Henry VIII*, 1.1.19; and *The Merchant of Venice*, 1.2.72–74.

21. David Bevington, *Tudor Drama and Politics* (Cambridge, Mass.: Harvard University Press, 1968), pp. 48–53.

22. Alan C. Dessen discusses hunting and outlaw costume in a paper, "Interpreting Stage Directions: Elizabethan Clues and Modern Detectives," delivered at the Shakespeare Association of America annual meeting, Minneapolis, April 8–10, 1982.

23. Hunter, "Flatcaps and Bluecoats," p. 35.

24. Charney, *Style in "Hamlet,"* p. 188.

25. Dessen, "Interpreting Stage Directions."

26. The term "alazon" is from Northrop Frye, *Anatomy of Criticism* (Princeton: Princeton University Press, 1957).

27. Turner, *The Ritual Process*, pp. 106–107.

28. *The Merchant of Venice*, 2.5.13; and *The Merry Wives of Windsor*, 3.3.147.

See also the Countess of Auvergne and her Porter in *1 Henry VI*, 2.3.1–2; and Capulet's Wife in *Romeo and Juliet*, 4.4.1. The motif is an enduring one; household keys are used as a visual attribute for Esther Summerson in Dickens' *Bleak House*.

29. Fleischer, *Iconography of the English History Play*, pp. 117–120; and Martha Hester Golden, "Stage Imagery in Shakespearean Studies," *Shakespearean Research Opportunities* 1(1965):10–20, citing other instances in Renaissance drama including *1 Edward IV, James IV*, and *If You Know Not Me You Know Nobody*. See Lawrence Stone, *The Family, Sex and Marriage in England, 1500–1800* (New York: Harper & Row, 1977), pp. 202–204.

30. Turner, *The Ritual Process*, p. 111; and *Dramas, Fields, and Metaphors: Symbolic Action in Human Society* (Ithaca, N.Y.: Cornell University Press, 1974), pp. 272–299.

31. On uncertainty of interpretation of costuming signals see Slater, *Shakespeare the Director*, pp. 2, 137–170.

32. *Henry VIII*, 3.2.276–280; and *1 Henry VI*, 1.3.36–56; see Craik, *The Tudor Interlude*, p. 57. On the symbolic use of color in costuming, in Roman comedy, and in the Tudor morality play as well as in Elizabethan drama, see also Laver, *Drama: Its Costume and Décor*, p. 29; Don Cameron Allen, "Symbolic Color in the Literature of the English Renaissance," *Philological Quarterly* 15(1936):81–92, esp. p. 15; M. Channing Linthicum, *Costume in the Drama of Shakespeare and His Contemporaries* (Oxford: Clarendon, 1936), chaps. 2 and 3; Eldred Jones, *Othello's Countrymen: The African in English Renaissance Drama* (London: Oxford University Press, 1965), pp. 49–60 and chap. 4; F. M. Kelly, *Shakespearian Costume for Stage and Screen* (London: Adam & Charles Black, 1938; 2nd ed., rev. Alan Mansfield, 1970), pp. 17–18; Smith, "Some Principles of Elizabethan Stage Costume," pp. 240–257; and E. K. Chambers, *The Elizabethan Stage*, 4 vols. (Oxford: Clarendon, 1923), 3:79–80.

33. Fleischer, *Iconography of the English History Play*, pp. 106–117; and Bridget Gellert Lyons, "The Iconography of Ophelia," *English Literary History* 44(1977):60–74.

34. Robert Greene, *A Groatsworth of Wit* (1592), in Alexander B. Grosart, ed., *The Life and Complete Works . . . of Robert Greene*, 15 vols. (London, 1881–86), 12:104.

35. See Gerstner-Hirzel, *Economy of Action and Word*, pp. 50–53.

36. Hunter, "Flatcaps and Bluecoats," p. 29, citing the Act of 24 Hen. VIII (1533), cap. 13, p. 1.

37. David Bevington, *From "Mankind" to Marlowe* (Cambridge, Mass.: Harvard University Press, 1962), pp. 94–95.

38. John Nichols, ed., *The Progresses and Public Processions of Queen Elizabeth* (London: printed for the editor, 1788–1805), 2:*204–*206, sig. Ee2ᵛ–Ee3ᵛ. Hunter, "Flatcaps and Bluecoats," pp. 30–31, also cites *Eastward Ho*, 2.2. See *The Plays of John Marston*, ed. H. Harvey Wood (London: Oliver and Boyd, 1939), 3:85–171, esp. p. 105.

39. For example, *King John*, 4.1.1; *Cymbeline*, 5.4.9; *Richard III*, 1.4.95; and *1 Henry VI*, 2.3.32. See Alan C. Dessen, "Elizabethan Audiences and the Open

Stage: Recovering Lost Conventions," *Yearbook of English Studies* 10(1980):1–20.

40. For instance, *Romeo and Juliet*, 1.5.1–7.

41. A. L. Soens, "Cudgels and Rapiers: The Staging of the Edgar-Oswald Fight in *Lear*," *Shakespeare Studies* 5(1969):149–158; and Alan C. Dessen, "The Logic of Elizabethan Stage Violence: Some Alarms and Excursions for Modern Critics, Editors, and Directors," *Renaissance Drama*, n.s. 9(1978):39–69.

42. Turner, *The Ritual Process*, p. 125.

43. See William C. Carroll, *The Great Feast of Language in "Love's Labour's Lost"* (Princeton: Princeton University Press, 1976), pp. 66–72.

44. Richard David, ed., *Love's Labour's Lost*, in The Arden Shakespeare, 4th ed. (London: Methuen, 1951), p. 95.

45. See for example John A. Hodgson, "Desdemona's Handkerchief as an Emblem of Her Reputation," *Texas Studies in Literature and Language* 19(1977):313–322; Lawrence J. Ross, "The Meaning of Strawberries in Shakespeare," *Studies in the Renaissance* 7(1960):225–240; and Lynda E. Boose, "Othello's Handkerchief: 'The Recognizance and Pledge of Love,' " *English Literary Renaissance* 5(1975):360–374.

46. Stephen Gosson, *Plays Confuted in Five Actions* (London, n.d. [1582], imprinted for Thomas Gosson), "The 2. Action," sig. C6. Quoted in W. Carew Hazlitt, ed., *The English Drama and Stage under the Tudor and Stuart Princes, 1543–1664* (London, 1869), p. 181.

47. Cf. Gerstner-Hirzel, *Economy of Action and Word*, pp. 39–42.

48. See Marilyn L. Williamson, "The Ring Episode in *The Merchant of Venice*," *South Atlantic Quarterly* 71(1972):587–594.

49. See Craik, *The Tudor Interlude*, chaps. 3 and 4; Bevington, *From "Mankind" to Marlowe*, pp. 91–97; Wickham, *Early English Stages*, 3:101 ff.; and Nancy K. Hayles, "Sexual Disguise in *As You Like It* and *Twelfth Night*," *Shakespeare Survey* 32(1979):63–72. The question of doubling to facilitate rapid costume change in Shakespeare is discussed in William A. Ringler, Jr., "The Number of Actors in Shakespeare's Early Plays," in *The Seventeenth-Century Stage*, ed. Gerald Eades Bentley (Chicago: University of Chicago Press, 1968), pp. 110–134; and Stephen Booth, "Speculations on Doubling in Shakespeare's Plays," in *Shakespeare: The Theatrical Dimension*, ed. McGuire and Samuelson, pp. 103–131.

50. On the donning or doffing of boots as a signal of travel in *Richard II*, 5.2.84; *2 Henry IV*, 5.1.53, 5.3.136; *The Taming of the Shrew*, 4.1.132; and *Romeo and Juliet*, 5.1.11; and in other Elizabethan dramatists, see Dessen, "Shakespeare's Patterns for the Viewer's Eye," in *Shakespeare's "More Than Words Can Witness*," ed. Homan, pp. 101–103; Fleischer, *Iconography of the English History Play*, p. 50; and Linthicum, *Costume in the Drama*, pp. 243, 246.

51. Thomas F. Van Laan, *Role-Playing in Shakespeare* (Toronto: University of Toronto Press, 1978), passim.

52. Bevington, *From "Mankind" to Marlowe*, pp. 158–163, 245–251.

53. David A. Samuelson, "Performing the Poem," in *Shakespeare: The Theatrical Dimension*, ed. McGuire and Samuelson, pp. 11–28.

54. Garber, *Coming of Age in Shakespeare*, p. 224.

55. Bevington, *From "Mankind" to Marlowe*, pp. 152–169.

56. This speech is assigned to Edgar in the Folio and to the Duke of Albany in the 1608 Quarto. The differences in text, while material, do not importantly affect the argument here.

57. *King Lear*, 3.4.106–108, 3.6.36, 4.6.80. See Charney, " 'We Put Fresh Garments on Him': Nakedness and Clothes in *King Lear*," in *Some Facets of "King Lear*," ed. Colie and Flahiff, pp. 77–88.

III. The Language of Gesture and Expression

1. Thomas Wright, *The Passions of the Minde in Generall*, corrected and enlarged (London, 1630), p. 176. Quoted in Joseph, *Elizabethan Acting*, p. 2. A number of quotations from Renaissance theorists on behavior in this chapter are cited in Joseph's book or in J. B. Bamborough, *The Little World of Man* (London: Longmans, Green, 1952); Lily B. Campbell, *Shakespeare's Tragic Heroes: Slaves of Passion* (Cambridge: Cambridge University Press, 1930, reprint ed., New York: Barnes & Noble, 1963); Lawrence Babb, *The Elizabethan Malady: A Study of Melancholia in English Literature from 1580 to 1642* (East Lansing: Michigan Stage College Press, 1951); Hardin Craig, *The Enchanted Glass: The Elizabethan Mind in Literature* (Oxford: Basil Blackwell, 1950), and "Shakespeare's Depiction of Passions," *Philological Quarterly* 4(1925):289–301.

2. R. A. Foakes, "The Player's Passion: Some Notes on Elizabethan Psychology and Acting," *Essays and Studies*, n.s. 7(1954):62–77. On the dangers of applying Elizabethan psychology too closely to the analysis of plays, see also Louise C. Turner Forest, "A Caveat for Critics against Invoking Elizabethan Psychology," *PMLA* 61(1946):651–672; and Albert L. Walker, "Convention in Shakespeare's Description of Emotion," *Philological Quarterly* 17(1938):26–66. Some abuses can be found in Ruth Anderson, *Elizabethan Psychology and Shakespeare's Plays* (New York: Russell & Russell, 1966), originally published in the University of Iowa Humanistic Studies, 1st ser., 3.4(1927):1–182 (see, for instance, pp. 145–176).

3. Joseph Hall, *Holy Observations*, par. 80, in *The Works of Joseph Hall, Doctor in Diuinitie, and Deane of Worcester* (London, 1625), p. 148. I am indebted to Wayne Shumaker for some notes on classical and continental theorists in *Fisionomia naturale*.

4. Beckerman, *Shakespeare at the Globe*, p. 144.

5. Bamborough, *Little World of Man*, pp. 59–67. On the use of animal symbolism to express the typical manifestations of pride, envy, wrath, and the like, see Morton W. Bloomfield, *The Seven Deadly Sins* (East Lansing: Michigan State College Press, 1952), passim. For decorum of classical character types in plays, infant in tantrum, youth as wastrel, soldier, man of affairs—dwelling "upon those qualities that are appropriate to a particular time of life"—see Horace, *On the Art of Poetry*, in T. S. Dorsch, trans., *Classical Literary Criticism* (Baltimore: Penguin, 1965), p. 85.

6. See Lawrence Babb, "The Physiological Conception of Love in the Elizabethan and Early Stuart Drama," *PMLA* 56(1941):1020–35.

7. Wright, *Passions of the Minde*, pp. 42–43. Discussed in Campbell, *Shakespeare's Tragic Heroes*, pp. 57–58.

8. Wright, *Passions of the Minde*, p. 27. The 1530 text reads *exhilerant* for *exhilarat*.

9. John Davies of Hereford, *Microcosmos: The Discovery of the Little World, with the Government thereof* (Oxford, 1611), p. 91. Reprinted in *The Complete Works of John Davies of Hereford*, ed. Alexander B. Grosart, 2 vols. (printed for private circulation, 1878), vol. 1, *Microcosmos*, p. 40.

10. William York Tindall, *The Literary Symbol* (New York: Columbia University Press, 1955), pp. 5, 8.

11. Wright, *Passions of the Minde*, p. 179. On literary conventions of gesture see Walker, "Convention in Shakespeare's Description of Emotion," pp. 26–66; and R. B. Gill, "The Renaissance Conventions of Envy," *Medievalia et Humanistica*, n.s. 9(1979):215–230.

12. Cicero, *De Oratore*, bk. 3, chap. 59, par. 223, in Loeb Classical Library, trans. Harris Rackham, 2 vols. (Cambridge, Mass.: Harvard University Press, 1942), 2:179. See Toby Cole and Helen Krich Chinoy, *Actors on Acting* (New York: Crown, 1949), pp. 22–25.

13. Sir Francis Bacon, "Of Boldnesse," *The Essayes or Counsels, Civill and Morall, of Francis Lord Verulam, Viscount St. Alban* (London, 1625), pp. 62–63. Reprinted in *The Works of Francis Bacon*, ed. James Spedding, R. L. Ellis, and D. D. Heath (London: Longman, 1858), 6:401–402.

14. Joseph, *Elizabethan Acting*, passim, and "The Elizabethan Stage and the Art of Elizabethan Drama," *Shakespeare Jahrbuch* 91(1955):145–160.

15. From the Epistle to *Promos and Cassandra*. Quoted in Beckerman, *Shakespeare at the Globe*, p. 139, and Campbell, *Shakespeare's Tragic Heroes*, p. 104.

16. John Bulwer, *"Chirologia" and Chironomia*," ed. James W. Cleary (Carbondale: Southern Illinois University Press, 1974), discussed in Joseph, "The Elizabethan Stage," pp. 145–160.

17. See Alfred Harbage, "Elizabethan Acting," *PMLA* 54(1939):685–708; S. L. Bethell, "Shakespeare's Actors," *Review of English Studies*, n.s. 1(1950):193–205; Daniel Seltzer, "The Actors and Staging," in *A New Companion to Shakespeare Studies*, ed. Kenneth Muir and S. Schoenbaum (Cambridge: Cambridge University Press, 1971), pp. 35–54; and especially the balanced appraisal by Foakes, "The Player's Passion," pp. 62–77.

18. John R. Elliott, Jr., "Medieval Acting," essay presented at the Seventeenth International Congress on Medieval Studies, Western Michigan University, Kalamazoo, May 1982.

19. For example see Styan, *Shakespeare's Stagecraft*, pp. 81–108.

20. Beckerman, *Shakespeare at the Globe*, p. 216; J. R. Brown, *Shakespeare's Plays in Performance*, chap. 2, and "On the Acting of Shakespeare's Plays," *Quarterly Journal of Speech* 39(1953):477–484; and Michael Hattaway, *Elizabethan Popular Theatre: Plays in Performance* (London: Routledge & Kegan Paul, 1982, pp. 72–79.

21. Bamborough, *Little World of Man*, p. 66; and Babb, "The Physiological Conception of Love," pp. 1020–35.

22. Bamborough, *Little World of Man*, pp. 64–67.

23. See Carolyn Ruth Swift Lenz, Gayle Greene, and Carol Thomas Neely, eds., *The Woman's Part: Feminist Criticism of Shakespeare* (Urbana: University of Illinois Press, 1980).

24. *Antony and Cleopatra*, 3.2.54–56; 4.2.35–37, 5.1.40–41; *2 Henry VI*, 1.1.113; *3 Henry VI*, 1.4.144–146, 2.5.72–88; *Richard III*, 1.2.156–163, 1.4.247–249, 4.3.7–8; *King John*, 4.2.163, 5.2.29–32.

25. *The Tempest*, 5.1.16–17; *As You Like It*, 2.1.65; *The Merchant of Venice*, 2.8.46.

26. Coppélia Kahn, "The Absent Mother in *King Lear*," read at the annual meeting of the Shakespeare Association of America, Minneapolis, April 9, 1982; and Stanley Cavell, "The Avoidance of Love: A Reading of *King Lear*," in *Must We Mean What We Say?* (New York: Scribner's, 1969), pp. 267–353.

27. See Leslie A. Fiedler, *The Stranger in Shakespeare* (New York: Stein & Day, 1972), pp. 43–81.

28. *As You Like It*, 2.4.25–39, 3.4.51, 3.5.50, 5.2.81.

29. Joseph, *Elizabethan Acting*, p. 73; and Babb, *The Elizabethan Malady*, pp. 83, 170. For examples of folded arms in plays of Shakespeare's contemporaries, see *The Fair Maid of the Exchange* (1607 ed.), sig. C2 and C3^v, and *How a Man May Choose a Good Wife from a Bad* (1602 ed.), sig. B3^v, both tentatively ascribed to Thomas Heywood. See Richard Knowles, ed., *As You Like It*, in A New Variorum Edition of Shakespeare (New York: Modern Language Association, 1977), p. 182. On other stage gestures of melancholy see Bridget Gellert, "The Iconography of Melancholy in the Graveyard Scene of *Hamlet*," *Studies in Philology* 67(1970):57–66; and Bridget Gellert Lyons, *Voices of Melancholy: Studies in Literary Treatments of Melancholy in Renaissance England* (New York: Norton, 1971), pp. 3–4; Erwin Panofsky's study of Dürer's *Melancholia I* in *The Life and Art of Albrecht Dürer*, 2 vols. (Princeton: Princeton University Press, 1943), 1:156–171; and, on Malvolio's crossgartering in *Twelfth Night*, Nancy K. Hayles, "Sexual Disguise in *As You Like It* and *Twelfth Night*," *Shakespeare Survey* 32(1979):63–72. See also T. W. Craik, "The Reconstruction of Stage Action from Early Dramatic Texts," *The Elizabethan Theatre V*, ed. G. R. Hibbard (Hamden, Conn.: Archon, 1975), pp. 76–91.

30. Other references by Shakespeare to the notion of the sigh's costing the heart a drop of blood and the wine's replenishing it include *2 Henry VI*, 3.2.60–63; *3 Henry VI*, 4.4.22; *2 Henry IV*, 4.3.89–112; *A Midsummer Night's Dream*, 3.2.97; *The Merchant of Venice*, 1.1.81–82; *Hamlet*, 4.7.122–123; and *Much Ado about Nothing*, 3.1.77–78. See Bamborough, *Little World of Man*, p. 128, and n. 40; and M. P. Tilley, "Good Drink Makes Good Blood," *Modern Language Notes* 39(1924):153–155.

31. Andrew Gurr, "Who Strutted and Bellowed?" *Shakespeare Survey* 16(1963):95–102.

32. *Antony and Cleopatra*, 1.3.19, 2.5.37–39.

33. See also *King John*, 4.2.106–108.

34. T. S. Dorsch, ed., *Julius Caesar*, in The Arden Shakespeare, 6th ed. (London: Methuen, 1955), p. 46, cites two contemporary illustrations of the folding of arms as a sign of melancholy: the engraved title page of Robert Burton's *Anatomy of Melancholy*, 3rd ed. (1628), and the engraved title page to *The Melancholie Knight* (1615) by Samuel Rowlands. The latter can be found in *The Complete Works of Samuel Rowlands*, 3 vols. (printed for the Hunterian Club, 1880), vol. 2.

35. Cf. also *The Tempest*, 1.2.222–224, where Ferdinand is described by Ariel as mourning the supposed death of his father, "cooling of the air with sighs / In an odd angle of the isle and sitting, / His arms in this sad knot." The actor presumably demonstrates the folded arms.

36. *Love's Labor's Lost*, 3.1.16–17; *Venus and Adonis*, l. 339.

37. Turner, *The Ritual Process*, p. 95.

38. See *2 Henry VI*, 3.2.141–144; *3 Henry VI*, 5.2.34–38; and *Titus Andronicus*, 5.3.151–153.

39. W. Wager, *"The Longer Thou Livest" and "Enough Is As Good as a Feast,"* ed. R. Mark Benbow (Lincoln: University of Nebraska Press, 1967), ll. 1293–96, 1422–24 in *The Longer Thou Livest*. Cited in Huston Diehl, "Inversion, Parody, and Irony: The Visual Rhetoric of Renaissance English Tragedy," *Studies in English Literature* 22(1982):197–209. Alan C. Dessen, "Interpreting Stage Directions: Elizabethan Clues and Modern Detectives," Shakespeare Association meeting, April 8–10, 1982, points to a stage direction in the "bad" (Q1) quarto of *Hamlet: "Enter Ofelia playing on a Lute, and her haire downe singing"* (G4ᵛ).

40. Andrea Alciati, *Emblemata* (Lugduni: Rovillium, 1588), p. 60; and Geffrey Whitney, *A Choice of Emblemes* (Leyden, 1586), Emblem 30. Cited by Fleischer, *Iconography of the English History Play*, p. 162.

41. See for example Fleischer, *Iconography of the English History Play*, p. 164.

42. Pierre de la Primaudaye, *The French Academie*, trans. Thomas Bowes (London, 1618; first French eds., 1577–90; partially translated into English, 1586, 1594, 1601), p. 471; and Nicholas Coeffeteau, *A Table of Humane Passions with Their Causes and Effects*, trans. Edward Grimestone (London, 1621), pp. 461–465.

43. David Garrick is said to have used a fright wig operated by strings to create the effect of hair standing on end; see Arthur Colby Sprague, *Shakespeare and the Actors* (Cambridge, Mass.: Harvard University Press, 1944), p. 382n43; and Charney, *Style in "Hamlet,"* p. 168.

44. La Primaudaye, *French Academie*, p. 497.

45. Coeffeteau, *Table of Humane Passions*, p. 602.

46. On kicking the rushes beneath one's feet as a sign of anger, as in *Antony and Cleopatra*, 3.5.16–17, see Joseph, *Elizabethan Acting*, p. 39.

47. *The Copie of a letter written by E. D. Doctour of Physicke to a gentleman by whom it was publisht* (1606), pp. 14–15; quoted in Bamborough, *Little World of Man*, p. 119.

48. John Davies of Hereford, *Microcosmos* (Oxford, 1611), p. 186; also in *Complete Works*, ed. Grosart, vol. 1, *Microcosmos*, p. 73.

49. Patrice Pavis, "Problems of a Semiology of Theatrical Gesture," *Poetics Today* 2.3(1981):65–93, esp. pp. 71–72; Daniel Seltzer, "The Actors and Staging," pp. 41–42; and Seltzer, "The Staging of the Last Plays," in *Later Shakespeare*, ed. John Russell Brown and Bernard Harris, Stratford-upon-Avon Studies 8 (New York: St. Martin's, 1967), pp. 127–165. Seltzer also notes signs of amazement or perplexity in *Cymbeline*, 5.5.109–115; and *The Tempest*, 2.1.311, 3.3.89–95, 5.1.217 S.D. See also Barbara Mowat, "The Beckoning Ghost: Stage-Gesture in Shakespeare," *Renaissance Papers 1970* (1971):41–54.

IV. The Language of Theatrical Space

1. Kernodle, *From Art to Theatre*, passim; Beckerman, *Shakespeare at the Globe*, passim; and G. K. Hunter, "Flatcaps and Bluecoats: Visual Signals on the Elizabethan Stage," *Essays and Studies*, n.s. 33(1980):16–47.

2. Turner, *The Ritual Process*, pp. 166–178.

3. Thomas Nashe, *Pierce Penilesse* (registered August 1592), quoted in Chambers, *William Shakespeare*, 2:188.

4. Alice S. Venezky, *Pageantry on the Shakespearean Stage* (New York: Twayne, 1951), p. 124. See Kernodle, *From Art to Theatre*, p. 137; Styan, *Shakespeare's Stagecraft*, pp. 24–25; and Irwin Smith, " 'Gates' on Shakespeare's Stage," *Shakespeare Quarterly* 7(1956):159–176.

5. Slater, *Shakespeare the Director*, p. 38, asserts (questionably) that Joan's appearance *"on the top"* is from the topmost hut in the De Witt sketch of the Swan Theater. Richard Hosley, "Shakespeare's Use of a Gallery over the Stage," *Shakespeare Survey* 10(1957):77–89, p. 86n8, speculates that *"the top"* refers to the gallery.

6. Kernodle, *From Art to Theatre*, pp. 141–142.

7. For instance, Samuel Kliger, "The Sun Imagery in *Richard II*," *Studies in Philology* 45(1948):196–202; and Richard D. Altick, "Symphonic Imagery in *Richard II*," *PMLA* 62(1947):339–365.

8. R. Holinshed, *The Third Volume of Chronicles* (1587), p. 501, col. 1, ll. 2–16, in Geoffrey Bullough, ed., *Narrative and Dramatic Sources of Shakespeare*, 8 vols. (London: Routledge & Kegan Paul, 1957–75), 3:403.

9. J. Dover Wilson, ed., *King Richard II* (Cambridge: Cambridge University Press, 1939), p. 194n186 S.D. The descent into the "base court" is seemingly derived from Holinshed's account of King Richard's arrest of the Duke of Gloucester in 1397, *The Third Volume of Chronicles* (1587), p. 489, col. 1, ll. 27–36; see Peter Ure, ed., *King Richard II*, in The Arden Shakespeare, 4th ed. (London: Methuen, 1956), pp. 114–115, but see also *La Chronique de la Traïson et Mort de Richart Deux roy D'engleterre*, ed. Benjamin Williams (London: English Historical Society, 1846), p. 59. A similar transformation from outside to inside a fortified location occurs in *1 Henry VI*, 2.1 and 2.2, at Orleans.

10. See Paul A. Jorgensen, "Vertical Patterns in *Richard II*," *Shakespeare Association Bulletin* 23(1948):119–134; Arthur Suzman, "Imagery and Symbol-

ism in *Richard II*," *Shakespeare Quarterly* 7(1956):355–370; and Dessen, *Elizabethan Drama and the Viewer's Eye*, p. 79.

11. See Ronald Watkins, *On Producing Shakespeare* (New York: Norton, 1950), pp. 87–88.

12. The stage direction *"trenches"* is borrowed from North's translation of Plutarch, and need not imply any elaborate setting in the theater. See Philip Brockbank, ed., *Coriolanus*, in The Arden Shakespeare (London: Methuen, 1976), pp. 126–128; and Bullough, *Narrative and Dramatic Sources of Shakespeare*, 5:511.

13. See Smith, " 'Gates' on Shakespeare's Stage," pp. 159–176; and Alan C. Dessen, "The Logic of Elizabethan Stage Violence," *Renaissance Drama*, n.s. 9(1978):39–69, esp. pp. 66–67. The Freudian implications of Coriolanus' entry into these gates are explored by Janet Adelman, " 'Anger's My Meat': Feeding, Dependency, and Aggression in *Coriolanus*," in *Shakespeare: Pattern of Excelling Nature*, ed. Bevington and Halio, pp. 108–124; and Robert N. Watson, *Shakespeare and the Hazards of Ambition: Heredity and Identity in Eight Plays* (Cambridge, Mass.: Harvard University Press, forthcoming), chapter on *Coriolanus*.

14. Francis Fergusson, *The Idea of a Theater* (Princeton: Princeton University Press, 1949), chap. 4.

15. Hunter, "Flatcaps and Bluecoats," pp. 20–21. See also Hunter, "Shakespeare's Earliest Tragedies: *Titus Andronicus* and *Romeo and Juliet*," *Shakespeare Survey* 27(1974):1–9; Ann Haaker, *"Non sine causa:* The Use of Emblematic Method and Iconology in the Thematic Structure of *Titus Andronicus*," *Research Opportunities in Renaissance Drama* 13–14(1970–71):143–168; and G. Harold Metz, "The Early Staging of *Titus Andronicus*," *Shakespeare Studies* 14(1981):99–109.

16. Hunter, "Flatcaps and Bluecoats," p. 21.

17. On the problems of staging the monument see Bernard Jenkin, *"Antony and Cleopatra:* Some Suggestions on the Monument Scenes," *Review of English Studies* 21(1945):1–14.

18. Chambers, *William Shakespeare*, 1:307, also posits a third door for the Courtesan's house.

19. See R. A. Foakes, ed., *The Comedy of Errors*, in The Arden Shakespeare, 5th ed. (London: Methuen, 1962), pp. xxxiv–xxxv, 38, 42, 44–45.

20. Styan, *Shakespeare's Stagecraft*, p. 21.

21. Reynolds, *On Shakespeare's Stage*, p. 70; and Harbage, *Theatre for Shakespeare*, pp. 26–27.

22. See James Black, "The Visual Artistry of *Romeo and Juliet*," *Studies in English Literature* 15(1975):245–256; and Goldman, *Shakespeare and the Energies of Drama*, pp. 33–44.

23. On the usefulness of "bad" quartos like that of *Romeo and Juliet* in determining stage action, see Slater, *Shakespeare the Director*, pp. 10–12, 14, 39, though she does not discuss the instance from 3.5. Richard Hosley, "The Use of the Upper Stage in *Romeo and Juliet*," *Shakespeare Quarterly* 5(1954):371–379; and Styan, *Shakespeare's Stagecraft*, p. 25, present the case for the main stage in the remainder of 3.5; but cf. John Cranford Adams, "Shakespeare's Use of the Upper Stage in *Romeo and Juliet*, III.v," *Shakespeare Quarterly* 7(1956):145–152,

who insists (unconvincingly) that the actors remain on the upper stage for the scene between Juliet and her family.

24. Garber, *Coming of Age in Shakespeare*, pp. 165–168.

25. Shakespeare depicts in the theater what he found in the chronicles. According to one authority, says Holinshed (*The Third Volume of Chronicles*, 1587, p. 165, col. 2, ll. 63–65, in Bullough, ed., *Narrative and Dramatic Sources of Shakespeare*, 4:33), as Arthur "assaied to haue escaped out of prison, and proouing to clime ouer the wals of the castell, he fell into the riuer of Saine, and so was drowned." John Foxe, *Actes and Monuments* (London, 1583, 1:250, col. 1, l. 26, cited in E. A. J. Honigmann, ed., *King John*, in The Arden Shakespeare, 4th ed., London: Methuen, 1954, p. 109), reports that Arthur died "leaping into the ditch thinking to make his escape."

26. *Hamlet*, 3.4.142. See Beckerman, *Shakespeare at the Globe*, pp. 201–203; cf. Charney, *Style in "Hamlet,"* p. 170; and George F. Reynolds, "*Hamlet* at the Globe," *Shakespeare Survey* 9(1956):49–53.

27. See Michael Neill, "Monuments and Ruins as Symbols in *The Duchess of Malfi*," in *Drama and Symbolism*, ed. James Redmond, Themes in Drama IV (Cambridge: Cambridge University Press, 1982), pp. 71–87: Reynolds, *Staging of Elizabethan Plays at the Red Bull*, pp. 88–92: Dessen, *Elizabethan Drama and the Viewer's Eye*, pp. 158–162; and Metz, "The Early Staging of *Titus Andronicus*," pp. 99–109.

28. Styan, *Shakespeare's Stagecraft*, p. 19.

29. Chambers, *The Elizabethan Stage*, 3:79–80, cites the evidence.

30. See, for example, *Troilus and Cressida*, 1.3.86; *The Winter's Tale*, 3.3.54–55, 5.1.173; *1 Henry VI*, 1.2.1; and *Coriolanus*, 5.3.183.

31. On the use of discoveries in dumb shows, some of them early, see Thelma N. Greenfield, *The Induction in Elizabethan Drama* (Eugene: University of Oregon Press, 1969), p. 131.

32. Beckerman, *Shakespeare at the Globe*, pp. 87–88. On the now-outmoded concept of the "inner stage," where whole scenes were thought to be acted as though Shakespeare's stage resembled that of the Restoration and eighteenth century, see Richard Hosley, "The Origins of the So-Called Elizabethan Multiple Stage," *Tulane Drama Review* 12.2(1968):28–50, and "The Discovery-Space in Shakespeare's Globe," *Shakespeare Survey* 12(1959):35–46.

33. See Inga-Stina Ewbank, " 'My name is Marina': The Language of Recognition," in *Shakespeare's Styles: Essays in Honour of Kenneth Muir*, ed. Philip Edwards, Inga-Stina Ewbank, and G. K. Hunter (Cambridge: Cambridge University Press, 1980), pp. 111–130; Daniel Seltzer, "The Staging of the Last Plays," in *Later Shakespeare*, ed. Brown and Harris, pp. 127–165; and Helene Keyssar, "I Love You. Who Are You? The Strategy of Drama in Recognition Scenes," *PMLA* 92(1977):297–306.

34. See James Edward Siemon, " 'But It Appears She Lives': Iteration in *The Winter's Tale*," *PMLA* 89(1974):10–16; William H. Matchett, "Some Dramatic Techniques in *The Winter's Tale*," *Shakespeare Survey* 22(1969):93–107; Nevill Coghill, "Six Points of Stage-Craft in *The Winter's Tale*," *Shakespeare*

Survey 11(1958):31–41; and Adrien Bonjour, "The Final Scene of *The Winter's Tale*," *English Studies* 33(1952):193–208.

35. On authorial stage directions see Slater, *Shakespeare the Director*, intro.; but cf. T. J. King, *Shakespearean Staging, 1599–1642* (Cambridge, Mass.: Harvard University Press, 1971), pp. 4–9, who argues that stage directions written by the prompter still possess textual authority inasmuch as they record details of performance by an acting company of which Shakespeare was a working member.

36. For example, *Richard III*, 2.3; *Richard II*, 3.4; *Macbeth*, 2.4; and *Coriolanus*, 1.1.1–47.

37. See Chapter I of this volume and Beckerman, *Shakespeare at the Globe*, pp. 164, 174–175.

38. See R. A. Foakes, ed., *King Henry VIII*, in The Arden Shakespeare, 3rd ed. (London: Methuen, 1957), p. 157n34 S.D.

39. *The Famous Victories of Henry the Fifth*, ll. 854–855 and 955–957, in Joseph Quincy Adams, ed., *Chief Pre-Shakespearean Dramas* (Boston: Houghton Mifflin, 1924), pp. 677–678. Cited in A. R. Humphreys, ed., *The Second Part of King Henry IV*, in The Arden Shakespeare (London: Methuen, 1966), pp. 240–241.

40. *1 Henry VI*, 2.1–2; *Coriolanus*, 1.4–5; and *Macbeth*, 5.8.34–35. The instance in *Macbeth* is not traditionally marked as a new scene, although it is by Kenneth Muir, ed., *Macbeth*, in The Arden Shakespeare, 9th ed. (London: Methuen, 1962), pp. 167–168; J. Dover Wilson, ed., *Macbeth* (Cambridge: Cambridge University Press, 1947); and some other recent editions. G. L. Kittredge, ed., *Sixteen Plays of Shakespeare* (Boston: Ginn, 1941), suggests in his notes to 5.8 that "a new scene might well be marked" at l. 35.

41. See Reynolds, *Staging of Elizabethan Plays*, pp. 147–154.

42. See for example the Fleury play of Herod, in David Bevington, ed., *Medieval Drama* (Boston: Houghton Mifflin, 1975), pp. 57–66; John W. Velz, "From Jerusalem to Damascus: Bilocal Dramaturgy in Medieval and Shakespearian Conversion Plays," *Comparative Drama* 15(1981–82):311–326; and John H. McDowell, "Conventions of Medieval Art in Shakespearian Staging," *JEGP* 47(1948):215–229.

43. Reynolds, *On Shakespeare's Stage*, pp. 33, 72; and Robert James Fusillo, "Tents on Bosworth Field," *Shakespeare Quarterly* 6(1955):193–194.

44. See Alan C. Dessen, "Elizabethan Audiences and the Open Stage: Recovering Lost Conventions," *Yearbook of English Studies* 10(1980):1–20, esp. pp. 18–20, and "Night and Darkness on the Elizabethan Stage: Yesterday's Conventions and Today's Distortions," *Renaissance Papers 1978* (1979):23–30, esp. pp. 29–30; also Kenneth Muir, ed., *King Lear*, in The Arden Shakespeare, 8th ed. (London: Methuen, 1952), p. 80. As Dessen notes, the scene has puzzled critics, such as A. C. Bradley, *Shakespearean Tragedy*, 2nd ed. (London: Macmillan, 1906), p. 260; and Marvin Rosenberg, *The Masks of "King Lear"* (Berkeley: University of California Press, 1972), p. 151. Others have felt obliged to assume that Kent is by convention simply not to be supposed there: for instance, George F. Reynolds, "Two Conventions of the Open Stage (As Illustrated in *King Lear*?)," *Philological Quarterly* 41(1962):82–95, esp. p. 87. Cf. Rose, *Shakespearean*

Design, pp. 28–30, who argues that by convention Edgar "does not notice Kent, also an outcast, sleeping in the stocks. But the audience sees that Edgar is not alone."

45. See Beckerman, *Shakespeare at the Globe*, pp. 159–160. Those who do not accept the continued presence of the table in scenes 5 through 7 include Agnes Latham, ed., *As You Like It*, in The Arden Shakespeare (London: Methuen, 1975), pp. 132–133; and *The Riverside Shakespeare*, ed. G. Blakemore Evans et al. (Boston: Houghton Mifflin, 1974), pp. 379–380. See Knowles, ed., *As You Like It*, p. 109, who finds the early setting of the table "thoroughly puzzling" and "totally unnecessary."

46. See Styan, *Shakespeare's Stagecraft*, p. 22.

47. Ibid., pp. 89, 123. See also Styan, "Sight and Space: The Perception of Shakespeare on Stage and Screen," in *Shakespeare, Pattern of Excelling Nature*, ed. Bevington and Halio, pp. 198–209.

48. See Barbara Hodgdon, "Shakespeare's Directorial Eye: A Look at the Early History Plays," in *Shakespeare's "More Than Words Can Witness,"* ed. Homan, pp. 115–129; and Kernodle, *From Art to Theatre*, p. 143.

49. See Fleischer, *Iconography of the English History Play*, pp. 246 ff.; Styan, *Shakespeare's Stagecraft*, p. 20; Hereward T. Price, "Mirror-Scenes in Shakespeare," in *Joseph Quincy Adams Memorial Studies*, ed. McManaway et al., pp. 101–113; and Robert Y. Turner, "Shakespeare and the Public Confrontation Scene in Early History Plays," *Modern Philology* 62(1964):1–12.

50. Dessen, *Elizabethan Drama and the Viewer's Eye*, pp. 144–145; see also Fleischer, *Iconography of the English History Play*, p. 206.

51. *A Midsummer Night's Dream*, 3.2, etc.; *The Tempest*, 3.2, etc.; and *Measure for Measure*, 5.1.322.

52. Beckerman, *Shakespeare at the Globe*, pp. 192 ff. See also Styan, *Shakespeare's Stagecraft*, pp. 103–105, on "The Ways of Eavesdropping"; M. C. Bradbrook, *Themes and Conventions of Elizabethan Tragedy*, 2nd ed. (Cambridge: Cambridge University Press, 1980), pp. 25–28; R. A. Foakes, *Shakespeare, The Dark Comedies to the Last Plays: From Satire to Celebration* (London: Routledge & Kegan Paul, 1971), p. 175, on *Henry VIII*; Jean Howard, "Shakespearean Counterpoint: Stage Technique and the Interaction between Play and Audience," *Shakespeare Quarterly* 30(1979):343–357; and Seltzer, "Staging of the Last Plays," pp. 145–146.

53. Douglas C. Sprigg, "Shakespeare's Visual Stagecraft: The Seduction of Cressida," in *Shakespeare: The Theatrical Dimension*, ed. McGuire and Samuelson, pp. 149–163.

54. See Lawrence, *The Elizabethan Playhouse*, 2nd ser., pp. 1–22; Reynolds, *Staging of Elizabethan Plays*, p. 166; Dieter Mehl, "Emblems in English Renaissance Drama," *Renaissance Drama*, n.s., 2(1969):39–57; Styan, *Shakespeare's Stagecraft*, pp. 42–43; and Lee Mitchell, "Shakespeare's Lighting Effects," *Speech Monographs* 15(1948):72–84. Alan Dessen usefully discusses nighttime effects in other Elizabethan dramatists; see "Night and Darkness on the Elizabethan Stage," pp. 23–30, and "Elizabethan Audiences and the Open Stage," pp. 3–5.

55. Paul A. Jorgensen, *Our Naked Frailties: Sensational Art and Meaning in "Macbeth"* (Berkeley: University of California Press, 1971), pp. 125–137.

56. *Othello*, 1.1.161, 184, and 1.2.55–85. See Passion Play I from the N Town Cycle in Bevington, ed., *Medieval Drama*, p. 516, l. 972 S.D.

57. Dessen, "Night and Darkness on the Elizabethan Stage," p. 28.

58. Kernodle, *From Art to Theatre*, chap. 1.

59. Reynolds, *On Shakespeare's Stage*, p. 97, quoting from Reynolds, "Some Principles of Elizabethan Staging," *Modern Philology* 2(1904–5):581–614, and 3(1905–6):69–97, esp. 3:74. See also John P. Cutts, " 'Till Birnam Forest Come to Dunsinane,' " *Shakespeare Quarterly* 21(1970):497–499, for an illustration of the symbolic use of properties in *Macbeth*.

60. Kernodle, *From Art to Theatre*, pp. 5 ff., 132. See also Lawrence J. Ross, "The Use of a 'Fit-up' Booth in *Othello*," *Shakespeare Quarterly* 12(1961):359–370.

61. Reynolds, *Staging of Elizabethan Plays*, p. 49.

62. W. J. Lawrence, *Pre-Restoration Stage Studies* (Cambridge, Mass.: Harvard University Press, 1927), pp. 299–324.

63. Garber, *Coming of Age in Shakespeare*, p. 159.

64. Styan, *Shakespeare's Stagecraft*, p. 22, believes Juliet's bed could be a four-poster with curtained hangings thrust on stage, or simply a curtain.

65. Heywood, *The Silver Age*, in *The Dramatic Works* (London: John Pearson, 1874), 3:154; and Middleton, *A Chaste Maid in Cheapside*, 3.2.0, ed. Charles Barber (Berkeley: University of California Press, 1969). Quoted with other Elizabethan instances in Reynolds, *On Shakespeare's Stage*, pp. 8–9; and *Staging of Elizabethan Plays*, pp. 65–68; and Styan, *Shakespeare's Stagecraft*, p. 22. See Richard Hosley, "The Staging of Desdemona's Bed," *Shakespeare Quarterly* 14(1963):57–65.

66. In *The First Part of the Contention betwixt the Two Famous Houses of York and Lancaster* (1594), we are actually shown the murder on stage; at the start of this long scene, "Then the Curtaines being drawne, Duke *Humphrey* is discouered in his bed, and two men lying on his brest and smothering him in his bed" (sig. E2). After they have done their work, the murderers close the bed-curtains on the orders of Suffolk and leave; the bed or at least the curtains evidently remain in view, for Warwick later bids the King "Enter his priuie chamber my Lord and view the bodie," whereupon Warwick "drawes the curtaines and showes Duke *Humphrey* in his bed" (E2ᵛ, E3). The quarto version of the next scene begins: "Enter King and *Salsbury*, and then the Curtaines be drawne, and the Cardinall is discouered in his bed, rauing and staring as if he were madde" (Fᵛ). In both texts the two scenes are linked by the bed or bed-curtained alcove.

67. *Antony and Cleopatra*, 2.2.31–32; and *1 Henry IV*, 3.1.4.

68. Michael Issacharoff, "Space and Reference in Drama," *Poetics Today* 2.3(1981):211–224, esp. p. 218.

69. John Webster Spargo, "The Knocking at the Gate in *Macbeth*: An Essay in Interpretation," in *Joseph Quincy Adams Memorial Studies*, ed. McManaway et al., pp. 269–277.

70. Dessen, "Elizabethan Audiences and the Open Stage," pp. 1–20; and James Black, "*Henry IV*: A World of Figures Here," in *Shakespeare: The Theatrical Dimension*, ed. McGuire and Samuelson, pp. 165–183. Rose takes a somewhat different approach to visual pattern in *Shakespearean Design*, pp. 49–59.

71. *1 Henry IV*, 2.4.1–83; and *2 Henry IV*, 2.4.13.

72. Cf. notes 52 and 53 above and accompanying text for a similar stage diagram representing a hard choice for Cressida.

73. See Dessen, "Elizabethan Audiences and the Open Stage," pp. 15–18.

74. See J. W. Saunders, "Vaulting the Rails," *Shakespeare Survey* 7(1954):69–81; F. D. Hoeniger, ed., *Pericles*, in The Arden Shakespeare, 3rd ed. (London: Methuen, 1963), p. 138; and Dessen, "Elizabethan Audiences and the Open Stage," p. 14.

75. Van Gennep, *Rites of Passage*, chap. 2.

V. The Language of Ceremony

1. Van Laan, *Role-Playing in Shakespeare*, intro., chap. 2.

2. J. E. Neale, *Elizabeth I and Her Parliaments, 1584–1601* (London: Jonathan Cape, 1957), p. 119. Quoted in Stephen J. Greenblatt, *Sir Walter Ralegh: The Renaissance Man and His Roles* (New Haven: Yale University Press, 1973), p. 52; and Bridget Gellert Lyons, " 'Kings Games': Stage Imagery and Political Symbolism in *Richard III*," *Criticism* 20(1978):17–30. See also G. Pellegrini, "Symbols and Significances: 'All Such Emblems,' " *Shakespeare Survey* 17(1964):180–187. Greenblatt, *Renaissance Self-Fashioning: From More to Shakespeare* (Chicago: University of Chicago Press, 1980), pursues the idea of role playing as virtually inescapable in the struggle for power and self-conscious identity made necessary by England's shift to Protestantism; see for example pp. 157–192. Greenblatt's work has affinities to that of Clifford Geertz, *Negara: The Theatre State in Nineteenth-Century Bali* (Princeton: Princeton University Press, 1980), who argues that the symbolic dimensions of state power are real forces; a ruler and his power are in effect created by the theatrical displays and rituals through which he acts out his role as governor. See also Jonathan Goldberg, *James I and the Politics of Literature: Jonson, Shakespeare, Donne and Their Contemporaries* (Baltimore: Johns Hopkins University Press, 1983), pp. 1–54.

3. Van Laan, *Role-Playing in Shakespeare*, chap. 2.

4. Venezky, *Pageantry on the Shakespearean Stage*, passim; David M. Bergeron, *English Civic Pageantry, 1558–1642* (Columbia: University of South Carolina Press, 1971), passim; and Gordon Kipling, "Triumphal Drama: Form in English Civic Pageantry," *Renaissance Drama*, n.s. 8(1977):37–56.

5. Van Laan, *Role-Playing in Shakespeare*, chap. 2.

6. On loss of identity see also Thomas F. Van Laan, "Acting as Action in *King Lear*," in *Some Facets of "King Lear*," ed. Colie and Flahiff, pp. 59–75.

7. G. K. Hunter, "Flatcaps and Bluecoats: Visual Signals on the Eliz-

abethan Stage," *Essays and Studies*, n.s. 33(1980):16–47, esp. pp. 25, 37.

8. *As You Like It*, 2.1.1–3; *Henry V*, 4.1.237; and *King Lear*, 3.4.33–44.

9. *Hamlet*, 1.2.78–82.

10. Van Gennep, *The Rites of Passage*, passim.

11. Turner, *The Ritual Process*, pp. 166–178.

12. *As You Like It*, 2.7.194–195; *King Lear*, 4.7.23; and *Hamlet*, 5.1.257–258, 5.2.400.

13. Fleischer, *Iconography of the English History Play*, p. 32.

14. See Lynda E. Boose, "The Father and the Bride in Shakespeare," *PMLA* 97(1982):325–347; Stone, *The Family, Sex and Marriage*, pp. 30–33, 88; and T. F. Thiselton Dyer, *Folk-Lore of Shakespeare* (New York: Dover, 1966, originally publ. Griffeth and Farran, ca. 1883), pp. 321–339.

15. Stone, *The Family, Sex and Marriage*, p. 31; Margaret Loftus Ranald, " 'As Marriage Binds, and Blood Breaks': English Marriage and Shakespeare," *Shakespeare Quarterly* 30(1979):68–81; and Garber, *Coming of Age in Shakespeare*, pp. 116–117 ff.

16. On marriage as an archetype of exchange see Claude Lévi-Strauss, *The Elementary Structures of Kinship* (Boston: Beacon Press, 1969), esp. chap. 29.

17. Boose, "The Father and the Bride," p. 342n5.

18. See Brownell Salomon, "Thematic Contraries and the Dramaturgy of *Henry V*," *Shakespeare Quarterly* 31(1980):343–356.

19. Ranald, " 'As Marriage Binds,' " pp. 75–76; and Boose, "The Father and the Bride," p. 344n10.

20. Boose, "The Father and the Bride," pp. 325–347.

21. Ibid., p. 338.

22. Stone, *The Family, Sex and Marriage*, p. 207, and *The Crisis of the Aristocracy*, chap. 10, sec. 7; Michael Neill, "Monuments and Ruins as Symbols in *The Duchess of Malfi*," in *Drama and Symbolism*, ed. Redmond, pp. 71–87; and Garber, *Coming of Age in Shakespeare*, pp. 213 ff.

23. See Hereward T. Price, *Construction in Shakespeare* (Ann Arbor: University of Michigan Contributions in Modern Philology no. 17, 1951), on the "motif of the interrupted ceremony," p. 28. See also Edward I. Berry, *Patterns of Decay: Shakespeare's Early Histories* (Charlottesville: University Press of Virginia, 1975), pp. 22–23; Barbara Hodgdon, "Shakespeare's Directorial Eye: A Look at the Early History Plays," in *Shakespeare's "More Than Words Can Witness,"* ed. Homan, pp. 115–129, esp. p. 118; and Andrew J. Cairncross, ed., *The First Part of King Henry VI*, in The Arden Shakespeare, 3rd ed. (London: Methuen, 1962), pp. lii–liii.

24. D. J. Palmer, "The Unspeakable in Pursuit of the Uneatable: Language and Action in *Titus Andronicus*," *Critical Quarterly* 14(1972):320–339. See also Albert H. Tricomi, "The Aesthetics of Mutilation in *Titus Andronicus*," *Shakespeare Survey* 27(1974):11–19.

25. *Hamlet*, 5.1; *Julius Caesar*, 3.2; *King Lear*, 5.3.234–331; and *Cymbeline*, 4.2.256–283. See Danson, *Tragic Alphabet*, p. 25.

26. Price, *Construction in Shakespeare*, p. 28 ff.; and Cairncross, ed., *The First Part of King Henry VI*, p. 83.

27. Lyons, " 'Kings Games,' " pp. 17–30. See also Soji Iwasaki, *The Sword and the Word: Shakespeare's Tragic Sense of Time* (Tokyo: Shinozaki Shorin, 1973), pp. 61–63.

28. On the vestiarian implications of an attack on royal authority (the rebels protest against "putting on so new a fashion'd robe" whereby John undertakes to "guard" or ornament with trimming "a title that was rich before," 4.2.10–27), see Honigmann, ed., *King John*, p. 97, citing J. W. Allen, *A History of Political Thought in the Sixteenth Century* (London: Methuen, 1928), p. 213.

29. See Ernest B. Gilman, "Shakespeare's Visual Language," *Gazette des Beaux-Arts* 96(1980):45–48, and *The Curious Perspective*, pp. 88–128.

30. James Black, "*Henry IV*: A World of Figures Here," in *Shakespeare: The Theatrical Dimension*, ed. McGuire and Samuelson, pp. 181–182. See also James Hoyle, "Some Emblems in Shakespeare's *Henry IV* Plays," *English Literary History* 38(1971):512–527.

31. Foakes, ed., *King Henry VIII*, pp. 128–129.

32. Venezky, *Pageantry*, chap. 1.

33. See Goldman, *Shakespeare and the Energies of Drama*, pp. 109–123.

34. *Henry V*, 1.2.234–297, 2.4.31–35; *Cymbeline*, 3.1.1–85; and *Hamlet*, 2.2.40–84.

35. Thomas Heywood, *Dramatic Works* (London, 1874), 1:165–166. See Stone, *The Family, Sex and Marriage*, p. 519; Martha Hester Golden, "Stage Imagery," in *Reader's Encyclopedia of Shakespeare*, ed. Campbell and Quinn, pp. 819–820; and Craik, *The Tudor Interlude*, p. 79.

36. Edward Hall, *The Union of the Two Noble and Illustre Famelies of Lancastre and Yorke* (London, 1548), the xx. year of King Henry the VI (1440), fol. lxiiii, ll. 30–31; in Bullough, ed. *Narrative and Dramatic Sources of Shakespeare*, 3:101.

37. See William Frost, "Shakespeare's Rituals and the Opening of *King Lear*," *Hudson Review* 10(1957–58):577–585.

38. Stone, *The Family, Sex and Marriage*, p. 171. For an instance in one of Shakespeare's sources see *The Painfull Aduentures of Pericles Prince of Tyre* by George Wilkins, ed. Kenneth Muir (Liverpool: University Press of Liverpool, 1953), p. 48: "euen in the instant came in *Pericles*, to giue his Grace [King Symonides] that salutation which the morning required of him." The passage was pointed out to me by my colleague Peter Blayney.

39. John T. Onuska, Jr., "Bringing Shakespeare's Characters Down to Earth: The Significance of Kneeling," *Iowa State Journal of Research* 56.1(1981):31–41, gives other examples of children kneeling before parents, including *Titus Andronicus*, 1.1.164, 373–392; *Pericles*, 5.1.217; *Romeo and Juliet*, 3.5.158; *1 Henry VI*, 4.5.32; *The Tempest*, 5.1.183; *Hamlet*, 1.3.57; *Richard III*, 2.2.105–106; and *The Winter's Tale*, 5.3.44, 119; see also 5.2.77.

40. See Beckerman, *Shakespeare at the Globe*, pp. 204–205.

41. Charney, *Style in "Hamlet*," pp. 175–176.

42. See Frances Ann Shirley, *Shakespeare's Use of Off-Stage Sounds* (Lincoln: University of Nebraska Press, 1963), chap. 2; Stauffer, *Shakespeare's World of Images*, chap. 2; Catherine M. Dunn, "The Function of Music in Shakespeare's Romances," *Shakespeare Quarterly* 20(1969):391–405; J. M. Nosworthy, "Music

and Its Function in the Romances of Shakespeare," *Shakespeare Survey* 11(1958):60–69; and John Hollander, "Musica Mundana and *Twelfth Night*," *English Institute Essays 1956*, ed. Northrop Frye (New York: Columbia University Press, 1957), pp. 55–82.

43. *Richard III*, 4.2; and *Julius Caesar*, 1.2.1–24.

44. *Macbeth*, 1.5–2.2. See Thelma N. Greenfield, "Nonvocal Music: Added Dimension in Five Shakespeare Plays," in *Pacific Coast Studies in Shakespeare*, ed. Waldo F. McNeir and Thelma N. Greenfield (Eugene: University of Oregon Press, 1966), pp. 106–121; R. A. Foakes, "Suggestions for a New Approach to Shakespeare's Imagery," *Shakespeare Survey* 5(1952):81–92; and Jorgensen, *Our Naked Frailties*, pp. 164–166.

45. *Henry V*, 1.1.44. See Jorgensen, *Shakespeare's Military World*, chap. 1; and Harbage, *Theatre for Shakespeare*, pp. 51–53.

46. For example, *King Lear*, 5.2.1–4.

47. Bevington, ed., *Medieval Drama*, pp. 169–177, 454–459, 499–514. On banqueting as ritual display of wealth and authority in primitive rituals, as in the potlatch, see Lévi-Strauss, *The Elementary Structures of Kingship*, chap. 5 and passim.

48. On the incorporating aspects of greeting rituals see van Gennep, *Rites of Passage*, chap. 3.

49. Charney, *Shakespeare's Roman Plays*, chap. 3. See also John Shaw, "The Staging of Parody and Parallels in *1 Henry IV*," *Shakespeare Survey* 20(1967):61–73; Robert Hapgood, "Speak Hands for Me: Gesture as Language in *Julius Caesar*," *Drama Survey* 5(1966–67):162–170; and Arthur Gerstner-Hirzel, "Stagecraft and Poetry," *Shakespeare Jahrbuch* 91(1955):196–211.

50. Arthur Suzman, "Imagery and Symbolism in *Richard II*," *Shakespeare Quarterly* 7(1956):355–370; Philip C. McGuire, "Choreography and Language in *Richard II*," in *Shakespeare: The Theatrical Dimension*, ed. McGuire and Samuelson, pp. 61–84.

51. Ure, ed., *King Richard II*, p. 24n50.

52. R. Holinshed, *The Third Volume of Chronicles* (1587), p. 501, col. 2, ll. 10–14, in Bullough, ed., *Narrative and Dramatic Sources of Shakespeare*, 3:404.

53. Sheldon P. Zitner, "Aumerle's Conspiracy," *Studies in English Literature* 14(1974):239–257; and Leonard Barkan, "The Theatrical Consistency of *Richard II*," *Shakespeare Quarterly* 29(1978):5–19.

54. Gilman, *The Curious Perspective*, pp. 122–128, and "Shakespeare's Visual Language," pp. 45–48. See also Barbara Hodgdon, "In Search of the Performance Present," in *Shakespeare: The Theatrical Dimension*, ed. McGuire and Samuelson, pp. 29–49; and Miriam Gilbert, "*Richard II* at Stratford: Role-Playing as Metaphor," ibid., pp. 85–101.

55. Onuska, "Bringing Shakespeare's Characters Down to Earth," n. 10.

56. Arthur Kirsch, *Shakespeare and the Experience of Love* (Cambridge: Cambridge University Press, 1981), chap. 4.

57. See Nevill Coghill, *Shakespeare's Professional Skills* (Cambridge: Cambridge University Press, 1964), chap. 1; Inga-Stina Ewbank, " 'More Pregnantly Than Words': Some Uses and Limitations of Visual Symbolism,"

Shakespeare Survey 24(1971):13–18; and Joyce Van Dyke, "Making a Scene: Language and Gesture in *Coriolanus*," *Shakespeare Survey* 30(1977):135–146.

58. See Frost, "Shakespeare's Rituals," pp. 577–585. Cf. Thomas B. Stroup, "Ritual and Ceremony in the Drama," *Comparative Drama* 11(1977–78):139–146.

59. Onuska, "Bringing Shakespeare's Characters Down to Earth," p. 38; Rosenberg, *The Masks of "King Lear,"* pp. 312, 336–345.

60. See Harbage, "Choral Juxtaposition in Shakespeare"; Dessen, "Shakespeare's Patterns," in *Shakespeare's "More Than Words Can Witness,"* ed. Homan, pp. 92–114; Maurice Charney, "The Persuasiveness of Violence in Elizabethan Plays," *Renaissance Drama*, n.s. 2(1969):59–70; David A. Samuelson, "Performing the Poem"; and William H. Matchett, "Some Dramatic Techniques in *King Lear*," in *Shakespeare: The Theatrical Dimension*, ed. McGuire and Samuelson, pp. 11–18, 185–208.

61. On Kent's return see Goldman, *Shakespeare and the Energies of Drama*, pp. 102–104.

62. Van Laan, "Acting as Action in *King Lear*," pp. 59–75. See also Terence Hawkes, "That Shakespeherean Rag," in *Shakespeare's "More Than Words Can Witness,"* ed. Homan, pp. 62–76; and Russell A. Fraser, *Shakespeare's Poetics in Relation to "King Lear"* (London: Routledge & Kegan Paul, 1962), pp. 61–84.

63. Ewbank, " 'More Pregnantly Than Words,' " pp. 17–18.

64. Quoted ibid., p. 13.

VI. "Maimed Rites": Violated Ceremony in *Hamlet*

1. Charney, *Style in "Hamlet,"* p. 175.

2. Fergusson, *The Idea of a Theater*, p. 138. See also Lynda E. Boose, "The Father and the Bride in Shakespeare," *PMLA* 97(1982):325–347, esp. p. 330, for analysis of a "collision" of rituals in the mixture of funeral and marriage.

3. Fergusson, *The Idea of a Theater*, pp. 114–119.

4. Kernodle, *From Art to Theatre*, pp. 5 ff. and passim; Fergusson, *The Idea of a Theater*, p. 116; and R. A. Foakes, "*Hamlet* and the Court of Elsinore," *Shakespeare Survey* 9(1956):35–43.

5. Danson, *Tragic Alphabet*, p. 24; see also Charles R. Forker, "Shakespeare's Theatrical Symbolism and Its Function in *Hamlet*," *Shakespeare Quarterly* 14(1963):215–229.

6. *Hamlet*, 1.1.148–149; 1.5.149–162. See Maurice Charney, "*Hamlet* without Words," in *Shakespeare's "More Than Words Can Witness,"* ed. Homan, pp. 23–42.

7. *Hamlet*, 1.1.50–52, 129; 1.4.57–61. See Charney, *Style in "Hamlet,"* p. 169.

8. See Maynard Mack, "The World of *Hamlet*," *Yale Review* 41(1952):502–523; and Harry Levin, *The Question of Hamlet* (New York: Oxford University Press, 1959).

9. See Maynard Mack, Jr., *Killing the King: Three Studies in Shakespeare's Tragic Structure* (New Haven: Yale University Press, 1973).

10. Fergusson, *The Idea of a Theater*, p. 114. See also Foakes, "*Hamlet* and the Court of Elsinore," pp. 35–43; and Rose, *Shakespearean Design*, pp. 95–125.

11. The literal reading of the 1604–5 second Quarto is: "*Florish. Enter Claudius, King of Denmarke, Gertrad the Queene, Counsaile: as Polonius, and his Sonne Laertes, Hamlet, Cum Aliis.*" The Folio text reads: "*Enter Claudius King of Denmarke, Gertrude the Queene, Hamlet, Polonius, Laertes, and his Sister Ophelia, Lords Attendant.*"

12. Charney, "*Hamlet* without Words," p. 36; George F. Reynolds, "*Hamlet* at the Globe," *Shakespeare Survey* 9(1956):49–53.

13. See Coghill, *Shakespeare's Professional Skills*, chap. 1, esp. p. 1.

14. Fergusson, *The Idea of a Theater*, p. 114.

15. Paul Hamill, "Death's Lively Image: The Emblematic Significance of the Closet Scene in *Hamlet*," *Texas Studies in Literature and Language* 16(1974–75):249–262, argues that Claudius' Elsinore is a castle of lechery, complete with riotous banqueting.

16. See Jacqueline E. M. Latham, "The Imagery in *Hamlet*: Acting," *Educational Theatre Journal* 14(1962):197–202; and Kent W. Cartwright, "Ceremony in *Hamlet*, *Lear*, and *Macbeth*," *Dissertation Abstracts International* 39(1979):6773–A.

17. See Francis Berry, *The Shakespeare Inset: Word and Picture* (London: Routledge & Kegan Paul, 1965), pp. 116–143.

18. See Thiselton Dyer, *Folk-Lore of Shakespeare*, pp. 340–361; and Bridget Gellert Lyons, "The Iconography of Ophelia," *English Literary History* 44(1977):60–74.

19. Lynda E. Boose, "The Fashionable Poloniuses," *Hamlet Studies* 1(1979):66–77.

20. Ibid., pp. 69–73.

21. Bridget Gellert, "The Iconography of Melancholy in the Graveyard Scene in *Hamlet*," *Studies in Philology* 67(1970):57–66; and John P. Sisk, "Ceremony and Civilization in Shakespeare," *Sewanee Review* 86(1978):396–405.

22. Fergusson, *The Idea of a Theater*, p. 138.

23. See Wendy Coppedge Sanford, *Theater as Metaphor in "Hamlet"* (Cambridge, Mass.: Harvard University Press, 1967), pp. 23–24.

VII. Epilogue

1. Owen Feltham, *Resolves: A Duple Century one new an other of a second Edition* (London, 1628), p. 65. Quoted in Huston Diehl, "Iconography and Characterization in English Tragedy, 1585–1642," *Comparative Drama* 12(1978–79):113–122. The *paragone* of ear and eye is to be found in Horace's *Ars Poetica*: "The mind is less actively stimulated by what it takes in through the ear than

by what is presented to it through the trustworthy agency of the eyes—something the spectator can see for himself." Trans. Dorsch, *Classical Literary Criticism*, p. 85.

2. Mario Praz, *Mnemosyne: The Parallel between Literature and the Visual Arts* (Princeton: Princeton University Press, 1970), and "Modern Art and Literature: A Parallel," *English Miscellany* 5(1954):217–245; and Wylie Sypher, *Four Stages of Renaissance Style* (Garden City, N.Y.: Doubleday, 1955).

3. Marco Mincoff, "Baroque Literature in England," *Annuaire de l'Université de Sofia* 43(1946–47):27. Cited in Hagstrum, *The Sister Arts*, p. xiv.

4. G. Giovannini, "Method in the Study of Literature in Its Relation to the Other Fine Arts," *Journal of Aesthetics and Art Criticism* 8(1950):185–195, esp. p. 190.

5. John M. Steadman, "Iconography and Renaissance Drama: Ethical and Mythological Themes," *Research Opportunities in Renaissance Drama* 13–14(1970–71):73–122, and "Falstaff as Actaeon: A Dramatic Emblem," *Shakespeare Quarterly* 14(1963):231–244. A similar point about the importance to the Renaissance of referential meaning derived from myth and biblical story is made by Svetlana and Paul Alpers, "*Ut Pictura Noesis?* Criticism in Literary Studies and Art History," *New Literary History* 3(1971–72):437–458. See also other articles in the same issue of *NLH*; Robert J. Clements, *Picta Poesis: Literary and Humanistic Theory in Renaissance Emblem Books* (Rome: Edizioni di storia e letteratura, 1960), p. 26 and passim; and Laurence Binyon, "English Poetry in Its Relation to Painting and the Other Arts," *Proceedings of the British Academy, 1917–18* (London: Oxford University Press), pp. 381–402, esp. p. 383.

6. Lessing, *Laocöon*, p. 55 and chap. 16. Discussed by Gilman, *The Curious Perspective*, pp. 3–5.

7. Rose, *Shakespearean Design*, p. 10.

8. Gilman, *The Curious Perspective*, pp. 1–15.

9. Turner, *The Ritual Process*, p. 129.

Index

Index

Index